The Commonwealth of Massachusetts
Department of the State Treasurer
One Ashburton Place
Boston, Massachusetts 02108-1608

Timothy P. Cahill
Treasurer and Receiver General

Dear Conference Participant,

I hope you will accept this book, *Women & Money,* to assist you in taking your first steps toward a more financially secure future.

Did you know that:

- Three out of four working women earn less than $30,000 per year?
- Women earn less and receive half the average pension benefits of men?
- Recent statistics show that a staggering 71% of the nation's 4 million elderly poor are women.

These facts make it vital that all women, regardless of salary or economic well-being, become more informed about how to secure their financial future. Young or old, rich or poor, married or single, working at home or outside the home, every woman needs to become her own financial guru.

I believe that empowering every person in the Commonwealth with an understanding of how to plan for the future is one of the best investments I can make as Treasurer. Attending a Money Conference and reading this book will provide a solid foundation on which to build your financial future.

Like any self-improvement project, this one will take more than one day. I urge you to use the knowledge gained at the Money Conference and this book as your travel guides on a journey toward financial independence. This journey might introduce you to a brokerage firm, credit union, consumer credit counselor, certified financial planner, your local banker, or any number of people and places you haven't encountered until now.

Stay in touch with us and let us know how you are doing. I'd appreciate your feedback on the conference and how best we might structure future conferences to support your continued financial growth. You can write to me at the State House, Room 227, Boston, MA 02133 or send e-mail to Treasurer_Cahill@tre.state.ma.us.

Thank you for making the Money Conference a part of your future!

Sincerely,

Timothy P. Cahill
Treasurer and Receiver General

The Money Conference for Women is underwritten by:

 LEHMAN BROTHERS
Where vision gets built.

...and funded by the following generous sponsors:

 Sovereign Bank

BLACKROCK

CITIZENS BANK®

NEW YORK LIFE
The Company You Keep®

WELLINGTON
MANAGEMENT

with special assistance from:

Western
New England
College

Women & Money

Your Personal Finance Guide

Dee Lee

FLYING PIG PUBLISHING
Harvard, Massachusetts

Women & Money
Your Personal Finance Guide

ISBN 0-9746110-0-X
Library of Congress Control Number: 2003113564

Design and composition by Lyn Rodger, Deerfoot Studios
Cover design by Lyn Rodger, Deerfoot Studios

Flying Pig Publishing
P.O. Box 304
Harvard, MA 01451

www.flyingpigpublishing.com

Printed in the United States of America.

Disclaimer: The opinions expressed in this book are solely those of the author and are based on the author's personal experiences. They are not intended to be the norm for all investors. Reasonable care has been taken in the preparation of the text to ensure its clarity and accuracy. The book is sold with the understanding that the author and publisher are not engaged in rendering legal, financial planning, or accounting services. Laws vary from state to state, and readers with specific financial questions should seek the services of a professional advisor. The author and publisher specifically disclaim any liability, loss, or risk, personal or otherwise, which is incurred as a consequence, directly or indirectly, of the use and application of any of the contents of this book.

Other titles by Dee Lee

The Complete Idiot's Guide to 401(k) Plans

The Complete Idiot's Guide to Retiring Early

Let's Talk Money

Table of Contents

Part Two: The Roles You Take On As Women

Introduction

I was driving home after being in New York on business and stopped at my favorite deli for a late lunch. After ordering, I checked my office for messages and was told the book deal was a go. Yes, I would write another book, this one for women about money.

Now I just needed to find out what women really wanted to know. So when my waitress came back for my order I flippantly asked her what she wanted to know about money. "Everything," came her quick response. She asked me why I was asking. So I told her about the book and explained I wasn't sure I could get "everything" in it but was going to try.

After she brought me my sandwich, she told me that she would be off shortly, and if I could wait, she would be back to give me a detailed answer. At the end of the shift, five women crowded around my table to give me advice on what should go into this project, what they wanted to learn that had never been taught to them. But then each focused on something different, a particular financial concern due to something happening in her life or someone close to her. This was my first focus group.

Over the next several weeks, there were three more organized focus groups of women of all ages and across economic lines. Interestingly, the needs were the same as in my group of waitresses. No one had a clue about what to do if she should be widowed or divorced. How would she handle the finances of caring for an elderly relative and saving for college at the same time? Thus the format of the book was conceived.

The first part of the book would be dedicated to financial planning, how to set your goals, and how to achieve them. The second part of the book would focus on the different roles we as women take on during our lifetime. What do we need to know when we are someone's wife, ex-wife, widow, daughter, mother, or partner? Some of you may even play all of these roles during your lifetime; others will take on two or three. You will need to know about all of them, however, so you can help your mother, sister, cousin, daughter, or friend deal with her financial life.

Added to each chapter are the stories of real women and the men they are coupled with struggling with financial decisions and the consequences of those decisions for themselves and their families. I met these women and their men at workshops, book signings, and in my role as a newspaper and magazine columnist. I have included lots of resources to help in your quest for financial freedom. Most of them are websites where you can log on and get more information on a subject. If you don't have a computer, head to your local library and spend some time learning to use the computers there.

Appendix A has the worksheets you will need to start your financial plan. I would suggest copying them so you can use them again and again. Do them in pencil. Neatness does not count, but accuracy does!

Appendix B is a glossary of sorts. What is there is five website links that will provide you with more information than I could fit in this book. You will need a computer to use the sites and for that I apologize to anyone who does not have access to a computer except through their library.

Every decision you make as an adult woman will have a financial component to it. I am hoping, with this book, to give you the skills you need to make good financial decisions and be successful.

Success is not a destination; it's a journey. Good luck with your planning, and I am so very pleased to be a part of it.

Dee Lee

Acknowledgements

No book is ever written in a vacuum. There are always so many others involved. Some play a small part; some give you ideas without even knowing they helped. Others such as the women in my focus groups and all of the women who have shared their stories with me over the years have helped make up the very fiber of this book.

A special thanks to Lyn Rodger of Deerfoot Studios whose handy work you see on every page for she formatted the book for me. The cover is her design as well. A special thanks to Lyn for working under a tight deadline once we got the first book order.

Thanks to Kurt Czarnowski of the Social Security Administration in Boston who now has the distinct privilege of having reviewed this book and the four before it. He was always willing to answer my questions about what women need to know about Social Security.

Now I need to acknowledge my two children, Jennifer and Bryan, for I am forever telling stories about them. All of them are true too! The role I took on, as mother, has definitely been the hardest job I have ever had for there was no job description that came with the job. It's also been the most rewarding job I have ever had! Love ya!

Now last on the page is Doug. Thank you for believing again I had another book in me. I did! Whenever I write, I don't cook. But I still like to eat and Doug doesn't cook! So we have been eating at McDonald's and making sandwiches. You have to understand that Mickey D's is the closest restaurant to us—and that is seven miles away. We're talking country here!

PART ONE

Achieving Financial Success

The first section of this book is all about strategizing your personal financial plan. A financial plan is not just about investing. A financial plan is about setting goals, figuring out what you want in life.

Then you will need a starting off point. What's your net worth and where do you spend your money? If you have a negative net worth you will need to get out of debt. Debt is a barrier to financial success.

To reach your retirement goals you'll need to learn about investing, taxes and retirement strategies. You'll need to use insurance and estate planning to protect the ones you love and the assets you have accumulated.

The first part of this book will help you with the basics of financial planning.

"We've done very little planning for the rest of our lives if we expect to live to age 90," Doris told me. She went on to tell me that she and her husband are over the hill, the big hill. I asked innocently enough which hill they were referring to, 50 or 60. "Sixty," she exclaimed. "Do we look like we're 60?" I said no, of course not. So for the record Doris is closer to 50 than she is to 60.

Doris and her husband Bill have been doing some reading and research about retiring earlier than 65 and wonder if that is at all possible for them. Recently a friend of theirs sold his business and retired at age 55. He has been lauding the virtues of early retirement ever since. Doris admitted that they were a bit envious of this fellow for he was just coming back from spending the last two months traveling. And during the last two months they have been going to work every day, cleaning house, doing yard work, grocery shopping, cooking meals; all those mundane things in life that must get done.

We are not planners Doris told me. We go along in life and things happen and then we react to them. For example their daughter was a junior in high school filling out college applications before they thought seriously about college planning and expenses. So 6 years after graduation they are still paying off school debt. And recently their daughter's college boyfriend proposed by putting an engagement ring in a Cracker Jack box. Again they were caught off guard when the word wedding came up even though she has been dating this young man since college. Now they are wondering about a home equity line of credit to pay for a wedding.

It is never too late to start planning I told her.

Chapter 1

Getting Started

· ·

In This Chapter

This book can change your life, if you want it to. In this chapter you will learn why it is so important for women to take charge of their financial lives and begin the financial planning process. Every decision you make as an adult has a financial planning component to it.

· ·

We are about to begin a journey together. At this point in the book, you are already looking for words of financial wisdom to guide you. You're ready for information, information that will lead you through the maze of financial planning. Let's start on the journey together.

What This Book Will Do for You

Maybe I should start by stating what this book *won't* do for you. It's not going to solve your money problems. Only you can do that. What I will promise you are the tools to help you solve your own money problems, in a format that will empower you to take charge of your finances. You're not going to be day trading by the end of the book, but you will understand what you need to do. By using the tools and resources presented here, you'll be able to start the financial planning process and get your financial house in order.

Success is a journey, not a destination.

Whenever I do a financial workshop, I let my audience know what my goals are for our time together. I also let them know what I expect from them. My goals for you as you read this book are to help you understand your financial situation and what you can do differently to make it better. My expectations are the same as any teacher's: I want you to take the tools I offer and use them. I want you to begin thinking about money as a tool, something that can empower you to do other things. I want you to enjoy reading my book. It would please me if you found it entertaining as well as educational, but I want you to use it. I want it to make a difference in your life.

Why Life Planning Is Essential

As adults, almost every decision we make has a financial component to it. Think about that for a few minutes. For example, I decide to go on a diet—something I do at least once a year. Do I buy a book on dieting? A trip to a bookstore tells me that there are more dieting books than financial planning books available. Do I join an organization such as Weight Watchers, or do I hire a cook and trainer and do it the way Oprah did? The bottom line here is that all of these options cost money. Which one I choose will depend on the resources I have and the resources I wish to dedicate to this goal. (If you are wondering which I chose, I am a card-carrying member of Weight Watchers.)

Money plays a big part in our lives. Not having enough money is a scary thing, but that fear can either be motivating or crippling. Only you decide which it will do to you. At one time in her life, Erin Brockovich, the woman played by Julia Roberts in the film of the same name, was flat broke with three kids to feed and rent to pay. It motivated her to find a job and do well at that job. She also got her debt under control and no longer allowed it to control her.

You need to conquer your money fears. That might sound a bit extreme, and even as I write, I am envisioning a group of women warriors wearing breast armor with swords drawn, slashing away at taxes and inflation and conquering all that is evil about money. More

---

Don't hesitate to go out on a limb sometimes—after all, that's where the fruit is.

important, however, they are in control of their money and are using it as a tool to achieve their goals and dreams. Once successful, they can then teach the younger women in their tribe about money, care for the older women, and even give some it away to help other tribes in need.

Money equates to power in some relationships. It tips the balance in favor of the person controlling the purse strings, the one earning the most or the person most knowledgeable about money. To create a better balance as a woman, you need to understand your financial situation and learn more about money. You need to do more than just balance the checkbook and pay the bills; you need to have an equal say in how the family's assets are invested.

What You Need to Know as a Woman

Financial planning is different for women. As with other industries that service women, the financial industry is just catching up with the fact that women are indeed different than men and have different needs. Nike had been manufacturing shoes for women, and they weren't selling. Then one day, during a brainstorming session, one of the women commented that Nike's problems were not going to go away until it realized that women were not little men.

And so it is with your finances. Let me share with you some facts:

✔ Women live longer than men (an average of seven years) and need to plan for a longer retirement period.

✔ On average, women earn less than men, sometimes doing the very same job.

✔ More than 50 percent of all marriages fail.

✔ After a divorce, on average, a woman will see her standard of living drop by as much as 30 percent.

✔ According to the AARP, the average age of widowhood is 56.

There are lots of ways to become a failure, but never taking a chance is the most successful.

✔ Ninety percent of women become wholly responsible for their finances at some point during their lifetime.

✔ Women are more likely than men to be in and out of the job market, spending an average of 11.5 years caring for children or an elderly relative.

✔ Women are less likely to receive a pension, and those that do receive a pension get only half as much as the average man.

✔ For every year that a woman stays home caring for a child, she must work five or more extra years to recover lost income, pension coverage, and career promotion.

✔ Social Security is the only source of retirement benefits for 50 percent of retired women.

✔ Women at all economic levels fear they'll become bag ladies.

✔ Most women lack the knowledge to adequately plan for retirement, yet 70 percent say they don't want to depend on their kids during retirement.

These are scary statistics! So, as a woman, you are different and have different financial needs than men. You are not a little man. You need to do the following:

✔ Learn about money: how to make it, save it, keep it, invest it, protect it, and pass it along to the next generation.

✔ Start saving for retirement with your first job because you may not have the luxury of 40 years in a career to save.

✔ Take charge of your finances, and if coupled, you need to share in managing the family's finances.

✔ Learn how to get out of debt and how to use debt properly to increase your net worth.

Nothing is ever gained without risk: you can't steal second base and still keep one foot on first.

✔ Learn about investing to make your money grow faster than taxes and inflation.

✔ Know where Social Security fits into your retirement picture.

✔ Understand your money situation so you can better function as a wife, a divorcee, a widow, a mother, daughter, or a partner.

✔ Know what you don't know and go learn about it.

Why Women Fail to Plan

Women don't plan to fail; they fail to plan. Most of us are ChPs, charted procrastinators. You buy the books, you read the books, and then you get stuck. You need to get over that next hurdle, and that's the action part. Occasionally, you need a boot in the butt to get there. I am, at this very moment in time, putting on my boots to provide that incentive.

Below are some excuses why people fail to plan. See whether you can see yourself in any of these:

✔ "It's not my responsibility to take care of this financial stuff. It's my husband's, my parent's, my employer's, my partner's, or Uncle Sam's."

✔ "I don't have enough money now to do the things I want to do. I'll have less if I contribute some of it to a retirement plan."

✔ "I'm planning on receiving an inheritance, so I don't need to plan."

✔ "I'm going to wait until I find the right guy before I start this financial stuff."

Have you ever found yourself making any of these excuses? It is so easy to procrastinate. Procrastination is the biggest obstacle you will face: your inability to get started, always thinking you have tomorrow to do it. Remember what your mother used to say about the road to

Take a chance! Even a turtle gets nowhere until he sticks his neck out.

hell being paved with good intentions. She was right! We're all guilty of it because it does take work and effort to plan.

> *Planning does pay off: According to a study conducted by the Consumer Federation of America with NationsBank, consumers who developed an overall financial plan reported roughly twice the savings as those without a plan. This was true at all income levels.*

Working Through the Financial Planning Process

There are six areas of financial planning that we will review together. The areas are all interrelated. What affects one area impacts the others as well. If nothing else, you should be aware of these areas and how they impact your financial strategies:

1. **Goal setting and organization of your stuff.** You've got to have a starting off point. We'll set goals together, and you'll make them realistic so they'll be achievable. I'm going to ask you to organize your important documents. That may mean you have to find them first. Often times, important papers are put somewhere safe, and we forget just where that safe place is.

2. **Risk management.** Risk management is a fancy term for using insurance to protect your assets from a loss you couldn't afford on your own. When you purchase an insurance policy, you are purchasing a financial product that provides you with peace of mind as well as the assurance that, if you suffer a loss, the insurance company will try to make you whole.

3. **Tax planning.** Uncle Sam has his hand in your pocketbook because he wants his fair share; at least he thinks it's a fair share. You'll learn how to shelter your income from taxes while saving for retirement.

Remember, early to bed and early to rise, 'til you make enough money to do otherwise.

4. **Retirement planning.** If you're 35, retirement seems so far away. At 35, you also think that 55 is old, but if you're 55, you think that 85 is old. Retirement planning should begin with your first job. So you need to figure out how much to save to reach your goals.

5. **Investment planning.** There is a lot more to financial planning than just investing. Investing is a tool you use to achieve the goals you set for yourself. You also need to understand how much risk you should be taking with your investments to achieve your goals.

6. **Estate planning.** Although death, especially our own, is not a popular subject, no one gets out of this world alive, so you might as well plan for it. There is a need to protect your assets from Uncle Sam's long reach, but more important, you need to have things in order for the ones you leave behind.

The Bottom Line

You now know what you need to do next, you need to take charge of your finances. And learn about the five areas of financial planning that we'll work on together in the first half of the book. For the most part, every decision you make as an adult woman has a financial component to it.

People do what they like to do or what they are paid to do. And just sometimes they are lucky enough that it's the same.

eanne and Brian Norton are a childless couple in their early 40s. They married late and started seriously saving late as well and wanted some help reaching their goals they told me. Like so many of us their lives have had ups and downs and it was in a down period when I met them.

Jeanne has a chronic illness that has taken away her ability to work full time. She's still able to do some work at home but is frustrated with her inability to contribute more to their savings and household expenses. Jeanne and Brian are enjoying the American dream; a house, two cars, two horses, three dogs and a multitude of barn cats. They have been together over 12 years now and have come from a negative net worth due to credit card debt and an upside down mortgage on a condominium to a net worth that is close to $500,000.

The Nortons realize that although they have done a great job of accumulating assets and savings they have done very little investing. Their first goal was to get out of debt, and the second goal was to purchase a home and pay it off as soon as they could. At age 30, retirement seemed so far away that neither Jeanne nor Brian took advantage of the retirement plans that were available to them at that time. So their third goal of an early retirement got put on the back burner.

Now in their 40s, they are thinking differently and are saving the maximum in their retirement plans. But because they started late they realize they must save more for retirement than if they had started 12 years ago. Their goals are modest they believe. They would like to retire early and have their nest egg provide an adequate income for both them and their animals in a warmer climate.

Chapter 2

Identifying What You Want from Life

In This Chapter

The fun part of this chapter is getting your reticular activating system working for you! Your brain cells are possibly all ready working on helping you achieve your goals and dreams. Dreaming is good for you and daydreaming about life's possibilities will help you achieve your goals.

We all have hopes and dreams, and our hopes and dreams are our goals. Some, however, are truly fantasies, such as Rosie O'Donnell's dreams about Tom Cruise. Nevertheless, Rosie's goals to be a financially independent woman and to adopt several children were real goals, goals she was able to achieve.

What Dreams Do You Have?

To start your financial planning process, you need to set your goals so you can then get the process in motion. Remember in *Alice in Wonderland* where Alice meets the Cheshire cat?

> "Alice asks the Cheshire Puss, 'Would you tell me please, which way I ought to go from here?'

The poor man is not he who is without a cent, but he who is without a dream. —Harry Kemp

"That depends a good deal on where you want to get to,' said the Cat. Alice's answer, 'I don't much care where.' His retort, 'Then it doesn't matter which way you go.'"

To get where you're going, you've got to know where you're going. That's what setting goals will do for you. Goals give you direction and a destination—they quantify what you want. Together, we'll work on realizing those goals. I'll help you plot your course and help you stay on course.

Here are some question you might want to ask yourself as you start this process:

✔ What are my dreams?

✔ What are my hopes?

✔ What do I value in life?

✔ Where do I want to be in 5, 10, or 20 years?

You do have the power to achieve your goals, and the first step to achieving them is to put pen to paper and write them down. Writing your goals down stimulates a part of the brain called the reticular activating system. This system begins a filtering process and, when activated, begins collecting information and routing it to the conscious part of your brain. So, when opportunity knocks, you will answer the door. That's the technical reason why writing your goals down works—because it makes you more of aware of them. So this wonderful thing that sits inside your skull, your

A study done by Harvard University asked graduating seniors what their goals were. Only 3 percent of the class actually could discuss their goals and dreams. At the twentieth reunion of this class, Harvard followed up and discovered that the 3 percent who had been able to formulate their dreams actually outperformed their classmates. Interestingly, that 3 percent carries over to the population as a whole. It is estimated that only 3 percent of Americans plan seriously for their futures, and of that 3 percent, only 20 percent ever develop a written plan and follow it through to a conclusion.

When you have a dream you've got to grab it and never let go.
—Carol Burnett

brain, works to help you achieve your dreams even as you grocery shop or sleep.

Let's start with something wild. I'd like to you to write down your dreams and goals, and if you want to include Tom Cruise in them, that's okay with me. I'm not going to be looking over your shoulder, so no one but you is ever going to see these. Write them all down. Then categorize them under one of two headings: fantasy or achievable dreams. Be careful here, they may overlap in real life.

Fantasy

Let's look at the fantasy page first. If Tom Cruise made it to this list, good luck to you! Is everything on this list a fantasy or do they simply appear somewhat outlandish to you? Putting down you would like to be a talk show host and earn $2 million a year may be a fantasy for most of us, but then again Rosie did it. Dating Tom Cruise also won't make it past the "I Wish List" But don't be afraid to write them down. Start to dream about it. What would it take to be a talk show host?

How about dancing with the president? Dancing with the president of the United States was a goal that someone shared with me recently during a workshop. The more we talked about this goal, the more it began to gel for her. She is a registered Democrat and has represented her state at the national convention many times. What would it take to get an invitation to an inaugural ball if her candidate were elected? Does she have the extra time and energy to spend campaigning in her state? Would her efforts be rewarded by an invitation to one of the many balls held in Washington? Could she envision herself in a grand, green velvet number with a square neck, wearing her best pearls and earrings? Could she see herself dancing at this ball, possibly even with the president?

It appeared achievable, and envisioning helped to bring it into focus. However, the process we used was to take the goal apart, breaking it down into achievable pieces. The brainstorming got her to think and to come up with ideas and new short-term goals she could use to achieve her bigger goal of dancing with the president. I then asked her

A dream is just a dream
A goal is a dream with a plan and a deadline

whether she would think she had failed if she were to get as far as the inaugural ball but not get the opportunity to dance with the president. She grinned and said, "Absolutely not." This was certainly more achievable than Rosie's fantasy about Tom Cruise.

So some of the things on this list may very well be achievable and can be put on the next list.

Achievable Dreams

Let's go to work on the second list, achievable dreams. This will be the hard stuff about money, family, and your life. Retirement is often number one or two on many people's lists. I often see a "comfortable retirement" listed. Now that certainly is a commendable goal, but you need to put some corners on it. Huh? That's right. Corners. This is a fuzzy picture, and you need to bring it into focus. What is comfortable? Comfortable for you may not be what I want in my retirement. Get specific here. When do you want to retire? Where do you want to retire? How much income would you like to have in retirement? See what I mean?

A more specific retirement goal would be to retire in 20 years at age 60, work two days a week, remain in your present housing, have an income stream equal to $50,000 in today's dollars, and be able to travel while you are healthy. Wow! Now envision what it might feel like not to have to get up on Monday morning, pack your lunch, and fight traffic to get to work. Feel the warmth of the tropical sun on your face while you are traveling in the Caribbean. Dreaming is okay and is recommended here.

Now you need to break this goal down into smaller goals to reach the goal of a comfortable retirement. Twenty years is a long time off, but the one thing age has taught me is that time flies. So you'll need to start working on this goal right now. How much more will you need to save each week in your retirement plan? Where will those dollars come from? To reach this new goal, will you need to change your present lifestyle to save more—for example, by giving up dining out?

Many of us spend half our time wishing for things we could have if we didn't spend half our time wishing. —Alexander Wollcott

Next, break your goals out into long-term and short-term. When do you want to achieve these goals? A long-term goal is five years away or longer. And it's the short-term goals that help you achieve your long-term goals.

✔ Commit to paper your dreams and hopes.

✔ Get them into focus by making them more specific.

✔ Break them down into parts so that they are achievable.

✔ Set up a time frame.

How Are You Going to Achieve Those Dreams?

This may sound simplistic, but you are going to do it by putting one foot in front of the other—baby steps to begin with. And I'm going to be with you all the way. As you look over your lists, one of the things that may jump out at you is how many of your dreams—if not all of them—have a financial element to them. As grownups, most of our decisions and our dreams all have a financial component attached to them.

Losing weight may have made your list. It always makes mine! And it is always on the Achievable List. Do you join an organization like Weight Watchers to help you? Do you join a gym or an aerobics class? How much more will it cost you in time and money for the food you will need to prepare? If you lose more than 10 pounds, you may even need new clothes or transition clothes until you reach your goal weight. All of this takes money, and you will need to figure out where it will fit in your budget.

What you need to do is prioritize your lists. What are the things you absolutely want to have? This is where you can cross Tom Cruise off the list and maybe the red Jaguar! With what is left, you further prioritize using a numbering system. I like to use 1 thru 4, with 1s being keepers and 4s being that would be nice to have. Your dream list is a work in progress because, as your life changes, so will your goals.

There are people who have money and people who are rich.
—*Coco Chanel*

Nothing here is cast in concrete, so have fun with your first homework assignment.

You certainly want to accomplish all the dreams on your list, and you may be able to do that—it just may take you a bit more time. When speaking with younger women, one of their concerns is "having it all." They certainly can have it all, just not all at the same time. So it may be with your dream list.

Women's Life Stages

As women, we will go through many stages in our lifetimes. In the past, things seemed simpler and appeared to lie in a straight path. We went to school, maybe landed jobs, got married, and had children. We then struggled as a family, caring and educating the children, and then retired and dealt with our old age. Today, our lives are more cyclical in that we move in and out of these life stages.

We start life out as daughters with our parents caring for us. We might become our own persons and have careers. Maybe we become wives or partners and perhaps even mothers. Sadly, we may reach a stage in which we are widows or ex-wives and must take full responsibility for ourselves and maybe our children. Many of us revert to the stage of being daughters, but this time, instead of being cared for, we are the caregivers. Often the pull of being a mother and a daughter at the same time creates an emotional and financial tug of war.

We may repeat some of these stages, and some may get skipped because we choose to do something different with our lives. Women remarry and have a second family, care for their own parents, and maybe even care for in-laws as well as going it alone and re-establishing their careers.

Each of these stages has a different financial impact on us, and with each of these stages, our dreams may change or go out of focus for a time.

Every woman is unique. We each have different opportunities, challenges, and crosses to bear. By planning, you can control your

Never let yesterday use up too much of today.

destiny, and by committing yourself to reaching your goals, you set your course for success.

The Bottom Line

Setting goals, whether long-term or short-term goals is a lot of work. There is a need to prioritize our goals so we'll be sure we can achieve them. Some goals are pure fantasy and fun and others will help us achieve financial success. As women we take on many different roles as we go through life and some of them may be repeated.

I'm tired of love: I'm still more tired of rhyme. But money gives me pleasure all the time. —Hilaire Belloc

laine introduced herself at a book signing and pointed out her husband Tom to me. They were looking to find out what else they could be doing to improve their financial situation.

Elaine and Tom are in their mid thirties and have been married for seven years and have been together for nine years. In those nine years they have accomplished a lot they told me. When they got married they had a negative net worth between them with credit card debt and school loans that needed to be paid off. Today they have a positive net worth with only a mortgage of $20,000 left on their condo. They bought the condo at a depressed price through an FDIC foreclosure with no money down. They are very proud of the fact that they did their homework and ended up with a wonderful place to live. Their plans are to pay it off and then sell it and use the money to purchase a single family home.

They are so frugal they made me feel guilty about buying a bottle of water to drink during the book talk. They have decided that children are not in their future plans. They want a comfortable retirement and possibly to retire early. Both Elaine and Tom are taking courses towards their masters degrees but are doing it one course a semester. Their respective employers are reimbursing some of the cost so they don't want to take too many courses for the reimbursements will only cover two courses a year.

They haven't been to a movie in years and they only buy second hand cars and furniture that is on sale. They are both contributing the maximum to their retirement plans but still feel there is more they can do.

They think they are doing all of the right stuff they told me. Their budget is in great shape and they are making every penny work for them. But still they worry about not having enough. I explained that worrying about not having enough is universal at all economic levels.

What's important is that Elaine and Tom understand their financial situation and have a handle on it.

Chapter 3

Figuring Out
Your Starting Point

. . . .

In This Chapter

This chapter will help you establish your starting off point on the financial planning journey you are embarking on. It will take some work on your part to get yourself organized but as you read through the chapter and begin to work on the worksheets in the appendix you will find with each task accomplished a sense of control over your financial picture.

. . . .

With any journey, there's a beginning. Where are you starting? That's what you need to find out next. To achieve the dreams you listed in the preceding chapter, we need to see what resources you already have, so we'll take a look at what you've got—your net worth.

Then we're going to look at one of your biggest assets, your ability to earn an income. We'll also get you to look at how and where your paycheck goes each week. The cash flow worksheet will help you figure out where the cash goes. These worksheets are in the appendix and I would recommend making copies to work from.

Net Worth

To figure out where you are, you need to figure out what you've got. So you'll need to work on the net worth statement located in

---

Money isn't everything. After all, there are checks, charge accounts, and credit cards.

Appendix A. This can be simple or complicated. It's going to depend on how simple or complicated your life is and how much stuff you own.

Your net worth is a snapshot of what you own at a particular moment in time. Next month it will be different because you will have spent some of the money in your checking account, your mutual fund may have appreciated, or you could have sold your home. In accounting terms, a net worth statement is your assets (what you own) minus your liabilities (what you owe). You subtract your liabilities from your assets to determine your net worth.

What You Own

Start with the plus column. What are the assets you own? You will need to list everything that is yours. Take the time to separate who owns what. This will be important for estate planning as well as divorce planning. You will also use a net worth statement when you are reviewing your insurance needs. Try to be as accurate as you can.

There is no need to list your household items individually; you can lump those together. Their worth is not the price you paid for them; it's the price they're worth today (what you could sell them for on E-bay). Your dishes may have been $50 a place setting, but if they are 10 years old, they have depreciated—gone down in value. The same is true with that recliner chair. It is worth less than the original purchase price. Now, it may be a different story with the value of your home because that, I hope, has increased in value—appreciated over time.

When you reach the section about investments, note that it is broken into "invested" assets and "use" assets. Your invested assets are those that help you reach your goals. The use assets are what you use to maintain your lifestyle. This is the column that holds your toys such as the summer house, the sailboat, and your jewelry. These assets do count when adding up your total net worth, but they usually are not the assets that contribute to that comfortable retirement.

We're told you'll never find the line "Money is the root of all evil" in the Bible. But you will find that it states, "Love of money is the root of all evil." There's a big difference.

What You Owe

Now for the negative column, what you owe. With all of that good stuff you own, your net worth was looking pretty good, wasn't it? Now you've got to fill in the "liabilities" column. Ouch! For some of you, things aren't looking too good right now.

Let's take a look at the kind of debt you've got. Is it a home mortgage you have or a student loan? This kind of debt is used to increase your net worth, so it's considered good debt. Yes, a student loan is good debt because it allowed you or your kids to further your education and increase your salary capabilities.

Some of the debt you may have is short-term debt: taxes that are due, a church pledge, that dental bill for a new crown, or credit card debt. Credit card debt that you carry beyond one month is bad debt because you are using credit to pay for items you have consumed, such as dining out and movies. Carrying that debt forward from month to month can get very expensive with the high cost of credit today.

A positive net worth is what you want here. You want to have more assets than liabilities, and you want to have more invested assets than use assets. A high net worth that consists primarily of toys and your primary residence might produce a great bottom line, but it's not going to help you realize those achievable goals such as sending the kids to college, getting out of debt, or providing for an early retirement. One of the hard things about being a grownup in this situation is that you may have to defer some of the toys and concentrate on increasing the invested assets.

A negative net worth spells trouble. In this case, you owe more than you own, to put it simply. This can happen if you have used your credit card to supplement your lifestyle or to buy things that don't appreciate. You might have gotten into a real estate deal in which the real estate didn't appreciate but actually depreciated, and your mortgage is now more than the real value of the property. This is a situation you need to turn around. As you evaluate your net worth, remember that it is just a snapshot in time, and you have the ability to alter it for the future.

Life is a struggle to keep earning capacity to yearning capacity.

Cash Flow

As we continue to figure out just where you are, you need to analyze your cash flow. Where does the money go each month? Here's where you figure that out. Unless you are planning to receive an inheritance, the only legal place I know of that you can come up with the cash to invest is from your income stream.

I purposely put together a long worksheet for you, the cash flow worksheet in Appendix A. This worksheet may take longer than the net worth statement to finish. You really need to do this over a month's time. Why, you ask? So that you understand not only where you are spending but also how you are spending your money.

I have found that, unless prompted, readers forget a category or two. Here accuracy counts, neatness does not. A large miscellaneous number means you haven't taken the time to figure out where the money has been spent. You'll never be able to analyze where you can save money unless you know where you are spending it. What consumes your income?

A $50 discrepancy each week can slowly add up to one heck of a lot of money over time. It equals $200 a month, $2,400 a year, $84,000 over 35 years. Now let's take this one step further. If you had invested that money in a retirement account, your $50 a week, assuming a 9 percent return, would have provided you with a golden nest egg worth close to $600,000. See why I think it's so important to find even the smallest discrepancies in your cash flow?

The first part of the worksheet asks you to list your sources of income. That should be easy to compile: your salary (use your gross salary here so you can keep track of your withholdings), alimony, child support, interest income, and dividends. You get the picture here. This is what flows into your hands.

Next let's look at the expenses—what flows out of your hands. The big stuff is easy. Your rent/mortgage payment and car payment are fixed monthly expenses that don't usually change. You know what those are. For things like telephone, utilities, and medical bills, try to

---

I don't know how much money I have in the bank. I haven't shaken it lately. —Milton Berle

get those numbers from last year's checking account and credit card records. Check out the discretionary expenses next. These are the extras in your life, and for some of you, they may actually be essential. It's your call here.

If you want to project your expenses for the upcoming year, take last year's expenses and multiply them by an inflation factor of 4 percent. To do that, just multiply last year's numbers by 1.04 to get your projection.

Why, you ask, should this take you a month? Well, when you go to the ATM and withdraw $100, you need to account for that somewhere. Maybe it was dry cleaning, gas, groceries, and a quick stop for coffee and a bagel. Putting down $100 in the miscellaneous category every week will never give you a clear picture of your cash flow. And if you're going to start saving money, it's got to come from your cash flow. Knowing where you are spending your money gives you the power to make changes in your spending habits so that you have a positive bottom line here.

As with the net worth worksheet, you want positive numbers here. You want your expenses to be less than your income so that there is money left over to save and invest. Now if that's where you're at, you have a positive cash flow and you're saving at least 10 percent of your gross income, congratulations. You get a gold star. But if you are living paycheck to paycheck and have nothing left over for savings, you need to set up a spending plan.

What happens if you have a negative cash flow—that is, your expenses are more than your income? You use your credit card to pay for everyday items such as groceries and gas for your car. You are over your head in debt, and if you're not careful and don't get a handle on the problem, you will find yourself drowning in debt. You'll learn more about getting out of debt and setting up your spending plan in the next chapter.

Knowing how much you have already accumulated and where you spend your money are two essential building blocks when putting together your personal financial plan. Even if you are using a financial

---

People who used to live from payday to payday used to be called shiftless; now they are called good managers.

advisor, he or she will ask you to complete a net worth statement and will want to know how you are spending your money.

Two very good software packages for helping you track your expenses and portfolios are Intuit's Quicken and Microsoft's Money (both companies have software packages that start at around $35). Also check out their web sites for help as well: www.quicken.com and www.msn.com.

Managing the Unforeseen: The Emergency Fund

Now that we are on the subject of money and I have your rapt attention, do you have any money set aside in a reserve fund in case there is an emergency in your life? Just thought I'd throw that question out to grab your attention.

So what's an emergency fund, you're asking? My grandmother called it her rainy-day fund and kept it hidden in the teapot of the good china, because the good teapot still had a lid and way back then she didn't need much of a cash stash to survive an emergency.

This is money to be used when a hurricane or a tornado blows the roof off your house, you lose your job, or your union calls a strike. The need could come in the form of a disability or an illness that keeps you out of work for an extended period of time, or it could be the immediate expenses of an untimely death in the family. You need to plan for the unexpected.

The experts agree that everyone needs an emergency fund, but they often disagree on how much you need in it. The conventional wisdom is to have at least three months' worth of living expenses set aside, and if you can do it, six months' worth stashed away is even better.

Three months of living expenses is not the same as three months of income. You need only cover the basics here. Take a look at your cash flow. What will it take to maintain your lifestyle, rent/mortgage payment, groceries, monthly utilities, childcare, insurance payments, and so on? That's the amount you'll need. If you are single or the sole breadwinner in a family, an emergency fund is extremely important

Money is like a sixth sense, and you can't make use of the other five without it. —Somerset Maugham

because you don't have the luxury of a second income to cushion some of the emergency. My recommendations are as follows:

✔ Bare minimum for anyone: *3 months*

✔ Children & 2 steady incomes: *3–6 months*

✔ Children & 1 steady income: *4–6 months*

✔ Children & no steady income: *6–9 months*

People who earn most of their money on commissions, such as a realtor or a small business owner, may not have a regular paycheck. You need to have an extra cushion here, even if you are single with no children. If you feel uncertain about your job status, a rather common feeling nowadays, you may want to increase the amount in your cash stash. Many people tell me they will use their credit card or a home equity line of credit if they have an emergency. Be careful here, for if you are out of work or your home has been damaged it is hard to open a home equity line of credit. If you are retired and have a regular pension and Social Security, a cash stash in the teapot will do just fine for you. But don't let the kids know it's there!

Your emergency fund is just that—money to be used for emergencies. When income stops coming in or drops, you will need this money to keep paying your mortgage and buy groceries. It's not mad money, a vacation fund or a Christmas Club. It's your family's first line of defense when something major goes wrong.

Keep it separate from your regular spending money accounts. This means it shouldn't be in your regular checking account where you can write a check on it easily. You do want access to it in case of emergency, but you're better off putting it in a money market mutual fund where it can earn some interest and still be available. Put three months worth of living expenses there and let it grow. A potential drawback here is that the minimum amount needed to open such an account is usually $1,000. Now many of you will be complaining that you don't want your money just sitting in an account not earning

---

Establish an emergency fund and you'll be surprised how quickly an emergency develops.

much. Well if you want to take some risk you can put it a balanced mutual fund or a short-term CD. But you do want it available if you need it, so it's got to be liquid, financial jargon meaning that you can easily turn it into cash.

So what if you don't have three months worth of living expenses stashed away. No excuses now, take a look at your cash flow. Where can you make a difference? What can you cut out or cut back on to be able to save more money. Can you put in some overtime? Can you take on a part time job? When the next raise comes along plan to save it and the first savings goal should be your cash stash.

How Much of This Stuff Should I Keep?

After plowing your way through your net worth and cash flow, you now have accumulated a pile of paperwork. So what do you do with all of this stuff? Here's the opportune time to get organized. You've been talking about it for years. Things just sort of pile up and then it takes days to find the papers you need.

A large, three-ring binder is a good beginning, especially if you don't have a lot of stuff. The first section is for your dreams. Put them up front where you can review and update them on a regular basis. Next, put in your net worth and cash flow worksheets. Then, as you update them, file them here so you can see how well you are doing. Keep the old ones because it's a real morale boast as your assets increase.

The next section of your three-ring binder should hold the inventory worksheet. Take some time to fill out the Inventory and Location of Important Documents worksheet in Appendix A. I promise you that it will save time and energy in the future when you are looking for something. More important, if something should happen to you, someone can easily come in and find the important papers that may be needed.

Next on the to-do list is a filing system. It doesn't need to be elaborate. You could just use your three-ring binder if you don't have much stuff. A simple crate with hanging folders will do nicely. If you have

Nowadays a woman is given a raise to enable her to live the way she is already living.

the space, a filing cabinet is a real plus. A desk with your computer on it and deep drawers to hold your files would be best. Envision an organized spot where most of the important papers in your life are in one place. It would be ideal to have an office area in your home where things are kept, maybe near the computer, especially if you use the computer to monitor your checking account or your portfolio.

Your filing system should be simple. Set up your filing system with main categories: personal documents, estate-planning documents, and so on. The more stuff you have, the more elaborate and detailed the system will need to be. If you do decide to use your computer to keep track of this information, make a paper copy and put a backup disk in the file.

This is also a good time to weed through your stuff, keeping what is necessary and tossing out what you no longer need. The Inventory and Location of Important Documents worksheet will give you a good idea of what should be kept. Common sense should prevail. If you are going to need anything in the future, you should keep it, but things like checks to the grocery store can be safely thrown away.

Master File

Set up a master file that contains lists of all of your assets and all of your important documents (wills, trusts, durable power of attorney, medical directives, and passports). List all of your advisors and their updated addresses and phone numbers. Do the same for insurance policies, credit cards, investment, and bank accounts.

Taxes: Maintain a separate file for each calendar year for your personal tax data: records of income, transactions such as property sales, itemized deductions, etc. IRAs or pension contributions should be noted in this file as well as having a folder of their own. Keep copies of Form 1099s, as well as any documentation for your deductions, such as cancelled checks.

Banking: When reconciling bank statements (and you should be doing this monthly), transfer any canceled checks needed for tax documentation to the current year's files. Keep all checks that relate to the

---

Middle class: The people who live in public like the rich do—and in private like the poor do.

house, e.g., new storm windows. You'll need these when you sell your home, to help establish its cost basis. File these in your real estate file. Keep all other checks for one year. Retain check ledger and bank statements for at least seven years.

Stocks, Bonds, and Mutual Funds: It's best to maintain a file for each account and a folder for each holding. Keep all cost information relating to investments so you can determine your cost basis when you sell them, to determine whether you had a profit or a loss. Keep copies of all 1099s—the form sent to you by the investment company indicating capital gains and dividends paid during the year. You'll need all those old 1099s to establish the cost basis for your mutual funds.

Insurance Policies: You want separate folders for each type of insurance you have. Keep the most recent policy in your current file, along with any endorsements or addendums. Also keep old policies that provide liability protection, such as your homeowner's policy, for at least three years, just in case you should find yourself facing a lawsuit. Records of pending and paid health insurance claims should be kept in a separate file labeled "medical insurance payments."

Credit Cards: Retain the loan agreements and any new information the card issuer may send out with your monthly statement. Retain purchase slips and billing statements for at least one year. Staple all pertinent charge slips to the warranties so if you have to return an item you can find the paperwork. Maintain a list of all card numbers and the phone numbers to call in the event a card is lost or, worse, stolen.

Real Estate Documents: Closing papers, settlement sheets, deeds, and titles should be maintained in a separate file for each property. Keep copies only. The originals should be in a safety deposit box or fireproof safe. Keep in this file any documents, such as canceled checks or receipts, for work that increases the cost basis of your real estate.

Ownership Papers: Purchase records, receipts, and other items pertaining to ownership of cars, boats, or other large equipment or appliances should be maintained in separate files, with the warranties and instruction books. If something goes wrong, you know where to look.

Certainly there are lots of things in life that money won't buy, but it's very funny—have you ever tried to buy them without money?
—Ogden Nash

Employment Records: Keep information relating to employee benefits, employee contracts, and copies of W-2s. Keep the W-2s until you are able to reconcile them with Social Security benefit statements.

Tax Returns: Keep copies of your tax returns for at least seven years. The IRS in most instances has three years to audit a return, unless they suspect fraud, in which case there's no time limit.

Warranties/Service Contracts/Instruction Booklets: File warranties and service contracts along with the receipts, in case you have to return an item or have it serviced. Maintain a file for instruction booklets, which you should update as you purchase new items.

Personal Data: Originals of personal records such as birth certificates, marriage certificates, adoption papers, military service documents, and divorce decrees should be stored in a safety deposit box or a fireproof safe. Original wills and trusts are best kept in another safe place, such as your lawyer's safe. This is because safety deposit boxes are often sealed upon death. Keep copies of wills, trusts, original durable powers of attorney, and medical directives in a safe but accessible place in your home.

Monthly Bills: Monthly phone, electricity, fuel oil, gas, and grocery bills can be filed in a house or maintenance file or individually. Keep for one year and then discard. You can keep lists of your annual expenses for comparison purposes.

Pensions and IRAs: Set up a permanent file for each retirement plan. File all annual statements showing contributions, distributions, and any rollovers. If you file IRS Form 8606, which is for a nondeductible IRA, keep copies in this file as well.

Miscellaneous: Now that so many people own video cameras, videotape your home and its contents, to create a permanent record of all of your valuables. This will be helpful in the case of a robbery or a fire. Store the video in a safety deposit box or a fireproof safe. If you don't have a video of your home and its contents, keep a list of your belongings in a safe place and take pictures of your possessions. I know how tedious it can be to draw up a list but, as you've probably now discovered, you own a lot of stuff and you need to take steps to protect it.

I've been rich and I've been poor. Rich is better! —Sophie Tucker

Organizing your stuff will give you a sense of accomplishment. But what's more important is that it will be a gift to your family. I would also recommend that, as you get on in age, you hold annual family meetings to let everyone know where your stuff is located. No, not where the car keys are, but where you keep your files. Tell them if you've changed or added advisors in the last year and give them updated lists. After completing the Inventory and Location of Important Documents worksheet, make a copy for your files and then give a copy to your attorney, a family member, or a trusted friend for safekeeping.

The Bottom Line

Lots of work ahead isn't there? You really do need to take the time needed to work on the worksheets. Your net worth statement is a jumping off place, the beginning of your plan. Understanding your cash flow and how and where you spend your money will be crucial to saving and investing. You have a general idea where everything is kept but as we age our brains become so cluttered with other stuff it is easy to forget where that really safe place was that we put the insurance papers. Spend some time sorting through the maze of paperwork.

No amount of cash is ever petty.

Notes:

Sarah came up to me after a workshop recently to tell me her story. Sarah was 33 and about to close on her first house and was very excited.

When her husband walked out on her 13 years earlier he left her with a one-year-old, a two-year-old, lots of debt, and all of her dreams shattered. She was forced to file for bankruptcy and ended up on welfare for over six years, struggling to get on with her life. She managed to go back to school and care for her babies and even save a small amount of money. The only savings vehicle she was allowed while on welfare was EE savings bonds which are tucked away in a safe place to be used for college expenses for the now teenagers.

Sarah was now taking advantage of a first time homebuyer program and closing on her first home. Her payments are going to be equal to her rent so she felt she could manage this major purchase. And once I explained she would get a deduction for the interest she paid, she was delighted with the prospect of tax savings. Her immediate reaction was, "Oh, I can put more away into my 401(k)."

Sarah is walking proof that even the worst debt problems can be overcome with patience and discipline.

Chapter 4

Help! I'm Drowning in Debt!

In This Chapter

This chapter is about debt, getting out of debt and fixing the problems you may have with debt. But it's also about ways to save more to reach your goals and how to use good debt to increase your net worth, your personal bottom line.

Credit cards are a wondrous creation, allowing us to rent cars, make plane reservations, buy presents over the Internet, pay for groceries, and buy shoes. Credit cards can also tempt us, easily luring us into debt. Even my dentist accepts credit cards as a method of payment when I have my teeth cleaned.

I'm in Way over My Head

So what did your net worth and cash flow worksheets reveal about you and your spending habits? If you have a positive cash flow and net worth and have a savings plan in place, you only need to skim this chapter. If those worksheets revealed bad debt or you sense that you are getting in debt over your head, read on.

Debt can slowly creep up on you, one credit card transaction at a time. It's insidious, and it becomes almost seductive. After one of my workshops last year, one of the participants told me her story.

It's costing Americans twice as much to live beyond their means as it did ten years ago.

Sandy had graduated from college with credit card debt, and it had continued to haunt her ever since. She felt like she was in over her head. During her junior year, she started to receive pre-approved credit card applications in the mail and, for a while, just threw them away. That winter, all of her friends were planning a wonderful ski trip over Christmas. They coaxed and cajoled until she finally gave in. She used her credit card to pay for the ski trip, maxing it out at her $1,500 limit. She began to pay just the minimum due each month, which was affordable, she told herself.

Then there was the spring break trip. The lure of the beach in Florida was too tempting, so she filled out an application for another card and then maxed that one out. This continued, and when she did graduate, she had a diploma, $15,000 in school loans, and $8,000 in credit card debt—a negative net worth of $23,000.

Five years later, Sandy's credit card debt was hovering at the $8,000 mark because she had only been paying the minimum each month and was still using her credit cards to pay for vacations. She asked if I could throw her a life preserver and pull her out.

The only person who could get Sandy out of debt was Sandy, I told her. I could certainly throw her a life preserver, but she had to use it to swim back to shore. First she needed to re-evaluate her dreams and goals. To get out of debt, she was going to need to take a cold hard look at her cash flow, painful as it was. Where was her money going each month? What triggered her spending and the use of her credit card? She would need to stop the credit card abuse and make lifestyle changes to have more money each month to pay off the debt and begin to save. She had nothing saved for retirement or an emergency. All of this would take discipline on her part, but I told her that I was confident she could do it.

The following are credit card danger signs:

✔ You don't know how much you owe.

✔ You're only making minimum payments each month.

A weekly budget is just something to help you explain why the money ran out about Tuesday. —Ervin L. Glaspy

✔ You have a negative net worth.

✔ Your cards are maxed out.

✔ You're opening new accounts to pay old debt.

✔ You are worried about your debt.

✔ You have been denied credit.

✔ Your creditors have begun to call.

✔ You are hiding the truth from family members.

Good Debt vs. Bad Debt

There is good debt, and there is bad debt. When Sandy graduated, she had both. Good debt is debt used to purchase an appreciable asset—an asset that will go up in value such as a house, growing your business, or paying for an education. Educational debt is considered good debt because an education helps you further your career and improves your opportunity for a higher salary and a better life. Good debt enables you to build your net worth over time. It also enables you to purchase an asset that would take years of saving to acquire, such as a house.

Bad debt is debt used to pay for consumable purchases such as vacations, food, clothes, and gasoline, on which you proceed to only pay the minimum each month rather than paying the card balance in full each month. There may always be times in our lives when we can't pay that balance in full each month, but that should be the exception instead of the norm.

According to Bank Rate Monitor (www.bankrate.com), consumers have over $3 billion outstanding in credit card debt and are paying an average of 14.5 percent on that debt. By carrying a $3,000 balance and only making the minimum payments each month, it would take you 37 years to pay off the card, and you would have paid close to $8,000 in interest. That's a lot of money!

The trouble with the average family budget is that at the end of the money there's too much month left. —A. James Grant

However, that would all be in after-tax dollars, so you would need to earn almost $11,000 to pay off that debt if you were in the 25 percent tax bracket. Ouch! The credit card companies are making a nifty profit on the backs of the consumer. If you are carrying your credit card balance month to month, you may soon be drowning in debt. Also beware of what your minimum payment is each month. You want to be sure you are paying down some of the debt each month as well as the interest charges. The Bank Rate Monitor's website has a nifty calculator that can help you figure out how long it would take to pay down your debt.

For more information on credit cards and credit card rates, check out www.bankrate.com. Bankrate.com provides some good calculators to help you figure out how long it will take to pay off your debt as well as financial planning articles and information about mortgages as well.

Credit card companies encourage you to be a "revolver," someone who does not pay off the balance each month. Nearly 60 percent of cardholders do this, and the balance they carry each month is over $8,000. Resist the temptations (that the credit card companies dangle in front of you) to put off paying your balance in full each month.

Credit card companies make the bulk of their profits from the revolvers. As a consumer, you may be paying the credit card company an annual fee to use the card, and then you are paying monthly interest charges to carry your balance. The credit card company did pay the bill for whatever you charged, but not out of the goodness of its heart.

If you charge those new school clothes at Wal-Mart, the credit card company reimburses Wal-Mart for your purchases, and that amount goes on your bill. For the privilege of allowing the merchant, in this case Wal-Mart, to accept your credit card, the merchant must also pay a fee to the credit card company, usually 3 to 4 percent of the purchase price plus an annual fee. Furthermore, you normally have a grace period before you must pay the credit card company for those new school clothes. It is usually about 25 days, and if not paid in full, the interest begins to accrue.

Debt is the worst poverty. —Thomas Fuller

These are not the only fees credit card companies can charge. There are late fees, which can be as high as $39. And being late can cause your interest rate to increase to as high as 27 percent. If you use your card to take a cash advance at an ATM machine, the interest rate may be higher, and the clock starts to tick immediately because cash advances usually don't have a grace period. So the credit card company makes money coming and going, most of it from the consumer.

OPT–OUT Mailing List

Want to stop those unsolicited credit card offers? Under a revision of the Fair Credit Reporting Act in 1998, credit-reporting agencies are required to take your name off those pre-approved offer lists if you contact them. To permanently stop these offers you can now do it all with one phone call that will reach the three major reporting agencies, Experian, Equifax, and Trans Union. You will be required to give personal information over the phone. This number is for stopping unsolicited card offers only! 888-567-8688

Ridding Yourself of Bad Debt Without Bankruptcy

Credit card debt creates anxiety and financial chaos. It plays havoc with relationships, and if you have children, it sends them the wrong message about money management. I can try to make it simple, but not easy, for you with the following five-step program:

1. **The desire to get out of debt.** This is the most important part of this program. Lip service is not acceptable here because this is going to be hard work on your part. It's going to require lifestyle changes and the breaking of bad habits. Are you ready?

2. **Assessing just how much debt you have.** Calculating your net worth will give you a good picture of your present debt load. If you haven't done your net worth worksheet, go back to Chapter 3, "Figuring Out Your Starting Point." That will help you determine

---

An old-timer is one who remembers when you did not start to shop for Christmas until after Thanksgiving.

how much debt you have and who you owe. Now take the list and break it down further. What interest rates are you paying for each card? The most current information can be found on your card statement. You may be surprised to find that the rates have increased since you first opened your account.

3. **Devise a workable plan.** You need a plan that you can live with. Put it in writing. You'll be more committed to it. Stop using your credit cards! Call your creditors and ask if they would be willing to lower their interest rate. Tell them you are planning to transfer the balance because you can get a better deal somewhere else. Review your cash flow worksheet from Chapter 3. Where is the money going to come from each month to pay down your credit cards? What are you willing to change or give up to make the goal of being debt free happen? Start out with baby steps, paying more than the minimum each month.

   For a psychological boost, look to pay off the card with the highest interest rate first or choose the one with the lowest balance so you can eliminate that one quickly. Some individuals have found that switching balances to a lower-interest-rate card also helps. But beware! More and more card companies realize that you are rate hunting and make it difficult to get a low rate for the balance transfer. Read the fine print of any new contract you sign, even if it means getting a magnifying glass to help. Software programs, such as Intuit's Quicken and Microsoft's Money, can help you prioritize and schedule payments by using their debt reduction programs.

4. **Perform plastic surgery on all but one of your cards.** This may be painful, but look what having these cards has done to you. Get the scissors out and cut them up. Do you remember in the *Wizard of Oz* when the Wicked Witch of the West melted before your eyes and you had a sense of relief that she was gone? I promise that you'll feel the same when you cut up your cards. Next, cancel

In God we trust, all others pay cash.

those cards. Cutting them up is not enough because it is too easy to backslide, call the card company, and order a replacement card.

Before canceling, check the fine print in your contract because some card companies actually raise your interest rate if you cancel a card while carrying a balance. In this case, pay off that debt and then cancel the card.

Now, what do you do with that last card? Your wallet will not be naked without it, I promise. Leave it at home in a safe place. You choose where. Maybe you should put it in your new filing cabinet or in your underwear drawer. Put it some place where it will take an effort to retrieve it. Carrying it in your wallet makes it too easy to use if temptation rears its ugly head and starts to whisper "Buy me, buy me!" Saying that the devil made you do it is not a viable excuse here.

Consider getting a debit card because, with a debit card, you can't spend what you don't have. A debit card is connected to your checking account or money market account, and the amount of the transaction is debited directly from your account.

5. **Seek some professional help if you just can't manage it on your own.** Contact the National Foundation for Consumer Credit (NFCC). This is a national network of nonprofit organizations that provide consumer credit education, debt counseling, and debt repayment programs. Many of its members are locally managed nonprofit agencies operating under the name Consumer Credit Counseling Service (CCCS). Contact the NFCC at 800-388-2227 or visit its web site at www.nfcc.org. The CCCS deals with credit card companies every day, so they may be able to negotiate a lower interest rate or even stop the interest on your debt. Their counselors can help you set up a budget and re-establish credit. These are nonprofit organizations that provide services on a sliding scale.

There was a time when a fool and his money were soon parted, but now it happens to everybody. —Adlai E. Stevenson

The Last Resort: Bankruptcy

Bankruptcy is the last resort when you are trying to solve your debt problems. If there is absolutely no other way to handle your debt, consider bankruptcy, but it is not the panacea it is so often thought to be. For families that have suffered a job loss or illness, however, bankruptcy may be their only option to get out of the abyss of debt.

More than 1.5 million Americans filed for bankruptcy last year, which can be filed under Chapter 7 or Chapter 13. Chapter 7 bankruptcy requires that most of your possessions be sold and that your creditors be satisfied. Chapter 13 sets up a court-approved repayment plan and allows you to keep your assets. The Consumer Credit Counseling Service is able to help you assess your situation to see which course of action would be best. Beware new bankruptcy laws pending in Congress may make it tougher to walk away from credit card debt.

Bankruptcy stays on your credit history for up to 10 years and can make everything from renting an apartment to buying life insurance more difficult because you have a bankruptcy listed on your credit history. Furthermore, there are some responsibilities in your financial life that you can't wiggle out of. Bankruptcy will not wipe out your obligation to pay child support, alimony, income taxes, or the repayment of your student loans. These payments will continue after filing for bankruptcy.

Getting another credit card after filing for bankruptcy will probably be easy because credit card companies know you can't file for bankruptcy again for six years. These companies know that your debt has just been wiped away, so your cash flow will have increased. Don't go there! If you get a clean slate, keep it that way.

What Does Your Credit History Look Like?

Checking your credit history should be like getting your teeth cleaned. You want to do it every year. You may think your credit history is perfect because you have never been late or missed any of your

If you think nobody cares you are alive, just miss a couple of mortgage payments.

loan payments, but recent studies have shown that perhaps as many as 50 percent of all credit histories have errors in them. And these errors could be a problem for you.

Today, your credit history is used as a measuring tool for more than simply applying for a loan. A potential employer may ask your permission to review your credit history. This is especially true in the financial industry, and if you refuse, your ability to land the job will be in jeopardy. When you purchase life insurance, the insurance company will want to see your credit history and whether you make payments in a timely fashion. Auto insurers are also looking at your credit history and basing auto insurance rates on a person's credit history and credit score. With a tight rental market in many metropolitan areas, landlords want to see prospective tenants' credit histories. Whether you're going to be able to pay the rent or not is foremost on their minds.

> *For more information about your rights as a credit consumer check out the Federal Trade Commission's website www.ftc.gov.*

Credit cards that have never been formally cancelled will appear on your credit history as an open line of credit, even if you have not used them in years. These can potentially cause problems because, if you are applying for a loan such as a school loan or a home mortgage, they will be entered into the credit formula as debt, even though there is nothing owed on them. You still have the ability to charge them to their limit.

Another reason you want to check your credit and probably in today's environment the most important reason to check your credit history is to check for identity theft. If someone has stolen your identity and is using your Social Security number the bogus credit cards will begin to show up on your credit history. So your first line of defense is to annually check your credit history for any fraudulent activities. And while you are checking your credit history inquire about your credit score. More and more creditors are using credit scores as a measurement factor in deciding if you should get a loan and what interest rate to charge you.

Maybe one reason budgets don't work is that we only work five days a week but we spend money all seven.

There are three major reporting agencies, and they do not share information with each other, so you need to check your history from all three agencies. If you find errors, you can write to the agencies explaining the error, and they have 30 days to correct the error. Send any supporting documentation as well. You'll want to check your report again after you have sent the corrections to be sure the changes were made.

If you have been denied credit in the past 60 days, you can get a copy of your credit history for free. The cost per agency is $8 in all states except Connecticut ($5) and Maine ($3). The first copy is free in Colorado, Georgia, New Jersey, Maryland, Massachusetts, and Vermont. To get your free credit history you will find it easier to do it by snail mail. The major agencies are as follows:

Equifax
P.O. Box 740241
Atlanta, GA 30374-0241
800-685-1111
www.equifax.com

Experian
P.O. Box 2002
Allen, TX 75013
888-397-3742
www.experian.com

Trans-Union
P.O. Box 2000
Chester, PA 19022
800-888-4213
www.transunion.com

Credit is what keeps you from knowing how far past broke you are.

Credit Scores

More and more we are hearing about credit scores and how important they are. Yes indeed you should get a copy of your credit t history but you need a copy of your credit score as well. A credit score basically measures your credit worthiness by applying a formula to data supplied by the credit reporting agencies.

Credit scores are like SAT scores. The higher the number the better the score. Scores range from 300 to 850 and each reporting agency has just a little different twist on the score and data.

Each agency has contracted with a fourth company, Fair Isaac & Co. that takes the raw data from the agencies and creates scores. And theses scores can vary as much as 100 points in some case for the same consumer. You remember what 100 points meant to you on SAT score—so it is with your credit score. The highest scores get the best rates when applying for a loan or a credit card.

A good credit score is 720 and above. An excellent score is above 730 and if you hit 800 and above you are in a rare club. If your score is below 580 you will be considered a poor risk and those good rates will be a dream.

There are several factors that impact your score:

✔ **Payment history:** are you on time or always a late? Are you paying off just the minimum or do you pay it in full each month?

✔ **Current credit use:** are you maximizing your credit line? This actually is a negative. You are rewarded for not using all of your available credit line

✔ **Length of credit history:** how long have you owned the card

✔ **Total amount of debt:** how much debt do you have

✔ **Recent inquiries:** too many is not good

✔ **Credit mix:** A mortgage and credit cards is better than all credit cards

Money isn't everything—sometimes it isn't enough.

To find out your scores you can buy them directly through www.myfico.com or go to the individual reporting agencies when you are inquiring about your credit history. Beware of companies that offer to increase your score. You can do that yourself by doing the following:

✔ Make sure your credit report is accurate

✔ Pay your bills on time

✔ Limit the number of accounts you have

✔ Cancel cards you do not use, zero balances can count against you

✔ Pay off your balances

Your credit score is just as important as your credit history. Check it out!

Identity Theft

This is a crime that is on the increase. The Federal Trade Commission recently released a survey showing that 27.3 million Americans have been victims of identity theft in the last five years, including 9.9 million people in the last year alone. Some individuals don't report it to the local police department or the FTC (the Federal Trade Commission at www.ftc.gov) Yup, that's who you need to report it to, but I digress. So those numbers could be low.

According to the survey, last year's identity theft losses to businesses and financial institutions totaled nearly $48 billion and consumer victims reported $5 billion in out-of-pocket expenses. With identity theft it becomes the victim's job to repair their reputation and credit.

According to the survey results, 52 percent of all ID theft victims, approximately 5 million people in the last year, discovered that they were victims of identity theft by monitoring their accounts. Another 26 percent—approximately 2.5 million people—reported that they were alerted to suspicious account activity by companies such as credit

Money ain't everything—but it sure comes in handy when you lose your credit cards.

card issuers or banks. Eight percent reported that they first learned when they applied for credit and were turned down.

It is very easy to steal another's identity. Your name, address, Social Security number, date of birth, credit card numbers, and checking account numbers are floating around everywhere. You need to protect all of those numbers. This type of crime has been around for years. The movie, "Catch Me If you Can," really happened and it happened 30 years ago.

What should you do if you find your identity has been stolen?

1. File a police report, they may not want the paperwork or the hassle but you need to do it. Get a copy of the report in case banks, credit card companies and others need proof of the crime.

2. File a complaint with the FTC, head to the their website, www.ftc.gov or call 877-ID-THEFT (438-4338) which is a toll free number. The FTC has good information on their website on to how to handle an identity theft, a booklet entitled "Identity Theft: When Bad Things Happen to Your Good Name" and sample dispute letters to help you close all of the bogus accounts.

3. Contact the fraud departments of the three major credit-reporting agencies and report that your identity has been stolen. Ask that a fraud alert be placed on your file and that no new credit be granted without your approval.

Equifax: 800-525-6285   www.equifax.com
Experian: 888-397-3742   www.experian.com
Transunion: 800-680-7289   www.transunion.com

How to prevent identity theft:

✔ Be vigilant about your Social Security number, do not write it on your checks

✔ Shred mail and paperwork that contain your vital information

✔ Don't leave mail in your mailbox for the mail carrier to pick up

---

People do not become rich by what they earn, but by what they save.

✔ Check your credit history annually

✔ Protect your pin numbers

✔ Protect your wallet—it is full of all your important information

Credit Cards That Pay You

Credit and credit cards are financial tools. If used properly they can monetarily benefit you. For most of us we can't live in today's world without a credit card. I for one don't carry much cash and like a record of everything I purchase so I use my credit card to pay for everything I can. Even the dentist.

So if you do have credit cards make them work for you. Think about using cards that reward you. To do research on this subject I used the Goggle search engine and typed in reward credit cards and rebate credit cards. Also another source is Bank Rate Monitor's website: www.bankrate.com.

Reward cards are the ones that offer you a reward for using the card. There are gas cards, car cards where you can accumulate the dollars to use to purchase a new car, or the ability to get good stuff, like magazine subscriptions, gift certificates, and travel gear. Now in order to make this work you really have to want the stuff offered. For instance you get an LL Bean card and you can redeem your rewards for Bean merchandise. If you are going to use a reward card make sure you get one that does not have an annual fee.

Rebate cards will send you money for using their card. Normally its one percent of the annual card usage. The first kid on the block was the Discover card years ago but many cards have moved into this territory. Discover offers 1 percent but there are many other cards out there, which do better than the 1 percent. They offer a better deal if you shop at preferred merchants or shop online going through their websites. You can save for college for the kids or your own retirement. There is the www.Upromise.com, www.theeducationplan.com, and www.babymint.com all willing to put away dollars for education

Remember when you looked forward to receiving the salary you can't live on today?

planning. And for retirement there is a card, www.nesteggz.com that will actually send the rebate to a retirement plan of your choice to help you save for retirement. I like the Upromise for you don't need to get their credit card to take advantage of the college savings and you can just register your current credit cards to get the bonus. Also grandma can register her cards for the Upromise rebates.

Airline cards. These all come with a fee of some sort. Look for a card that is not linked to a particular airline for it will give you more flexibility in choosing dates to fly for there are no black out dates as there are with the direct airline cards.

If you are going to use credit make it work for you.

Creating a Spending Plan

Setting up a budget is akin to starting a diet, so we're not going to set up a budget here. Instead, we're going to set up a spending plan that allows you to spend freely whatever is left over after the essentials in your life are taken care of. However, those essentials must include a savings plan. Saving and investing must become as essential as heat and electricity. Spending plans are very individual because an item such as a gym membership may seem frivolous to one person and absolutely essential for another.

Let's begin by reviewing your cash flow. Hopefully, you have spent some time wading through it and really have a handle on where you are spending your money each month. There are your fixed costs. There is no way to get around them immediately. Maybe you can refinance your mortgage and get a lower mortgage rate. Maybe you can share your apartment with a roommate to lower your rent. However, the basics in your life are the price you pay for your lifestyle. So, unless you are willing to move, the fixed costs are what you have to work with for now. However, once we get beyond the rent/mortgage and car payment, there are areas where you can make small changes and reap big rewards in savings.

Good judgment comes from bad experience and a lot of that comes from bad judgment.

You'll need to take a closer look at each item on your cash flow statement. Is that item essential to you? Can that item be eliminated or its usage reduced in some way? For example, let's look at your utility costs. Is there a way to save money in this area of your spending plan? Can you lower the thermostat in the winter to 69 degrees and raise it in the summer when you are using the air conditioner? Do you turn off lights and fans that aren't being used? If your water is metered, do you have leaky faucets, do you water your lawn daily, take long showers, or run the water while brushing your teeth? Small changes on your part can turn into immediate savings. Tackle the telephone bill next. Where can you make changes? Can you e-mail your friends or look into a lower-cost long-distance carrier? Do you need all of the features you currently have? Do you see where I'm going with this?

Do this with each item in your cash flow list. If you analyze it, you may find some easy ways to make an immediate impact on your savings. Be ruthless. Stopping for coffee and a bagel each morning at Dunkin' Donuts can prove expensive over time. It's $1.50 for the coffee and $1 for the bagel. Every day for a week would equal $12.50, which translates to $50 a month and $600 a year. Of course you need your coffee, but can you make it at home and carry a thermos with you to work? Can you buy bagels by the dozen, keep them in the freezer, and pop one into the toaster in morning? Now you'll have to purchase the coffee beans and the bagels, but this small lifestyle change could save you over $450 a year. Those dollars can go to pay down debt or go into your retirement plan, and if we assume a 9 percent return in 20 years, it could be worth $25,000, in 30 years it could be worth $62,000. Small change does add up!

> *The Ouch Factor: Popular thinking has it that, to benefit from a new fitness regime, you must do it until it hurts. I don't believe in doing anything until it hurts, and that includes exercise, dieting, and budgeting. Be sure to budget some money for fun things and to occasionally reward yourself for sticking to your budget.*

If you are sharing your life with someone, budgeting and saving should be done together. You'll keep each other on your toes. One area

---

Experience is something you don't get until just after you need it.

that usually produces immediate results is reviewing the food items. Yes, you still need to buy groceries and eat, but do you need to eat out or stop and pick up dinner so often? Close to 50 percent of every dollar we spend on food is for restaurants or take out. Eat at home more and pack your lunches. You'll eat healthier and save money—not a bad combination. I guarantee that making small changes in how and where you spend money will demonstrate big results, but all of this will take time and energy on your part. You will need to expend the time to produce the savings. A web site that finds the best deals in nine categories of recurring bills, including utilities and insurance, is: www.lowermybills.com.

Next look at how much you need to save and invest to achieve your goals. Do you want to contribute 10 percent to your retirement plan, 2 percent to your emergency fund, and 3 percent to the college fund for the kids? Your 401(k) contribution can be deducted from your paycheck pretax. You won't see it, and you won't miss it. Start by contributing 1 or 2 percent. Then every couple of months, increase the contribution until you reach your goal of 10 percent. Set up an automatic investment or savings plan for the emergency fund and college fund. Again, start with a small amount and increase it as cash becomes available. Also whenever you get a raise share it with your retirement plan. For example you get a 4 percent increase, increase your retirement plan contribution level by 2 percent.

Painless Ways to Save

This has been a tough chapter to struggle through. I promise the rest is easier after this. This chapter requires a lot of work on your part, work that will continue every day of your life because I've asked you to change your habits and perhaps those of your family. They like eating out at McDonald's and getting the Happy Meal toys, and you're going to have to say no and appear to be the bad guy on occasion—not an easy thing to do.

It's so easy to be wise. Just think of something stupid to say, then don't say it.

The savings chart below will give you some idea as to what your savings can do for you in the future. I chose a 9 percent return, which is moderately aggressive, and a 20-year time span. If you invest your savings in your 401(k) plan or if you use one of the new 529 college

Ways To Save

Old Way	New Way	Annual Savings	Invested in a college savings plan (529) or retirement plan for 20 years & assumes a 9% return
Carrying $3,000 credit card debt at 18%	Paying the bill off in full monthly	$540	$30,000
Buying 2 bottles of water daily: **$1 each**	Purchase at a discount store: **25 cents**	$548	$31,000
McDonald's weekly outing for a family 2 Happy meals, 2 Big Mac value meals: **$14.50**	Hamburgers, baked potatoes, milk, salads & cookies at home: **$6**	$442	$25,000
Dinner for two adults with fancy wine: **$60**	Dinner at home with cheap wine: **$14**	$2,400	$133,000
Cigarettes — 2 packs a day: **$4.50 a pack**	Hard to do, but give it up! **$0**	$3,300	$183,000
Movie tickets, popcorn & soda for two adults: **$23**	Video, popcorn & soda at home: **$5**	$936	$54,000
Gym membership: **$90/month**	Running shoes and free weights: **$190**	$890	$49,000
Lunch out: **$7**	Lunch from home: **$2.60**	$1,100	$63,000
Chinese take out for 4 with fortune cookies: **$36**	Chinese dinner at home, no fortune cookies: **$10**	$1,350	$75,000
Car wash: **$7**	Car washed at home: **50 cents**	$338	$19,000
Shirts at dry cleaners: **$1 each**	Home laundry: **10 cents each**	$234	$13,000
Dunkin' Donuts coffee & bagel: **$2.65**	Dunkin' Donuts coffee brewed at home & a bagel from the freezer: **60 cents**	$492	$25,000
		TOTAL SAVINGS	*$700,000*

The younger we are, the more we want to change the world. The older we are, the more we want to change the young.

savings plans that allow the money to grow tax deferred for the kids, you can see what some small changes can produce over time. Instead of heading to McDonald's twice a week, cut it back to once a week, and you could have $25,000 in the college fund. I'm not asking you to give up your bottled water. Just shop for it smarter and buy it in bulk, and you'll have $31,000 in your retirement nest egg. Make small changes in your lifestyle, and it will add up over time to more than small change!

The Bottom Line

Debt can be a tool to help you achieve your dreams of home ownership, starting a business or a college education for yourself or your kids. But debt if used improperly can really mess up those same dreams. If you have "bad" debt make every effort to get it under control before it takes control of you. Remember "good" debt helps you increase your bottom line!

Ginger Rogers did everything Fred Astaire did, but she did it backwards and in high heels.

ancy wanted to know if she and her husband had accumulated enough assets so that they could be assured a comfortable retirement. Her husband retired at age 62 last year and started to collect his Social Security benefits. Nancy is still working. After raising the children she went back to work and was hoping to hit the 20-year mark so she could collect a larger pension from her employer. Her job also provides the health insurance they need because you cannot apply for Medicare until you are 65 years old. That they found out after Kevin retired and went to apply for Social Security and Medicare. So if she were to also retire they would need to purchase health insurance until they were both eligible for Medicare.

Nancy has been recently diagnosed with a chronic illness that could eventually leave her disabled. But she wants to continue to work to get that larger pension and Kevin wants her to retire now so that she'll have some time to enjoy the fruits of their years of work and saving. Kevin is also concerned about being the caregiver, a role he never thought anything about until Nancy's illness. The vows we take when we marry, "in sickness or in health" mean little more to us at that time than bringing someone chicken soup when they have the flu. Growing old just quietly creeps up on us.

Nancy and Kevin asked for some help with their financial planning. They think they have done a good job of picking stocks and have used a buy and hold strategy that has worked very well for them. They figure they want an after tax income in retirement of $65,000. Part of that will come from their pensions but the rest will need to come from their portfolio. So questions have come up in retirement that they should have planned for earlier they told me. Should they be thinking about selling their stocks and buying mutual funds and living off the distributions they asked.

A bigger issue they had was long-term care insurance. Should that be on their radar screen they wondered. Growing old ain't for sissies they told me. They're right! And neither is planning for the unexpected. But that's what Nancy and Kevin have started to think about and in doing so have acknowledged one of the most often overlooked components of the financial planning process—insurance.

Chapter 5

Protecting Yourself and Your Assets: Buying Insurance

In This Chapter

This chapter is all about learning how to be a smart consumer when buying insurance. Insurance is a financial product that we use to protect our assets and our dependents if we are not around to provide for them.

You're now ready to begin learning about the five areas of financial planning. The first is risk management, which is a fancy term for using insurance.

Insurance is risk protection. Insurance is all about protecting your assets from catastrophic happenings such as death, fire, floods, disabilities, and illness. You purchase insurance to cover a possible risk that may never occur and that you hope will never occur. Most people hate to buy insurance because they think its just money thrown away. They are buying a financial product that they are hoping never to use. To collect on the insurance, something bad must happen.

According to Webster's dictionary, "risk" is the possibility of loss, injury, or damage and includes the probability of such a loss. Risk management, then, is an understanding of these probabilities, such as the chance that you may be involved in a car accident or become disabled and never work again in your chosen profession. Recognizing

---

The safest way to double your money is to fold it over and put it in your pocket. —Kin Hubbard

and understanding your risks is the first step in your risk-management program. Next, you'll need to evaluate the risk and decide how to manage it.

Managing Everyday Risks

There are four ways to manage risk: avoid, control, transfer, or retain.

✔ **Avoiding risk.** This may seem simplistic, but it certainly is the best way to deal with risk. You don't cross the street against the light, you don't drive in a blizzard, you don't build your house on the river's edge, and you don't let your kids play with matches.

✔ **Controlling risk.** This requires a bit more work. You must take measures to reduce the possibility of loss. If you do drive in a blizzard, you have a four-wheel-drive vehicle, four good snow tires, and air bags to protect you. Having smoke and heat detectors in your home to alert you to a fire and give your family enough time to get to safety is another example of controlling risk.

✔ **Transferring risk.** This is what you do when you purchase insurance; you allow the insurance company to assume the financial liability of a loss that you cannot afford on your own. The loss of your home could financially devastate you, so you transfer that financial risk by paying the insurance company a fee (the premium) to assume the risk for you.

✔ **Retaining risk.** This is accepting responsibility for some or all of the risk. Most common is the use of deductibles. By using deductibles, you agree to self-insure the small claims. If you skid in your own driveway during a blizzard and hit your snow blower, causing $475 worth of damage to your front bumper with a $500 deductible, you would pay for the damage yourself. Co-insurance and elimination periods are also ways to retain risk. There are instances in which we choose to self-insure. For example, if you have six months' worth of living expenses set aside, you may

---

Yogi Berra's observation of the nation's economy: "A nickel ain't worth a dime anymore."

choose to purchase only long-term disability insurance because you have enough in assets to cover a short-term disability.

Insurance can be a complicated product to purchase because you are entering into a contract with an insurance company that only wants to pay out on a claim under certain circumstances. To properly protect yourself and all that you love, you need to learn to read the fine print of those contracts.

What Kind of Insurance Do You Need?

Insurance is a financial product that we buy to protect our families and ourselves. No more, no less. So, why is it that so many of us are underinsured? We all need insurance coverage of some kind. The obstacle is often the insurance company or the insurance salesperson. They can be tough to deal with. However, this is a product you need, so learn as much about it as you can. In addition, when shopping for insurance, you need to decide how much of the risk you want to transfer to the insurance company and how much risk you can afford to retain yourself.

Insurance products, insurance companies, and insurance agents are regulated by individual states. To find out what state agency is regulating insurance in your state, go to the web site of the National Association of Insurance Commissioners (NAIC) at www.naic.org and click on your state.

The basics of insurance are easy: Insure yourself against catastrophe and self-insure the small stuff yourself. If you have anyone who depends on you and needs your income for support, you need life insurance. That's the big stuff. Buying an extended warranty on your TV, on the other hand, is an example of the small stuff you can handle yourself; so don't bother to buy it. Beware that many insurance companies are denying insurance to individuals who file several claims over a short time frame. During a storm a tree falls on your

Money would be more enjoyable if it took people as long to spend it as it does to earn it. —Ed Howe

deck and damages furniture worth $700 and your deductible is $500, I would suggest that you not bother to file a claim.

The rest of this chapter is devoted to helping you wade through the basics of the various types of insurance you will need at some point in your lifetime.

Health Insurance

We all need health insurance. Gone are the days when my grandfather could barter with the local doctor and keep him in potatoes all winter for delivering my twin uncles. The first thing you are asked about when you enter an emergency room is your insurance, not where does it hurt. So we've established that everyone needs health insurance. However, not everyone has it, and many young adults just starting out think it is an expense they can forego. Wrong! Your health is part of the big stuff you need to insure.

There are three types of health insurance available for most of us today:

✔ **Health maintenance organizations (HMOs).** These are organizations of healthcare personnel and facilities that provide a broad range of benefits on a prepaid basis. They are the most common delivery system of healthcare today, with many variations. The two most common are the group practice model and the individual practice association. In a group practice model, the HMO hires or contracts with physicians and other healthcare professionals to provide medical treatment at a central facility. With an individual practice association, on the other hand, the HMO contracts with individual physicians who treat HMO members in their neighborhood offices. HMOs can be very restrictive, and all of your referrals must come from your primary care physician.

✔ **Preferred Provider Organizations (PPOs).** These generally manage healthcare benefits through a predetermined network, a group of doctors, hospitals, and other healthcare providers that have agreed to provide services at specially negotiated rates under

Old insurance salesmen never die—they just lose their premiums.

contract with an insurance company. Enrollees in a PPO can choose a network based on their geographic location. Most doctor visits and prescriptions have a modest co-payment. Benefits are reduced if an out-of-network healthcare provider or facility is used.

✔ **Indemnity plans.** These can be purchased individually or by a business as a group plan. They are, in essence, a plan that reimburses you for your medical expenses. They usually have a deductible, which is the amount you pay, and those deductibles are increasing. After you have met the deductible each year, the plan will reimburse you for 80 percent of your costs.

No matter what type of health insurance your employer offers or you have purchased on your own, read the fine print of the contract and know what services are covered. How long are your kids covered on your policy—until they reach 18 or until they are finished with college? Are your stepchildren covered if they live with you? If both you and your spouse have health insurance, which policy covers the kids? Is there a lifetime limit on your coverage, meaning that, if there is a catastrophic illness, will your insurer continue to pay the bills? Some insurers stop coverage at $250,000. If you are switching policies, are you covered immediately by the new policy for pre-existing conditions? For example, if your son has asthma and is a regular visitor to the emergency room, will that be covered? And here's a biggy that I have seen undermine many financial plans of young couples; Does your policy include maternity care?

The best way to cut your health insurance costs is to stay healthy and practice preventive medicine. Exercise, eat well, take a multivitamin, stop smoking, and get enough sleep. These practices won't prevent everything, but you'll know you are doing something to help the bottom line. To find out more about your health insurance and physician, check out www.healthgrades.com. To get quotes for health insurance, check out www.ehealthinsurance.com or www.healthaxis.com.

Inflation is when you never had anything, and now even that's gone.

Disability Insurance

Disability insurance is used to cover the loss of your income if you should become disabled. That sounds simple enough, doesn't it? Do you need it? Yup, you do. If you are in a car accident and are out of work for six months, who or what is going to pay the bills? If you can tell me someone will take care of you forever should you become disabled, you don't need to read further. Perhaps you are relying on your spouse's income to support you during a disability. For the rest of you, start shopping for disability insurance.

This is a difficult call for workers because the odds are small that you will become disabled, but it can happen. Short-term disabilities are easy to self-insure. If you break your leg in a car accident, you may be out of work for six weeks, not six months. If you have two weeks of sick time, you'll only need to dip into your savings for four weeks of living expenses before you're back to work.

However, what if it's more serious? What if you have a broken back as well as the broken leg, and you need six months in a rehab facility so you can walk and drive again? Where will the dollars come from to cover your expenses? This is not a scare tactic, although that is not beneath me as a planner. I want to present the whole picture to you.

If you are permanently disabled, Social Security does kick in with some long-term benefits, but the dollar amounts are very small. The average Social Security disability benefit for 2003 is $833 and if you are married with one or more children the benefit would be $1,395.

> If you pay the disability insurance premiums and incur a disability, the benefit you receive is free of income taxes. If your disability insurance is part of the benefits package at work and your employer pays the premium, the benefits you receive during a disability are taxable income to you.

Okay, you're convinced. Now, where to get the coverage? Check with the benefits department at work for group disability insurance offered through your employer. That is going to be the cheapest insurance you'll find available to you. Do you need both short-term and long-term? Maybe not. If you are married and your spouse's income

---

You know inflation is out of hand when piggy banks cost more than they hold.

could cover family expenses for three months, or if you followed the advice in Chapter 3 and you have an emergency fund set up with three months' worth of living expenses, you may not need short-term disability insurance. It's the long-term coverage you really need. It usually kicks in after 90 or 180 days, so figure how long you and your family can make it without any of your income coming in.

Disability insurance only insures you for 45 to 70 percent of your income, and there may be some income caps as well. The insurance company wants you to return to work, and if you were receiving 100 percent of your income as a benefit, there may be no incentive on your part to try to return to work.

If you can't get insurance through your employer, consider getting it on your own. Find an insurance agent you trust and ask him or her to do some research for you. If an agent sells you a policy, he or she does earn a commission on the sale. Disability insurance can be hard to find and expensive for individual policies. Use the Internet to do some research on your own as well and when considering a policy look to the larger insurance companies that have more experience with disability insurance.

Property and Casualty Insurance

You need property and casualty insurance to protect the tangible assets you own—your home and its contents, cars, boats, your vacation home, and so on. It normally covers for loss, medical costs, and liability. Even if you live in an apartment, you'll want to insure your stuff to protect against loss or theft. Your landlord will have insurance on the building but not on your stuff.

Homeowner's Insurance

Your home may be the largest asset you'll ever own, and it is critical to protect it with insurance. Sure, you need to practice the other modes of risk management such as avoiding loss and controlling loss, but if there is a tornado, you want to have insurance because you cannot

---

In the old days the biggest deduction from a man's pay envelope took place after he got home.

move your home out of the path of a funnel cloud. This section is devoted to homeowners, but even if you are a renter, you need to have coverage to protect your possessions. Depending on where you live in the United States, your insurance needs will be different. If you live in California, you'll want earthquake insurance; if you are in Florida, you'll want to be covered for floods and hurricanes. If your home is

If you live in a designated flood area, be sure you have flood insurance. According to the Federal Insurance Administration, less than a third of homeowners in those areas are properly insured for floods. Don't be one of them. A designated flood area could be an area around a creek that floods every hundred years or so.

damaged or destroyed, you'll want to be able to rebuild. Read your policy carefully and ask a lot of questions.

There are several basic types of homeowner's insurance:

✔ **HO1.** This is basic and inexpensive insurance with limited coverage, naming the perils it will cover such as fire or lightening, windstorms or hail, smoke damage, explosion, riot or civil commotion, vehicles, aircraft, theft, vandalism or malicious mischief, damage by glass that is a part of a building, and damage due to a volcanic eruption. No, I did not include that to see if you were paying attention. That's part of the coverage, but after a volcanic eruption, I doubt there would be much left to repair.

✔ **HO2.** This expands HO1 and adds things such as weight of snow and ice, electrical damage due to surges and appliance malfunctioning, and heating or air conditioning damage. It is still limiting.

✔ **HO3.** This is the most widely purchased type of homeowners insurance. It covers all risks and perils of HO1 and HO2 on buildings and specified risks on personal property. There are several major exclusions: flood, earthquake, war, and nuclear accidents. And more and more we are seeing mold as an exclusion or it is limited to a dollar amount of coverage.

Banks will lend you money if you can prove you don't need it.
—Mark Twain

✔ **HO4.** This policy is for renters and covers risks to personal property only, not the physical property.

✔ **HO5.** Provides even broader coverage than HO3 and is much more expensive and difficult to find.

✔ **HO6.** Provides coverage for condominium owners only. It covers personal property and loss of use and the inside structures of the condominium. The building structure is covered by insurance that the condominium association must purchase.

✔ **HO7.** This is for older homes that may be in the historic district of a city.

You want to be insured for at least 80 percent of the replacement cost of your home. If it is totally destroyed and you are not properly insured, the insurance company does not have to reimburse you in full for the loss.

Also, be sure you have a replacement-cost provision, which compensates you for the full cost of replacement or repair of damaged or destroyed property without any deduction for depreciation. For example, if the pipes in an upstairs bathroom burst one winter while you are at Disney World, the bathroom lands in the kitchen, and you need to replace the kitchen appliances, you'll want to be fully reimbursed for the new appliances. Without this provision, the insurance company adjuster will estimate what your 10-year-old appliances were worth when the pipes burst and will reimburse you only that amount.

> *Owning a big dog could increase your insurance costs. Owning a big dog with a history of biting could have your insurance company refusing coverage. The breeds deemed to be the most dangerous are Rottweilers, Dobermans, Pit Bulls, Presa Canarios, Chows and wolf hybrids.*

Now look at your net worth statement. (I told you it would be important.) Do you have antiques, a stamp collection, or very good jewelry? Do you know what they are worth? Have you had them

An economist is a person who talks about things you don't understand and makes you believe it's your own fault.

appraised? You want to be sure that everything you own is properly insured. (Your basic HO3 will limit the dollar amount paid to you if there is a loss.) These articles need special coverage in the form of a floater/rider/endorsement that is attached to your homeowner policy.

> More and more of us are working out of our homes these days. If you're one of them, let your insurance company know. You want to be insured if your office equipment is stolen or damaged. A rider to your homeowner's policy will cover you.

It's not very expensive to add to the policy. And it's a good idea, no matter how anal it sounds, to keep the receipts for items you have bought in a fireproof place along with a home video of your home's contents.

Auto Insurance

You can't register a car in most states unless you have auto insurance. This really does protect you. Yes, it is a budget buster to have to pay auto insurance annually, but you don't want to drive without it. Your auto insurance covers injury to you and your passengers, your legal liabilities if you are in accident, medical costs and property damage.

Auto insurance is broken down into two parts: compulsory and optional (that is, what you have to have and the extras you can purchase). If possible, you want more than compulsory because, if you are injured or have injured anyone else, you will wish at that moment you had spent the extra bucks. Auto insurance is regulated by your state insurance commissioner, and as any of you who have lived in more than one state know, each state places different requirements and rates on auto insurance.

Shop around for the best deal. If you are a member of AAA, you are eligible for discounts. If you have taken drivers' education courses, you are eligible for a discount. And as always, know what you are purchasing! Check out www.quickeninsurance.com and www.insure.com for comparative rates.

"I know inflation is really here. I dropped a dollar bill the other day and was arrested for littering."

Umbrella Liability Insurance

If you have purchased homeowners or auto insurance, you have some liability coverage. If you are liable for an accident (you cause it) and someone decides to sue you, this part of your insurance kicks in. But what if the person decides to sue for $1 million and the maximum coverage on your auto insurance is $300,000? Where does the rest of the money come from if the jury decides in the other person's favor? From your assets! And your future wages can be garnished as well.

Sadly, umbrella liability coverage is needed in our world today. This insurance is purchased in face amounts of $1 to $5 million. This is a *Cover Your Assets* (CYA) type of insurance. As the image of an umbrella implies, it does cover you when your other coverage is not enough. So if you get sued for $1 million because of negligence in a car accident, $300,000 less your deductible would come from your auto insurance, and the rest would come from your umbrella policy.

We live in a society in which people are sued for frivolous reasons, and worse, juries often award exorbitant damages. Do you remember the woman who sued McDonald's for $8 million and won? She bought a coffee and proceeded to place it between her bare legs as she drove off. She claims there was no warning that the coffee was hot! So what can you do? Be sure you are adequately protected. Review your lifestyle. Do you have a dog that sometimes nips, a snowmobile, a speedboat that your kids can take out on the lake, a business in your home with clients or employees coming and going? If so, you may need the added protection of an umbrella policy. A $1 million policy can be had for less than $300 in annual premiums.

Life Insurance

Life insurance is an awkward subject to discuss because it also means discussing death. Frankly, there is no way any of us are getting out of this world alive. We just don't know when it will happen. With that in mind, you really need to plan as if you might die tomorrow when assessing your life insurance needs. This may all sound morbid, but you need to be practical and pragmatic here.

I think I've finally pinpointed when we lost control of our economy. It was when we discovered that fifty weeks of work couldn't pay for a two-week vacation.

Life insurance is a financial product that should be used to protect against the loss of your future income stream for your dependents. The protection is to cover the risk of your dying. Today, however, life insurance is sold for many other reasons as well. It can be used as a way to leave an inheritance for your children or to protect a business should a partner die. Here, however, we're primarily interested in protecting your dependents.

Let's determine how much life insurance you need. There are a lot of simple methods that insurance salesmen use. It might be eight times your present income or $100,000 of insurance per dependent. See if you can be a bit more precise. Look at your net worth. What do you have in assets that would be available for your spouse and children to use should something happen to you? How much life insurance do you have through your employer? Do you have young children that will need childcare? Do you have an emergency fund to meet any short-term cash needs that may occur immediately after your death? For example, this might include the cost of a funeral, for which, conservatively, you'll need at least $6,000.

Next, review your cash flow. If you're married, could your family survive without your income? Do you know what your spouse's earning potential is over the next 20 years? How much does it take to maintain the family's lifestyle? Take a good hard look at those numbers.

Recently Social Security sent you a benefits statement that contained your Social Security benefits along with the survivor benefits for your children should you die. Find it! Call Social Security (800-772-1213) or visit their web site at www.socialsecurity.gov to find out what your family will receive in benefits if you should die. This monthly benefit will replace part of the loss of your income.

If you do not pay into Social Security, the state, county, or federal government retirement plan you belong to has a benefits program for your dependents should something happen to you. Part of your planning process should be to know what these benefits are and to put the information in your master file.

An economist is a fortuneteller with a job.

When purchasing insurance, there are some decisions you need to make. Do you want the mortgage paid off with the life insurance proceeds? Do you want to finance the kids' college education?

Now, get ready to do some math or to get some help from your insurance agent, who should be willing to do a needs analysis for you. There is also an Insurance Needs worksheet in the Appendix that will require you to do the math. What would your family's expenses be for the next year following your death including the funeral expenses? What are the long-term expenses the family will face, such as college funding? If you have two kids and you want to send them to a state school, it could cost $75,000 for each of them in 10 years. The mortgage may be $100,000. This alone adds up to $250,000 that you may need covered when you die. Then there is the income you provide minus the Social Security benefit your family will receive. Multiply that annual number by as many years as your family will need it. For example, it could be $22,000 times 13 years, which adds up to another $286,000. So, in rough numbers, you would need $500,000 of life insurance. Now, if you can't afford that much insurance, you begin to look at how your family could live differently once you are gone. Does your spouse downsize and sell the house? Do the kids pay for their own education?

> *To get more help in figuring out how much life insurance you need, check out the following web sites: www.youdecide.com, www.quickeninsurance.com, and www.msn.com or head to the Appendix to use the Insurance Needs worksheet.*

Term Insurance

There are two basic types of life insurance available to you: term and cash value. Term is pure insurance, and cash value offers insurance and a savings program.

Term insurance offers a death benefit—and nothing more—for a specific time frame referred to as the term. This is the least expensive life insurance available when you are young, and as you age, the premiums increase. Term insurance is well suited for short-term needs such mortgage protection, getting the kids through college, or until

---

President Harry S. Truman used to quip that he was looking for a one-armed economist, one who never could say, "On the one hand this, but on the other hand that."

the at-home spouse returns to work. Term insurance is easy to purchase, and you can get quotes via the Internet.

Term insurance is available in several forms. You can purchase a one-year term policy, and the following year the premium will increase. Today, however, level-term policies are available that allow you to contract with the insurance company for 5-, 10-, 15-, and 20-year policies. You pay for the insurance on an annual basis. A decreasing-term policy is also available and is often used as mortgage insurance because the amount of insurance needed decreases every year. Don't bother with it! Purchase a regular term policy because you'll want to cover more than just the mortgage if you were to die.

I am of the opinion that most people do not need anything but pure insurance, and term will suffice nicely. However, when purchasing term, you want to keep in mind that, after the term is up, you may not be considered insurable if during the 10 years you survived cancer or a heart attack and would like to continue your insurance. As we get older, our families grow, our net worth increases, our responsibilities lessen, and our need for life insurance protection also lessens. For quotes on term insurance, check out www.quickeninsurance.com, www.insure.com, and www.insweb.com.

Cash Value Insurance

Cash value insurance also comes in a variety of forms. It is more expensive than term insurance because it offers a forced savings or investment component as well as insurance. The savings component grows tax deferred, and it takes 20 years or longer to realize a substantial savings component, the cash value.

In later years, you can use the cash value to pay future premiums, or you can borrow against it. If you choose not to repay the loan, your death benefit will be reduced by the amount of the loan. If you cancel your insurance contract and have any

> *If you own your own life insurance and you die, the proceeds will go to your designated beneficiary but become a part of your taxable estate. If your spouse or children own the policy, the proceeds go to them and is not considered part of your taxable estate.*

I'm living so far beyond my income that we may almost be said to be living apart.

accumulated cash value, it will be returned to you. There are three types of cash value insurance available:

✔ **Whole life.** A whole life policy is the most traditional cash value policy, and it has been around for a long time. It's a product designed to cover you for your "whole" life. It will pay the face value of your policy to your beneficiaries at the time of your death. You also build up savings over the years that you own the policy. The savings rate is very low.

✔ **Universal life.** This is a variation of whole life insurance became popular when interest rates were very high, and it was offered as an alternative to the low interest that whole life policies paid.

✔ **Variable life.** Still another version of whole life that allows you to invest the cash value portion of your policy in specific stock, bond, or money market portfolios. The owner of the policy makes the investment decisions, and your cash value is determined by how well the investment choices perform.

> *Don't get caught in a "churning" scheme. Unscrupulous agents will churn your insurance policies by suggesting a new cash value life insurance policy to replace your old one, not because you need a different policy but because they get a hefty commission for new business.*

Long-Term Care Insurance

It's important to understand that long-term care is not just nursing home care. It's not just for the elderly either, although as we age, we become more likely to need this kind of care. Christopher Reeve is an example of someone young needing long-term care, but it is a rare occurrence.

Long-term care insurance may be an important part of your risk management program. Do you need it? It will be a personal lifestyle decision because there are no fancy formulas with which to figure out whether you need this type of protection. In the latest census, about

---

Life insurance is a great thing. It's the only way we have of being remembered after we are gone. The extent of your memory depends on how long the money lasts.

1.5 million of our elderly population lived in nursing homes. That's only 4.5 percent of the population age 65 and older. Of that number, almost three fourths were women. The number of elders in nursing homes has been declining, so the odds are small that you'll ever need this type of insurance. Nevertheless, read on.

Nursing homes are very expensive. According to the AARP, the average cost nationwide is close to $55,000 annually, and both the West and East coasts have a higher average of $75,000 a year. That's almost $206 a day. Now I know that sounds very expensive and it is for you can get a very nice hotel room for $206 a night and probably chocolate on your pillow as well. Hear me out here! Alaska has the highest LTC cost in the nation. According to a survey done by GE Capital the average annual cost is $163,400. After a couple of years there you could buy the nursing home! Another little tidbit, Alaska has the smallest number of people over 65—only 36,000.

The government encourages you to purchase long-term care insurance because it would like to get out of the business of funding long-term care through the Medicaid program. Part of the cost of the premium is treated as a medical expense and is deductible if you are over age 40. The older you are the larger the amount you can deduct.

Many middle-class Americans try to make themselves appear to be poor so that they would qualify for the Medicaid program, but from my experience, it's not worth it. If you are a gambling person think of the odds, less than 5 percent. If you have assets over $100,000 and own a home, buy the insurance. It's really cheap protection. And if your kids are worried about you losing your home because of nursing home expenses let them pay the premiums for you.

If you are struggling to make ends meet in retirement, living on your Social Security benefits and a small pension, you don't need to struggle to pay for the insurance because the government will take care of your long-term nursing needs through the Medicaid program.

For more information on long-term care, check out the AARP's web site at www.aarp.org. Get their publication, "Long-Term Care Insurance—To Buy Or Not To Buy" (D17186). Write to AARP Fulfillment

Judge your success by what you had to give up in order to get it.

at 601 E St. West, Washington, D.C. 20049. You also can find help at the Health Insurance Association of America's web site at www.hiaa.org.

Another good resource is *The Complete Idiot's Guide to Long Term Care Insurance* by Marilee Driscoll.

The Bottom Line

Annual insurance costs for the various kinds of insurance you need takes a big chunk out of your budget each year. A smart financial consumer needs to figure out their insurance needs and then shop for the insurance.

We could learn a lot from crayons: some are sharp, some are pretty, some are dull, some have weird names, and all are different colors . . . but they all have to learn to live in the same box.

*M*arian was determined to learn all about this financial stuff she told me. She had not really thought too much about financial planning until her new roommate moved in.

Marian is almost 30, teaches school and loves her job. She knew there might be a financial trade-off when she chose a career in teaching over working for corporate America when she graduated from college. But she thought with the extra vacation time and summers off it more than compensated for the lower pay scale. She was also somewhat aware that down the road there would be a pension if she stayed long enough in teaching.

And she was feeling very good about being smart enough to start saving for retirement using a 403(b) eight years ago and averaging $2,000 a year in contributions. She is proud of the fact that she no longer uses credit cards to supplement her income. Her only debt she told me was a school loan that will be paid off very soon. She also coaches sports so that brings in extra income and she received some savings bonds and stocks from her grandmother recently.

So life was good until her new roommate challenged her thinking about the future. Marian is now wondering if she should take a summer job where she can earn an extra $7,000 a year? Should she be contributing more money to a different 403(b) plan? And should she be thinking about buying a house and using Grandma's gift as a down payment?

All these questions have tax implications that Marian will need to understand and fully consider before choosing from her options.

Chapter 6

Pay Only What's Due Uncle Sam, No More!

In This Chapter

Taxes! A subject you only want to face once a year. But in this chapter you're going to learn that good tax planning is done all year.

"In this world, nothing is certain but death and taxes," wrote Benjamin Franklin in 1789. Not much has changed since then, has it? By taking good care of ourselves and wearing our seatbelts, we may be able to outwit death until we are very old. But taxes, well, they're like that little pink bunny—they just keep going and going and going. Congress is always tweaking them, dropping this tax, creating that tax, and they do it annually. So the tax planning that works for this year may not work for next year. You, as the taxpayer, must assume the responsibility of keeping abreast of tax law changes. We have had major tax law changes in 1997, 2001 and 2003. Each change has affected you and your planning.

You can't escape paying taxes unless you are very poor, and I don't want you to be very poor. I'd rather you were in a high tax bracket and paid lots of taxes because you would be making lots of money. Taxes are the price we pay to live in a civilized nation. And we do live in the best country in the world. Trust me on that one! We may rant and rave

---

Too bad you can't invest in taxes—they are the only thing sure to go up.

about our tax system and our government, but given the alternatives, I'm staying right here. The rest of this chapter will be about tax planning and learning what you can do legally to minimize your tax consequences.

Understanding Your Tax Bracket

The more you make, the more they take. Our tax system is based on a graduated tax, but moving into the next tax bracket does not mean that all of your income is now taxed at the higher rate. Only the additional income you earn above your current base will be affected by the higher bracket.

Your marginal tax bracket is the percentage in taxes you pay on each additional dollar earned above your base bracket. This is the rate you pay on the last dollar you earned for the year. If your new raise pushes you into the 28 percent tax bracket, don't turn down the raise because you don't want to pay the extra taxes. If your new raise puts you into the 28 percent bracket, only income above the 25 percent base will be taxed at the higher tax rate of 28 percent. Some of your income is taxed at each of the rates below the 28 percent bracket. Currently our tax rates are, 10, 15, 25, 28, 33, and 35 percent. They are scheduled to remain in effect through 2010. Now I am not making any promises here for every time we have a change at the White House we have a change in the tax laws.

The more money you make, the more you pay in taxes—this is a sorry fact of life. Some of this is due to the fact that the tax brackets increase as your income increases. In addition, you lose some of your tax advantages, such as exemptions for dependents or deductions, that are phased out as your income increases.

Now, if the state you live in also taxes your income—and most states do—add that tax rate in when you're planning. And you do need to do tax planning because, if you do not have enough taxes withheld from your paycheck or pay enough in estimated taxes, the IRS will penalize you, as will your state income tax division. There are

Put a good tax on beer and that would take care of the unemployment fund. —Will Rogers

seven tax-free states: Alaska, Florida, Nevada, South Dakota, Washington, and Wyoming.

If you are in the 25 percent marginal tax bracket for federal taxes and you live in a state that has a 5 percent income tax, your combined marginal tax rate is 30 percent. If your certificate of deposit has earned $1,000 for the year, your tax liability for the CD will be $300. So don't run out and spend your $1,000 because Uncle Sam has his hand out for his share, leaving you just $700 to spend.

The dollar amounts at which tax brackets occur change every year because they are indexed for inflation. The minute I put them here in the book, they will be outdated. As a taxpayer, you should at least understand what you are paying in taxes. You don't have to be able to quote tax code here; just know where to find the information when you need it. As you earn more income, your taxes may become too taxing (that's a pun!) to handle yourself, and you'll need to hire someone. You should still understand what you are signing, however, when the tax preparer hands you the completed 1040. More important, you should be able to review it and see if there are mistakes in it.

> *The IRS can be reached at www.irs.gov. To order tax forms, call 800-TAX-FORM (800-829-3676). For tax help, call 800-TAX-1040 (800-829-1040). These numbers are usually busy, so call early in the morning or in the late afternoon. To find out what publications the IRS offers, ask for publication 910, "Guide to Free Tax Services." You can download any of their publications via the Internet.*

There are also some good books out there. *J.K. Lasser's Tax Guide* and the *Ernst & Young Tax Guide* are easy to read and informative. Now reading a tax guide is a lot like reading the phone book so be forewarned. In searching for a good tax web site, I found many to choose from, but here is one that listed all the sites you'll ever need for your tax planning: www.el.com/elinks/taxes.

In filling out an income tax return, let an accountant instead of your conscience, be your guide. —Will Rogers

Tax Deductions

There are numerous deductions and exemptions for which you might be eligible. You can actually use these to lower your taxable income, so you'll want to keep good records. You subtract your deductions and exemptions from your gross income to get your taxable income. But you have to know which ones are available to you, and this is why a good guide or tax preparer is important. If you have dependents, you can take an exemption for each one. This could include your elderly parents you have been helping out financially as well. If you provide more than half their support, you may be eligible to claim them as dependents on your tax return.

Deductions are tricky. There are income limits associated with deductions. Make too much money and you lose the ability to use them. You need to list all the deductions you can take on Schedule A and add them up. Then compare this amount against the standard deduction the government allows and use the larger number that would be more beneficial to you. For many taxpayers they find it is so easy to file the 1040EZ. No hassle and little work and you don't need to hire anyone to help you. An IRS study concluded that taxpayers overpaid on average $423 in taxes when using the short form. Take the time to compare the forms to see which gives you the better tax deal.

Tax Credits

Tax credits are actually worth more to you than a deduction. A deduction is something you subtract from your gross income. A tax credit reduces the amount of taxes you owe, dollar for dollar. But what the government giveth, it often just dangles in front of our noses. There are income limits associated with these credits. If your income is too high, you can't use the credit.

You have to admire the Internal Revenue Service. Any organization that makes that much money without advertising—deserves respect.

Dependent and Childcare Credit

The dependent and childcare credit is available if you work outside your home or are a full-time student. The expenses must be for:

✔ A dependent under age 13

✔ Any person who is physically or mentally incapable of caring for themselves and they must qualify as your dependent

✔ A spouse who is incapable of self-care

The maximum amount of expenses that the credit can be applied to is $2,400 if there is one qualifying child or dependent and up to $4,800 if two or more dependents are being cared for. If your income is under $10,000, you can deduct 30 percent; if it is over $10,000, it is modified by one percentage point for each $2,000 of income. For taxpayers of incomes over $28,000, the credit is 20 percent.

Now, if you find that confusing, you are not alone! Our tax code is baffling because there are so many nuances within each code section. The government really needs to address this area because it hasn't been updated in years; although childcare costs have escalated, the credit has remained the same. You need a math degree to file your own taxes these days.

Child Tax Credit

Next we have the child tax credit, which is available for children being supported by you if they are under age 17. The credit begins to phase out if your income as a single parent is over $75,000, married filing jointly the limit is $110,000, and married filing separately $55,000. The credit is reduced by $50 for every $1,000 of income over the threshold income limit.

Now the credit was $600 per child for the years 2003 and 2004. The new tax law of 2003 accelerates the credit amount to $1,000 for those years and then guess what? Back down it goes. For the years 2005 thru 2008 it will be $700, goes up to $800 in 2009, then reaches the $1000 mark in 2010 and you guessed it. It all changes again, it

I feel very honored to pay taxes in America. The thing is, I could probably feel just as honored for about half the price.
—Arthur Godfrey

sunsets in 2010 and goes back to $500 per kid. Only Congress in its infinite wisdom could have thought up this one!

Education Credits and Deductions

The government is finally offering some relief for parents paying for college expenses. There are two education credits, the Hope Scholarship credit and the Lifetime Learning credit, now available, but the credit is phased out for single parents with incomes between $41,000 and $51,000 so if you earn over the $51,000 magic number you are not eligible to take the credit. For married parents filing jointly you can get all of the credit if your income is under $82,000 and still get some of the credit if your income is between $82,000 and $102,000. These credits are mutually exclusive, which in tax speak means that you can't use them for the same kid in the same tax year. So you'll need to do some planning here. The income limits are indexed to inflation.

The Hope Scholarship credit is a tax credit of up to $1,500 per student for qualified tuition and fees paid only during the first two years of a college education. So if you have two kids in school and you qualify your tax credit could be $3,000. The credit is worth 100 percent of the first $1,000 in tuition expenses and 50 percent of the next $1,000 for a maximum credit of $1,500 per student. The credit will be indexed for inflation.

The Lifetime Learning credit is not just for kids. Anyone who is enrolled in undergraduate or graduate courses or is just taking courses to improve his or her job skills can use the credit.

The Lifetime Learning credit is a credit of up to 20 percent of qualified tuition and fees paid during the taxable year on behalf of a student. The limit here is $2,000 per tax return. So if you have two kids in college no matter how much their education has cost you the Lifetime Learning credit limit is $2,000. This dollar limit is currently fixed and will not be indexed for inflation. Unlike the Hope credit, the Lifetime Learning credit can be claimed as long as the student is in school and can be used for both undergraduate and graduate school. So this credit is useful for the grown-up going back to school as well.

Next to surviving an earthquake, nothing is quite as satisfying as getting a refund on your income tax.

If you fall through the cracks because you make too much money there is a new tuition deduction you can claim for 2003. There is a $3,000 deduction for college costs waiting for you. Here the income limits are a bit higher. If you are single and making under $65,000 you are eligible to take the deduction and married filing jointly the magic number is $130,000. There is no phase out allowed here. A credit is usually worth more to you than a deduction but this deduction is unique in that you can claim the whole $3,000 even if you only had $3,000 in expenses. Caveat; you cannot use both the tuition deduction and the credits in the same year. It's either or!

Once the kids are out of college there is still help available. There is a deduction for interest paid on school loans. The old rule was that the deduction was only good for the first 60 months of the loan but that's changed and now it is good for the life of the loan. You can use the short form or the long form 1040 to use this deduction. Income limits determine who can take the deduction and who can't. If you are single the deduction is phased out if your income is between $50,000 and $65,000 and married filing jointly its $100,000 and $130,000.

Adoption Credit

The adoption credit is based on the cost of adopting a child. You may be able to take a tax credit of up to $10,000 for qualifying expenses paid to adopt an eligible child, which includes a child with special needs. Qualifying expenses include reasonable and necessary fees, court costs, attorney fees, and traveling expenses. The credit is phased out for income levels between $150,000 and $190,000. You cannot utilize the adoption credit if you are adopting your spouse's child.

Earned-Income Credit

The earned-income credit is the only credit given as a payment. The credit is available for low-income families, usually with children. If you do not have a qualifying dependent but are between the ages of 25 and 65 with a very modest income, you may be eligible for the earned-income credit.

If I have caused just one person to wipe away a tear of laughter, that's my reward. The rest goes to the government. —Victor Borge

Capital Gains Tax

The long-term capital gains tax is designed to get you when you have made a profit on an asset that you have held for at least one year and that has appreciated since you bought it. The lower your tax bracket, the lower the capital gains tax. In 2003 major changes to the tax code were made and the capital gains tax was cut from 20 percent to 15 percent for most long-term capital gains. For taxpayers either in the 10 percent or 15 percent tax bracket the capital gains tax rate is now 5 percent. These reduced rates apply to sales occurring after May 5, 2003 and before January 1, 2009.

The reduction of the capital gains tax increases the benefit of transferring appreciated assets to children over the age of 13. Why would you want to give the kiddo your stock? Your grandson got into the college of his choice and you want to help with the expenses. You have been holding onto some GE stock now worth $11,000 for many years that has a basis of $1,000 (basis is the price you paid for an asset). If you sell it to help him with college you will pay a tax of 15 percent on the $10,000 profit for a tax of $1,500. If you gift him $11,000 of the appreciated stock he will take on your cost basis of $1,000 and when he sells it his tax rate would probably be 5 percent and he'll pay only $500 in taxes.

> *How long should you keep your tax return? The IRS has three years (the period of limitations) after you have filed your return to audit your return, so you'll want to keep tax returns for at least four years (but if you have the space, seven years is better). Keep all of your W-2s until you have the opportunity to reconcile them against your Social Security statement for those W-2s are your proof of Social Security withholdings.*

Now, if you have an investment that loses money and you sell it, you have a capital loss, and the loss is allowed to offset your capital gains. If you suffer more in losses than you have made in gains, you will be able to use the loss against ordinary income up to a maximum of $3,000 for the year. If you still have losses left over, they can be carried forward to be used in another year.

Taxes are strange; you pay this year's taxes with the money you earned last year but spent the year before.

Cashing Out the American Dream

The old tax provision for the sale of your primary residence was that you could roll over any capital gains into a new house as long as you did so within two years of the sale and the new home was more expensive than the old home. Also available back in the olden days was a one-time capital gains exclusion of $125,000 on the sale of the primary residence of people over age 55. Both are gone now!

The new tax regs are a better deal. Married couples filing a joint tax return can exclude up to $500,000 of gain from the sale of their primary residence. Individual taxpayers may exclude up to $250,000. To qualify for the exclusion, the taxpayer must have owned the property and used it as his or her primary residence for at least two of the last five years (this ownership period does not have to be consecutive).

For a husband and wife filing a joint return, the exclusion is available if either spouse meets the ownership requirement and both spouses meet the use requirement. This exclusion is available to all taxpayers once every two years. This exclusion is particularly welcome for older taxpayers who want to downsize. They may have lived in their homes for over 30 years and would realize large capital gains when they sell.

Taxing Dividends

Dividends have always been taxed as ordinary income. All that has changed with the new tax law of 2003. Congress will now tax dividends at a 15 percent maximum rate on certain dividend income. Dividends that are eligible for the 15 percent rate are any dividends from a domestic corporation, mutual funds, qualified foreign corporation and partnerships. Dividends paid by a money market mutual fund or a REIT generally do not qualify. As with almost all of the provisions of the 2003 tax act, the lower rates on dividend income will expire by the end of 2008.

When you put the two words "The" and "IRS" together, it spells "theirs"!

Tax Favored Investments

Depending on the investments you choose, you may be able to defer your taxes, or perhaps no taxes will ever be due. Examples of tax-free investments include tax-free municipal bonds, the new Roth IRA, the Coverdell Educational Savings Accounts known as ESAs, and EE Savings bonds when used to pay for a college education.

In a tax-deferred investment, you can put off paying the taxes to some time in the future. Examples of tax-deferred investments would be retirement plans (both employer sponsored and for the self-employed) as well as EE Savings bonds, new prepaid 529 college savings plans, and annuities. You will owe taxes when you begin to withdraw the money.

Another subtle form of tax deferral is when you hold onto an investment and it appreciates over time, such as with a stock. You don't owe taxes on that asset until you actually sell it, and if you hold it for longer than a year, it will be taxed at the capital gains rate.

Deferring taxes when possible is always a good tax strategy. The first place to look for tax-deferral opportunities is where you work. What does your employer provide? A 401(k) plan, a 403(b), a 457 plan, the Federal Thrift Savings Plan for Federal employees, or a SIMPLE IRA?

Contributing to your retirement plan at work using pretax dollars is a great way to reduce your current tax liability. Here, you get your cake and can eat it, too. The income earned on investments you have made with pretax dollars compounds tax deferred until you begin to withdraw the money in retirement, and then and only then will you owe income taxes on the money.

If your marginal tax bracket is 25 percent, for every dollar you contribute to your plan, it actually is only costing you 75 cents. Such a bargain! If you want to invest that same dollar in an after-tax investment, you would need to actually start with $1.33 because you would have to pay the 25 percent tax first before you have the dollar in your hand to invest.

The only place you find success before work is in the . . . dictionary.

Tax planning is essential to your overall financial plan. Learning about deferring taxes and what tax bracket you are in can help you achieve your goals.

The Bottom Line

Taxing subject! Knowing the tax laws or hiring someone who knows the tax laws to help you with your tax planning each year is your best defense when it comes to lowering your tax liability. Keeping good records is a must for you always want to be able to back up any deduction you take on your tax return.

A dollar will not go as far as it used to, but it will go faster.

*R*ecently, I was in McDonald's with my husband eating supper (yes, supper at Mickey D's—since I started writing this book, I've had no time to cook. Besides, their salads are good and healthy!). This had been our third time there that week, and the elderly woman who mops up the floors commented on that. She told me we were good customers because we didn't leave her a big mess to clean up. I casually commented that, indeed, we had been there three nights but so had she. How many nights was she working? As many as they would let her, came her reply. She also worked in another McDonald's 10 miles away and had to drive to that one, costing her a gallon of gas to make the round trip.

Maria is working two jobs at two McDonald's to keep her house, she told me. She asked me why I was eating at McDonald's, and I told her about the money book for women. She looked at me with tears in her eyes and asked, "Where were you when I needed you 10 years ago when my husband and I retired?"

Her husband had been a career military man and ranked as a sergeant; when he retired, he took his full pension. They bought an RV and traveled back to many of the military bases on which they had lived over the years. They were enjoying retirement! That lasted for a couple of years until he had his first heart attack. After the second, Maria was afraid to travel with him, so they settled into a small town. Then came the third and fatal heart attack.

When her husband died, the pension died with him for he had taken a 100 percent payout, not the joint life and annuity option, which would have given him less money during his lifetime but would have provided Maria with a pension for as long as she lived. Instead, Maria is working two jobs for minimum wage so she can keep a roof over her head while collecting meager social security benefits.

Chapter 7

Planning for the Golden Years or the Golden Arches

● ●

In this Chapter

This chapter will help you envision your ideal retirement. Each of you want and need something that is uniquely yours. Just as no two fingerprints are identical neither is the retirement experience. If you are coupled your experience will be different than your spouse's.

● ●

What Does the Ideal Retirement Look Like?

Retirement planning now ranks as the number one money concern for women, but less than 50 percent of women have begun to save using their retirement plans at work. Younger women seem to be better at this than older women.

My lady from McDonald's thought she was going to have the ideal retirement. What she didn't understand was the obstacles that could derail her planning. So what's your ideal retirement going to look like, and do you have a backup plan?

For each of us, the ideal retirement is going to look and feel different. You want something to retire *to* rather than just quitting what you

---

You can be young without money but you can't be old without money. —Tennessee Williams

are doing. Most people do best when there is some structure to their lives. Every day in retirement would be a Saturday! Now, some of you may be jumping up and down at that prospect, and the rest of you are wondering what you are going to do after day 23.

What does your ideal retirement look like? Maybe retiring at age 60, working two days a week because you want to, staying in your own home with a $50,000 income stream and several trips already planned for the upcoming year with your friends? That sounds good to me. The only thing I might add would be a garden to play in with my summers free to entertain grandkids.

Your ideal retirement might be an RV with one of those little cars being pulled from behind. Maybe a condo in Arizona for the winters and a cottage by the sea on Cape Cod. Maybe a new career, going back to school or joining the Peace Corps. Start thinking about it!

Achieving the Ideal Retirement

Plan now, play later! That's my mantra for retirement. A survey conducted by the State Teachers Retirement System of Ohio found that 76 percent of those surveyed thought retirement planning should start before age 50, 34 percent thought it should start before age 35. I believe that retirement planning should start with your first job. Now, don't beat up on yourself if you haven't started; you didn't get this book until recently. The financial part, however, should start as soon as you get your first W-2 and have to file a tax return. While you are accumulating the funds to provide a comfortable retirement, you need to be planning the rest as well.

The AARP did a study and found that most people actually spent more time planning their summer vacation than they did their retirement. A summer vacation may last two weeks; you could be looking at spending about one third of your life retired, 25 years or more.

There is what I call the soft side of retirement, which is as important as the financial side. It is preparing yourself emotionally and psychologically for retirement. You have to ask yourself the following:

Taking it with you isn't nearly as important as making it last until you're ready to go.

✔ When are you going to retire?

✔ When does your spouse want to retire?

✔ Where are you going to retire?

✔ What are you going to do when you retire?

Now, all of these have a financial component to them, and without enough assets set aside, you may not have choices here.

When Will You Retire?

When you are going to retire depends on how much you have set aside. For some potential retirees, however, working is preferable to retiring. There are many 65-year-olds happily employed, collecting their Social Security benefits and a paycheck each month. I recently interviewed a 75-year-old woman about her plans for retirement, and she gave me a one-word answer, "Death!" She tried retirement and found it boring. Her kids wanted her to baby-sit, her husband wanted her to cook, and her mother, who is still alive, wanted her to come and visit every day. She still does all of those things but only on the weekends now.

If you decide to retire early, there are many things you need to plan for. Will you be able to tap into your retirement plans for income? Do you have enough in assets if you can't? Medicare doesn't start until you reach age 65, so you'll need health insurance.

When does your spouse want to retire? The conventional pattern has been for women to marry older men, which means that they reach retirement age before we do. Retirement is a personal option, and certainly, if you are coupled, you make joint decisions, but if you don't want to retire with him, don't. There could be more problems with you retiring early and being unhappy about it. Often times especially for women, the later years in our careers are when we are making the greatest contributions to work, and we're at our peak earning levels. If you will receive a pension from your employer, the pension formula often builds on the last years of your career.

An economist is a man that can tell you anything—he'll tell you what can happen under any given conditions, and his guess is liable to be just as good as anybody else's, too. —Will Rogers

So your husband can learn to do the grocery shopping and to cook. It will give him plenty of time to play golf and do the guy things he's talked about doing for so long. A word of advice: If he does take over the housework, do not—and I repeat, do not—criticize his vacuuming or his cooking. If you do, it becomes your job again. If dinner is always meat and potatoes, have a salad for lunch and fruit for breakfast to cover the basic food groups.

Where Will You Retire?

According to the AARP, most retirees stay put. At least, they do right after they retire. Your home may be your largest asset, and with the favorable tax-law changes, you may wish to sell it and downsize. The IRS allows you to exclude up to $500,000 from capital gains tax on your primary residence. Now your home would have to be worth a lot to take advantage of the whole exclusion. This could make cash available for your retirement planning.

You may decide that the winters in the north are too harsh and seek a warmer climate for at least part of the year. If you're planning any major moves, test the waters. If you think Arizona is the place to live and have visited there in the winters, try a month in the summer before you pack it up and move.

Don't discount your support system of family and friends where you live now. They may be hard to replace in a new environment—especially the grandkids! Studies have shown that retirees who are coupled and move do very well until the death of the first spouse. Then the surviving spouse may move back home to be near family. Single retirees actually do better in a move for they are cognizant of the need to build a support structure of friends.

Check out the health systems wherever you are thinking of moving. How far away are doctors and hospitals? As we age, these become more important to us. Check out the recreational facilities, the shopping, and the

> For more help on finding the Shangri-La for your dream retirement, try the following web sites: www.usa-retirement.com, www.retirementnet.com, and www.bestplaces.net.

The worst thing about growing old is having to listen to a lot of advice from one's children.

traffic. How do you plan to spend your time in retirement? Does the new area you are considering have enough activities available for you? If your family is far away, how easy is it for you to get to an airport? And how easy is it for them to travel to you?

What Will You Do When You Retire?

If you don't know, you are not ready to retire. What have you dreamed about? Just leaving your job to get away from it all is not enough. Do you have enough money for retirement, or are you going to need to look for part-time work? Do you have hobbies and sports that you are passionate about? Travel is wonderful, but most of us can't afford to be traveling all of the time.

What is it that will make you want to get up in the morning and start the day? As human beings, two of things that motivate us are our need to be needed and our need to be productive. Volunteering is a great way to fulfill these needs. Libraries, museums, churches, schools, and hospitals all need volunteers and offer flexible schedules to accommodate you. Check out the AARP's web site for more information, www.aarp.org.

More and more colleges are offering discounts for seniors, and some schools offer free classes. Retirement for some seniors is a time to try a second career. Going back to school for a computer course may help you connect with your kids and grandkids.

Are You on Track?

Retirement is a fairly new phenomenon. When my grandmother retired, she went to live with one of my aunts who had a dairy farm and Gram worked just as hard on my Aunt's farm as she had done on her own before my grandfather died. She got a bit more rocking-chair time with the babies, but there wasn't much playtime.

Today, retirees are expecting to have it easier in retirement than they did during their working years. Many are planning on leisure

Years make all persons old—a few wise.

time and travel. Unless you have enough money set aside, that ain't going to happen!

According to the American Savings Education Council (ASEC) in Washington, DC, 60 percent of women have never tried to figure out how much money they need to save for retirement. Even worse, 40 percent of women have not begun to save for retirement.

So how much money will you need for retirement? A lot! The first thing you need to review is your cash flow from Chapter 3, "Figuring Out Your Starting Point." If you haven't filled out the cash flow worksheet, you'll need to now. What does it take to maintain your current lifestyle? Is this the lifestyle you'll want in retirement? With a little bit of effort on your part, you will be able to calculate whether your savings are on track to reach your retirement goals by doing the BALLPARK E$TIMATE worksheet from the American Savings Educational Council (ASEC), located in Appendix A, "Worksheets."

> *Women spend 75 percent more time planning their wedding than they do their retirement.*

If you are coupled, try doing the worksheet together or each of you do one your own and then try together. If you finish the worksheet and the results indicate that you must save more than is available from your paycheck each week, redo the worksheet. This time, add part-time work if you left it off the first time or raise your projected retirement age from 60 to 65. This will increase your years of savings and your Social Security benefits. If this still doesn't work, raise the retirement age to 70.

The BALLPARK E$TIMATE worksheet was adapted from the ASEC's web site. To do this worksheet online, check out www.asec.org/ballpark. If you have check-paying software such as Quicken, you already have the ability to figure how much more you'll need to save in the planning section of the software. You will also find retirement-planning calculators at both www.quicken.com and www.moneycentralmsn.com as well as on many of the mutual fund company's websites.

If you don't want to work, you have to work to earn enough money so that you wont have to work. —Ogden Nash

Obstacles Along the Way

Many things can push you off course when you're planning for retirement. Storms take many forms in our lives. Let's work our way through some of the financial ones first. I will cover the various types of retirement plans available for you in detail in the next chapter.

Changing Jobs Frequently

The average American worker will work for seven different employers during his or her career. An employer can require that you wait a year before you are eligible to contribute to the company's retirement plan such as a 401(k). Not being able to contribute to an employer's plan and missing out on the employer's potential matching funds will mean less in your retirement nest egg in the future. Be sure you check out using IRAs while you are waiting for the enrollment period to open up for you. Also make some noise as an employee and request that your employer revisit the policy of making employees wait before they can contribute to the plan.

Let's assume a 9 percent return and the amount you would have contributed is $3,000 a year. You could have accumulated an additional $300,000 in your nest egg had you been allowed to enroll in the retirement plan the first day on the job with each new employer.

Single or Newly Married

If you are single or newly married and are not ready to start your family, do some advance planning. Contribute the maximum to the plans available to you right now. Those dollars will have the advantage of long-term growth, and your money will be working for you even if you are not contributing anything to the plan while at home with the kids.

Loss of a job can certainly mess with your retirement planning—especially if you didn't know it was coming. If you have been contributing to your plan and have a nest egg, it will be very tempting to take the money out of the plan. When you leave your employment, you are allowed to take your 401(k) with you. If it is over $5,000, your

The mint makes it first, and it's up to us to make it last.

former employer has to give you the option of leaving it with the plan. If it is under $5,000, you just might get a check in the mail from them and it will have 20 percent less in it for the plan provider by law is required to withhold taxes on the money sent to you directly.

Taking the Money and Running

Over 60 percent of workers take the money and run even though taxes are due, as is a 10 percent penalty if you are under age 59 ½. Hopefully, you have an emergency fund stashed away that will see you through this crisis, and you can keep your retirement nest egg growing.

If your 401(k) is worth $5,000 and you decide to take it, you won't have much left after taxes. Your former employer is required to withhold 20 percent for taxes before you ever see the check. And then come tax time, if you are in the 28 percent bracket, you will owe another 8 percent for taxes. If you live where there is a state income tax, that will be added to it as well, and then there is the 10 percent penalty if you are under age 59 ½. So you could lose over 40 percent to taxes, leaving you just about $3,000 to spend.

Keeping that $5,000 in your retirement account and assuming a 9 percent return, in 25 years, it could grow to $43,000. That's enough to buy you a red convertible for your retirement years. Okay it would have to a used red convertible but used is the better way to go!

Long-Term Disability

A long-term disability or a permanent disability can halt your retirement savings very quickly. You may even need to tap into what savings you had put away to survive without your income. Planning for a long-term disability by purchasing a long-term disability insurance policy is the best way around this obstacle. Make sure you have enough money in your emergency fund to cover any short-term illnesses that may occur and spend your money on the long-term disability policy.

A woman making money is like a bee making honey; she can make it, but they won't let her keep it.

Death of a Spouse

The death of your spouse can be catastrophic to your future. If your spouse's income was larger than yours, you may feel you just don't have anything extra to contribute to your retirement plan right now. Be sure both you and your spouse are properly insured. Life insurance should be used to cover the loss of an income stream. Also check those beneficiary designations; you should be the beneficiary on his retirement plans and he on yours. If there was not much saved for retirement, you will need to begin to do it on your own. It is never too late to start saving!

Divorce from Your Spouse

Many women will tell you that a divorce is harder to deal with than the death of a spouse. Retirement planning gets tricky during a divorce. If your income has been less than his over the life of the marriage and your retirement savings are less than his, you will want to ask for part of his retirement savings. You want half of the combined qualified retirement savings. You should also look to receive part of his pension if he is eligible for one. Alimony is considered income to you, and if that is the only income you are receiving, you are eligible to contribute to an IRA for yourself.

Children and Grandchildren

Children can be the delight of our lives and are an awesome responsibility. Because we are the primary caregivers for our children, women are more often in and out of the job market when children are young so that we can be home with them. But that also takes us out of the retirement savings market as well. If this happens to you, be sure you check out your eligibility to set up a spousal IRA for the years you are at home. If you are self-employed and working at home, be sure you check into the various types of self-employment retirement plans.

Boomerang kids are another issue. You know the ones I mean here. They left home once but keep bouncing back again and again,

When a man retires, his wife gets twice the husband, but only half the income. —Chi Chi Rodriquez

sometimes with children of their own. They have it pretty good living at home—meals, laundry, and a clean house. Don't make it too convenient, or they will never leave. I am a big believer in charging the kids rent and setting rules if they ask to come back home to live. There will always be extenuating circumstances, but once they get on their feet, don't make it too easy.

What about those wonderful grandchildren you love so much? I recently met a woman who, at 68, had to go back to work so she could afford the things she and her 12-year-old grandson needed. They couldn't make it on her savings and Social Security benefits. Over 11 million grandparents are raising their grandchildren. Many other grandparents are providing daily childcare so that their adult kids can go to work. Again, there may be no other way to handle the situation, but at least you are now aware. Make it a choice if you want to baby-sit the grandchildren. Check out www.aarp.org/grandparents for more help with being a care-giving grandparent.

There is a housing development in Boston reserved for grandparents raising their grandkids. The adult children are drug-addicted, in jail or have died leaving the grandparents to raise the kids. Many other cities are looking to the Boston housing development as a model.

The Bottom Line

Knowing what can derail your retirement planning gives you the ability to plan better. Life happens to us so often while we are busy planning for it. But being aware of the "what ifs" in life gives you a heads up.

The dime isn't entirely worthless; it makes a fairly good screwdriver when you need it.

Notes:

"The only retirement plan my current job offers is a shopping cart and a Hefty bag" Christine told me. She went on to explain that she's been doing this financial planning stuff but she's not sure she's got it right yet.

Christine is a single, baby boomer pushing 50. When she was a girl she remembers asking her father about business and finance. His answer was so typical of the men of that generation. "I'll take care of you, honey and when I'm not around your husband will take care of you," he told her. Her father did keep his part of the bargain. He left her some money last year and she is fully invested in mutual funds. She would also like to be saving additional money from her cash flow.

Christine's concerns mirror that of most baby boomers. She's worried that she won't be able to save and invest enough on her own to have a quality retirement. Compound that with being single and childless she is concerned about the need to hire caregivers in her later years. In retirement she would like to travel and perhaps even return to school to pursue an advanced degree. And if there was anything left over after she has played in retirement she would like her nieces to inherit it.

Christine does have an IRA, but she's not always been diligent about contributing to it on a regular basis. She has never stayed long enough in any job to be vested in their pension plan so her retirement planning consists of what she'll receive from Social Security, her IRA and her personal savings. Will it be enough she wonders or is the shopping cart a reality?

Chapter 8

Providing the Glitter for the Golden Years

- -

In This Chapter

This chapter is about just that, the glitter. What retirement plans are available for you to help you reach your retirement goals and how you can best use them. Read on to learn how to increase the size of your nest egg.

- -

What's going to provide the glitter for your golden years? More importantly, *who's* going to provide the glitter for those golden years? You? Your employer? The government? The responsibility really is yours! Social Security is a back up, and maybe you'll work somewhere long enough to get a pension, but ultimately, the buck stops with you. And hopefully, there will be some bucks.

Chapter 7, "Planning for the Golden Years or the Golden Arches," afforded you some insight as to how much more you need to save and what could sidetrack you along the way. This chapter will address the tools you'll use to meet your retirement goals.

Congress changed the rules in 2001 with the Economic Growth and Tax Relief Reconciliation Act to allow employees to contribute more for retirement as well as making it easier to move retirement money between different kinds of retirement plans.

When saving for old age, be sure to put away a few pleasant memories.

Employer Sponsored Retirement Plans

Your employer may offer the best retirement tools available to you. More and more employers are offering employees the ability to contribute money pre-tax to retirement accounts that give you the opportunity to grow your money tax-deferred until you begin to withdraw the funds in retirement.

401(k) Plans

More than 44 million workers are saving for their retirement using a 401(k) plan. This is a defined contribution plan set up by the employer. It allows the employee to make contributions to the plan through payroll deductions, and the employer may or may not make contributions to your account.

401(k) plans are self-directed, meaning the employee makes the investment decisions, choosing among choices the employer has provided in the plan. They are qualified retirement plans, and the contributions are permitted to grow tax deferred until the proceeds are withdrawn.

The law and your employer's plan limit how much you can contribute to these plans. For 2003, the maximum contribution limit is $12,000. Your employer's plan may restrict the amount you can contribute. So if you are earning $15,000 and there is a second income to support you, you can contribute $12,000 to your 401(k) plan. The maximum pre-tax limit will eventually increase to $15,000.

Many employers offer a match to employees. A typical match is 3 percent and dollar for dollar. So if you contribute 3 percent of your income, your employer will also contribute 3 percent. If you decide to increase your contribution, your employer will still only give you the 3 percent. If you are eligible for a 401(k) plan at work with a company match and are not utilizing it, you are leaving free money on the table. That's right, you are walking away and leaving money on the table, money your employer won't make available to you in any other way than through the 401(k) plan.

As inflation makes your money worth less and less, it's no comfort to reach into your pocket and find that you have nothing to worry about.

With the 2001 tax law came more changes. There is now a catch-up provision for anyone reaching age 50. Another bonus besides being eligible to join AARP. Now not all employers have added the catch-up provision to their plans. So even if the new tax law permits a catch-up they don't have to offer it. For 2003 the maximum catch-up contribution is $2,000 and will eventually reach $5,000 in 2006.

Contribution Limits for 401(k), 403(b) and 457 Plans

Year	Limit	Catch-Up Limit*
2003	$12,000	$2,000
2004	$13,000	$3,000
2005	$14,000	$4,000
2006	$15,000	$5,000

After 2006, the maximum pre-tax contribution limit as well as the catch-up provision will be indexed in $500 increments for inflation.

*Both the 403(b) and 457 plans have another catch up provision as well.

There are 401(k) regulations that are common to all plans. Your employer can require you to wait up to one year before allowing you to enroll in the plan. The money in the plan compounds tax deferred, and for that privilege, you normally don't have access to the money until you reach age 59 ½. Pulling it out before age 59 ½ could trigger a 10 percent penalty that is imposed by the IRS. The rules require that mandatory distributions must begin at age 70 ½ and are taxed as income.

Some plans let you borrow from your account. You are permitted to borrow up to one-half of the amount in your account with a limit of $50,000, and the loan must be repaid within five years. One of the pitfalls of borrowing from your 401(k) plan is that if you lose your job because of downsizing or you quit to take a new position, the loan

You can't build a reputation on what you are going to do.
—Henry Ford

amount could be due and payable within 60 days or less. Ouch! So think before borrowing.

Upon leaving your job, you do have access to the money in your 401(k). You can do a direct transfer to a rollover IRA, a direct transfer to your new employer's plan if it allows transfers, or if there is more than $5,000 in your account, your employer has to allow you to leave the money there. The transfers should all be made between the plan trustees, and you should not take possession of the money.

Your last option when you leave a job is to take the money and run. This is not a good idea though; if you do, your employer is required to withhold 20 percent for taxes. If you are in the 28 percent bracket and live in a state where you will owe state income taxes, your tax liability could be close to 35 percent, and then there is that 10 percent penalty that just won't go away. So you could lose almost half of your money to taxes and penalties. It's better to keep those dollars working for you in a retirement plan.

For more information on 401(k) plans, pick up a copy of *The Complete Idiot's Guide to 401(k) Plans* co-authored by me, Dee Lee. Almost every mutual fund company has a 401(k) site that offers help and calculators. Also check out what's available on the web as well; some places to begin, www.quicken.com, www.mpower.com and www.401khelpcenter.com.

403(b) Plans

403(b) plans are offered to employees of nonprofit institutions such as schools or hospitals. These plans are also referred to as TSAs, tax-sheltered annuities. A 403(b) is an agreement between the employee and the 403(b) provider, and all the employer does is to withhold the contributions for the employee and forward them to the provider. No one is minding the store here because the employer takes on no responsibility except to transfer the employee's money to the chosen provider.

Originally, only annuities were used for these plans, but today, you can find good mutual fund choices as well. And you *should* be looking for the mutual fund choices! The contribution limits for the employee

Definition of prosperity: that period from Friday's paycheck to Saturday's shopping.

is the same as for the 401(k) plans (new tax laws made contributions levels equal for 401(k) Plans, 403(b)s and 457 plans). For 2003 it is $12,000 with a catch up provision equal to $2,000 if you are over age 50.

> *Annuities have a "penalty-free withdrawal" clause that allows you to move 10 percent of the balance each year without incurring surrender charges. Some companies make it very difficult for you to move your money. Read that very small print in the contract before you sign on.*

Your account is allowed to compound tax-deferred, so the same rules apply here as in other qualified retirement plans. A 10 percent penalty usually will be levied if you take your money out before age 59 ½. Upon a job change, you should be able to roll your 403(b) into an IRA, or into a new employer's plan but check the fine print because some annuities have a back-end surrender charge, and even if the regulations allow a rollover, they don't. Withdrawals usually must begin at age 70 ½.

403(b) plans have another catch-up election, allowing participants who did not take advantage of earlier contribution years to "catch up" and put away extra money. The IRS rules are very complicated, so you'll need to get some help from the plan provider. I would suggest checking out the IRS publication 571, "Tax-Sheltered Annuity Programs for Employees of Public Schools and Certain Tax-Exempt Organizations." You can contact them at 800-829-3676 or online at www.irs.gov.

You should be able to invest your 403(b) money anywhere that will accept your account. The IRS ruled in 1990 that participants in a 403(b) plan could transfer out of their plan into mutual funds of their choice using a 403(b)(7) plan. This does not require a change of jobs. Only the accumulated savings can be transferred, and there may be surrender charges if you are transferring out of an annuity. You would only make this change to get better choices for your account.

Your plan administrator may not know or understand 403(b)(7) plans. Transferring your account may not be easy, but it will be worth the effort if your choices are better.

You can't escape the responsibility of tomorrow by evading it today.
—Abraham Lincoln

Participants in 403(b) plans should have choices, and those choices should include mutual funds. School districts and hospitals can make it very difficult or even impossible for participants to use another source other than the one they endorse. Petition your employer to make mutual funds available; sometimes it only takes 10 employees wanting a new provider for your employer to include it on the list. Sites that can help you with your 403(b) are www.403bwise.com; also check out the 403(b) forum at www.morningstar.com and www.mpower.com. More and more mutual fund companies are responding to the needs of 403(b) participants and offer good material on their sites as well.

> *According to the Spectrum Group, just 42 percent of public school teachers utilize 403(b) plans, and most public school teachers are women. Take advantage of your 403(b) and make it work of you.*

457 Retirement Plans

457 deferred compensation plans are available for state, county, or city employees. An employee may elect to contribute up to $12,000 for 2003 and you guessed it if they are over the AARP membership age, an extra $2,000.

Like the 403(b) plans there is another "catch-up" provision for participants as well as the one provided by the new tax law. If you have not made contributions over the years you were eligible to contribute and are within three years of retirement, you can stash away more money. Again, complicated stuff, so talk to the plan provider and check their website for more information. They will be very happy to help you set up a catch-up plan.

Mandatory withdrawals must begin by age 70 ½ and withdrawals are taxed as ordinary income. Plan assets compound tax deferred, but unlike the other two plans, employees can get at their money without a penalty before age 59 ½ if they terminate service or retire. At that time, they can choose to leave the money until a later date or they can begin withdrawals. They can also roll their money into an IRA or another retirement plan if they find a new job.

People get into debt trying to keep up with those who already are.

Most plan providers have good informative websites and www.mpower.com is one of the few noncommercial websites I have found for 457 plans.

Self-Employment Retirement Plans

SIMPLE-IRAs

The Savings Incentive Match Plan for Employees (SIMPLE) was designed for the small employer with fewer than 100 employees that has no other qualified retirement plan. With the SIMPLE-IRA, an employee will have his or her own IRA set up and may make elective contributions up to the lesser of $8,000 or 100 percent of his or her compensation. The $8,000 limit will be indexed in the future. That's right if you earn $8,000 you can put away $8,000. Here again if you are 50 or over you are eligible for a catch-up of up to $1,000.

The employer must contribute some money to a SIMPLE-IRA for the employee and has the option either to match the employee's contribution dollar for dollar up to 3 percent of compensation or to use an alternative matching contribution method of making a flat 2 percent contribution of the employee's compensation.

There is immediate vesting of the employer's contribution, which means that it belongs to the employee immediately. Withdrawals taken before the age of 59 ½ will be subject to an IRS penalty. Withdrawals made within the first two years that an employee is in the plan are not subject to the 10 percent penalty; instead, they are subject to a 25 percent penalty. Ouch! They don't want you messing with your retirement dollars! These plans are easy to set up but must be set up by October 1 of the preceding year. Most large mutual fund companies have standard plans they can offer you and good information as well.

This is a great plan for a self-employed individual for you are both the employee and employer.

A woman doesn't own her wealth—she owes it.

SEP-IRAs

A SEP-IRA is a simplified employee pension plan that uses an IRA format. A SEP is by far the easiest self-employment plan to use and set up. A call to your favorite mutual fund company will get you an application as well as help in calculating how much you can contribute each year.

Your annual contribution rate is the lesser of $40,000 or 25 percent of compensation. The maximum amount of compensation that can be used in determining contributions is $200,000. The contributions are deductible for the tax year for which they are made and can be made when you file your tax return.

If you have employees, they must be included in the plan, and they would receive the same percentage of compensation that you choose for yourself. You make contributions directly into their self-directed IRA accounts, and they make the investment choices. A feature that is useful for small business owners is that, if you are having a lousy year, you are not required to contribute to the SEP for you or your employees.

An employee is anyone who is at least 21 years of age, has performed services for you, and has received at least $400 in compensation. Plan assets compound tax deferred, and you can't take the money out before you reach 59 ½. Yup, there is a 10 percent penalty here also.

This is an easy plan to administer and it's flexible.

Self-Employed 401(k)

Self-employed 401(k) plans are the newest retirement plan available. As a result of the Economic Growth and Tax Relief Reconciliation Act of 2001 (Who thinks up these names?), self-employed individuals and owner only businesses can now use a 401(k) plan for retirement planning. You can employ no other employees other than your spouse and this includes sole proprietors, partnerships, corporations and S Corporations. The contribution limits are the same as for regular 401(k)

Today a dollar earned is a nickel saved.

plans, for 2003 it is $12,000 with a $2,000 catch up provision for anyone over 50. Most of the mutual fund companies and brokerage houses have IRS pre-approved plan designs so they make it very easy for you to set up.

The IRA Sisters

There are five IRA sisters and two IRA cousins. The IRA cousins are the SEP-IRA and the SIMPLE-IRA, which were covered in the preceding sections.

All have a family resemblance, and all are unique in their own way. IRAs, individual retirement arrangements, are a personal retirement savings tool available to everyone who has earned income. The maximum annual contribution is limited to $3,000. All of the IRAs have the same contribution limits and if you are 50 or over you are eligible to contribute another $500 to your IRA. All IRAs allow for tax-deferred growth of your assets. Rollover IRAs are unique in that you don't contribute to them directly; you roll (transfer) your retirement savings from an employer retirement plan into a rollover IRA when you change jobs or retire. IRAs may be supplemental to your employer-sponsored plans, or they may be all you have going for you in the way of retirement savings.

Congress set up these plans to encourage retirement savings, so once the money is in the IRA, it is going to be difficult and costly to get it out before the retirement age of 59 ½. You will be assessed a 10 percent penalty if you take the money out before age 59 ½ unless you either meet some hardship rules, become disabled, die, or start systematic withdrawals before you reach the magic age of 59 ½. Systematic withdrawals are also known as using the rule of 72t and are based on your life expectancy and the amount of money you actually have in the IRA.

Mandatory withdrawals from IRAs must start by April 1 of the calendar year in which you reach age 70 ½. The IRS is pretty strict about you starting to take mandatory withdrawals; the penalty for not

A living wage it has been said, is a little bit more than you are making right now.

making a timely withdrawal is 50 percent of the missed withdrawal. Uncle Sam has his hand out and is looking for those tax dollars. Remember that you were allowed to contribute the money with pretax dollars, so the IRS does not want that money to sit around forever, compounding tax deferred.

Congress has made it a bit easier to get at the money in your IRAs before reaching age 59 ½ under certain circumstances. Let me gently remind you, however, why you put this money away in an IRA in the first place. It was for your retirement and to enjoy the benefit of tax-deferred compounding. Unlike borrowing from your 401(k) plan, you cannot repay the money once you remove it from the IRA. You will not owe the 10 percent penalty when you withdraw the money for the reasons below, but you will owe income taxes on it.

The IRS has some good information on IRAs. Call them at 800-829-3767 and request publication 590, or download it at www.irs.gov.

If you become disabled, you are eligible to withdraw the funds in your IRA and if you have very large medical expenses or are unemployed you can use the IRA distribution to pay premiums for health insurance. Your medical and dental expenses must be in excess of the 7.5 percent floor for your deductible medical expenses. The health insurance premium exception is allowed only if you have received at least 12 weeks of unemployment benefits.

An IRA can be used to pay for post-secondary education expenses for the taxpayer, taxpayer's spouse, children, or grandchildren. There is also a first-time homebuyer withdrawal allowed with a lifetime limit of $10,000 to build or buy a "first" home that will be the principal residence of the individual, his or her spouse, or any child, grandchild, or ancestor of the individual or spouse.

Traditional IRAs

Traditional IRAs have been around for a long time. They offer you the ability to put away up to $3,000 in your retirement account and get a tax deduction. If your employer does not offer a retirement plan or

One good thing about living in the past, it's cheaper.

you are not eligible to participate in a plan if there is one and you have earned income, you can make a tax-deductible contribution of up to $3,000 to your IRA. If you only earn $1,500 during a year, you can actually contribute $1,500 to your IRA for the year.

For 2003, if you or your spouse is an active participant in an employer-sponsored retirement plan and you still want to contribute more to your retirement savings, you can also use a deductible IRA. There are income limits, however. If you are single and your adjusted gross income (AGI) is less than $40,000, you're golden and can deduct the full $3,000, but if your income is between $40,000 and $50,000, the deduction is phased out. If you're married filing jointly, the limit is phased out between $60,000 and $70,000 of AGI. I know it's not fair that the married filing jointly is not twice as much as the single tax-payer limit. Congress on the other hand thinks it is!

Rollover IRAs

This IRA is set up to receive distributions from qualified retirement plans such as your 401(k), a 403(b) plan or a 457 plan. If you are in between jobs, it can become a holding tank for your retirement money until you decide if you want to transfer the money into your new employer's plan. There is no time limit on money held in a rollover IRA. If your new employer does not allow transfers, no sweat! If you change jobs again and the newest employer allows transfers, you can roll it then. Do not co-mingle any of your other IRA funds with your rollover IRA because you will lose the ability to transfer it back into an employer sponsored retirement plan.

Spousal IRA

This is an IRA funded for a spouse with little or no income by a spouse with at least $3,000 in income. The combined income must be at least equal to the amount contributed. They must file a joint tax return for the year the deduction is taken. A Roth IRA may also be used for the spousal IRA, but there is an income limit to deal with.

Retirement is the period of life when you stop quoting the proverb that time is money.

Eligibility is phased out once joint AGI is between $150,000 and $160,000. If you are a spouse who is at home taking care of children or an elder relative, you may want to consider a spousal IRA for those years you are out of the job market.

If you stayed at home raising kids between the ages 30 and 45 you were out of the job market for 15 years, those 15 years could put a big hole in your retirement planning. But if you used a spousal IRA over those years and contributed on average $3,000 you would have contributed $45,000 to your spousal IRA. Now if we assume a 9 percent return once you reach age 65 you could have $500,000 in your nest egg. Not bad!

Nondeductible IRAs

This is definitely the Cinderella of the IRA sisters, sort of hanging out by herself waiting for a date. If you don't qualify for any of the other IRAs due to income limitations, you can always plunk down $3,000 for a nondeductible IRA. It behaves like the other IRAs in this section; the earnings compound tax deferred, and but when money is withdrawn from the account only the earnings are taxed as ordinary income because the contributions were made with after-tax dollars. Penalty-free withdrawals before age 59 ½ are allowed if the money is used for first-time home purchases or for higher-education expenses.

Nondeductible IRAs should be used when you are looking to create more tax-deferred investing for your retirement portfolio or you are hoping to convert your IRAs eventually to Roth IRAs.

> *Beneficiary designations are very important. Be sure yours are up-to-date. If there has been a marriage, divorce, death, or birth, you may want to change the beneficiary designation. If you are not named as the beneficiary on your husband's retirement account, you won't be entitled to the money if he should die even if his will says he leaves everything to you!*

Money will not buy you happiness but it makes misery more comfortable.

Roth IRA

Let's take a look at the newest sister of the IRA group. It has features that the others do not. With a Roth IRA, you use after-tax dollars to make your contribution, but when you withdraw the funds in retirement, you will not owe income tax on the withdrawals. You must have earned income to contribute to a Roth, and you can continue to contribute past age 70 ½. But as with all the IRAs, you are limited to a $3,000 annual contribution.

There are some other rules you must live with. Withdrawals from the account will be free of income taxes if the owner has held the Roth IRA for at least five years and has attained the age of 59 ½. Other withdrawals allowed after the five-year holding period would be for a disability or a first-time homebuyer distribution. With a Roth IRA you are always permitted to get at your contributions without a penalty.

The minimum distribution rules do not apply to the Roth IRA, and funds can stay in the account past the owner reaching age 70 ½. The value of Roth will continue to grow tax-free for your heirs if you choose not to withdraw the funds. Your heirs can choose to stretch the withdrawals of the inherited Roth IRA over their lifetime. If your estate is very large, the Roth IRA proceeds may be subject to estate taxes.

As with all good things, there are limitations. Contributions are phased out for single taxpayers if your adjusted gross income (AGI) is between $95,000 and $110,000 and for married couples filing jointly with an AGI between $150,000 and $160,000. These income limits have not changed in many years.

Roth IRAs are good choices for saving for retirement. The younger you are, the sweeter the deal, and you can convert a regular IRA to a Roth IRA. The proceeds of your IRA will be taxable in the year you make the conversion, but there will not be a 10 percent penalty due if you are under age 59 ½. Here I go again with the limitations. This is easy: if your AGI is over $100,000, whether you are single or married, you cannot convert your IRAs. I don't make the rules, Congress does and I try to interpret the rules but this one makes no sense to me, and it has not changed in years.

Dollars do better if they are accompanied by sense.

A conversion works best if you do not need to take money out of the IRA to pay the taxes that will be due. You want to be able to leave the IRA intact. You can choose to convert only part of your IRA. This feature will allow you to convert only the amount you can afford the taxes on.

If you are under age 35, my blanket advice would be to convert as soon as you can and as much as you can. If you are older than 35, look to the online calculators at the various mutual fund web sites for help. If you want to use the Roth IRA as a wealth transfer tool, it makes sense to convert and pay the taxes up front. For more help on Roth IRAs check out www.msn.com, www.quicken.com and www.rothira.com.

The following table shows what an annual $3,000 contribution to an IRA can do over time. I have assumed a 9 percent return for your money, which is in a portfolio that is invested heavily in stocks. If you start your IRA at age 35 and contribute $3,000 a year for 30 years (until you reach age 65) your IRA nest egg could have grown to $409,000. Add two more years of saving and investing until you reach full Social Security age of 67 and you would have close to a half a million dollars in that nest egg!

IRA Nest Egg

Age	50	55	60	65	70
25	$254,000	$409,000	$647,000	$1,000,000	$1,600,000
30	$153,000	$254,000	$409,000	$647,000	$1,000,000
35	$88,000	$153,000	$254,000	$409,000	$647,000
40	$46,000	$88,000	$153,000	$254,000	$409,000
45	$18,000	$46,000	$88,000	$153,000	$254,000
50	0	$18,000	$46,000	$88,000	$153,000
55		0	$18,000	$46,000	$88,000

The drive-up bank window was established so the real owner of the car can see it once in a while.

The High Cost of Waiting to Start

It is never too late to start. (You've heard that before.) But there is a cost to waiting. The older you are when you start saving, the harder it is to catch up if you can ever catch up. And you heard me say this before: start saving for retirement with your first job.

Let me show you a chart that will help put it in prospective. First I need to set the stage. The Chicks from Dixie all invested in IRAs at different times in their careers. Now just work with me here!

Natalie started out at age 25 investing $3,000 a year in a Roth IRA. She had been to one of my seminars and had heard me talk about saving for retirement. She thought she would just do it until she got married and had kids. Then she would do some real planning when her Prince Charming came along.

Well, Prince Charming never found his way to her doorstep. Natalie never married (Maybe she fooled around a little bit!) but kept contributing $3,000 annually into her IRA account. She found saving and investing seductive as her account grew, and she loved looking at her quarterly reports and checking her investments online.

Her sister, Emily, at age 25 thought she'd do the same—just save until Prince Charming showed up which was 10 years later. When he did, she got married. Once the kids came along, there was no extra money to put away in her IRA. Then her Prince Charming, who had a roving eye, ran off with the last Chick from Dixie, Martie. As a single mom, life was a struggle. But Emily refused to withdraw the money from her IRA no matter how desperate things got.

She was really a cheapskate at heart and did not want to pay that 10 percent penalty to get at her money, and she was only able to invest those first 10 years. Over the years, she never opened any of her statements. She just let them pile up and used them as kindling to start fires in her wood-burning stove. (She was very thrifty as well as stubborn!)

Martie had a great time playing. She could see no reason for saving when there were so many great things in life to buy. She loved her

I got all the money I need if I die by four o'clock.
—Henny Youngman

credit cards, and they loved her back. They traveled together every-where. Their glitter attracted Prince Charming, who came trotting after her thinking she was wealthy. Little did he know that it was only rhinestones and not diamonds!

Prince Charming helped Martie run up those cards to their max, and then he took off on his horse, Discover, when the creditors started knocking on the door. This left Martie to face the music alone. Her friend, Natalie, dragged her to a women and money conference where an epiphany occurred. She struggled to get out debt and began to save, starting at age 35.

Martie has not done as well as Emily, who actually invested less money. But Martie is not complaining because she is pleased with her nest egg. What Emily had going for her was time, and she was pleas-antly surprised when she opened the envelope at her retirement party to find out how much money she had. Natalie, well, she did just fine didn't she? Now that she's a wealthy and wise old woman, she is instructing her nieces on what to do with their IRAs and what to include in a prenuptial agreement if Prince Charming should show up.

So let's take a look at what the Chicks from Dixie actually ended up with in their IRAs. Natalie invested $129,000, Emily invested $30,000 and Martie invested $99,000. Emily stopped investing the year Martie started and Martie never caught up. The earlier you can contribute to your retirement plan the more flexibility you will have in your retirement planning. By the way, Emily did forgive Martie after she saw that she had more money in the end!

A country superstar is someone who gets rich by singing about how wonderful it is to be poor.

IRA Contribution

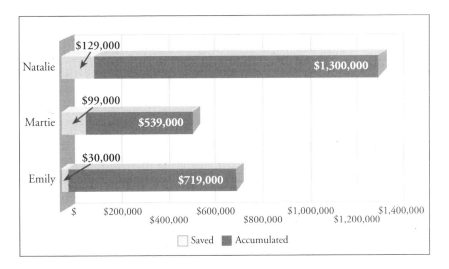

Natalie: $129,000 — $1,300,000
Martie: $99,000 — $539,000
Emily: $30,000 — $719,000

Axis: $ $200,000 $400,000 $600,000 $800,000 $1,000,000 $1,200,000 $1,400,000

Legend: ☐ Saved   ▨ Accumulated

Making the Money Last As as Long As as You Do

The good news is that we are all living longer; the bad news is that we are all living longer. To make your money last as long as you do, you will need to plan. There it is again, that four-letter word popping up in each chapter—plan.

Go back and review your cash flow worksheet that is in Appendix A. How much is it going to take to maintain your current lifestyle? Check the retirement savings worksheet in Appendix A. Have you accumulated enough assets to retire? If not, you may need to postpone retirement. There is a big gap between wanting to and being able to retire.

For example, if you are 60 and postpone retirement to age 65, you will receive a larger Social Security check, you will have five more years to save and invest, and you will have fewer years in retirement to provide for.

Two things are essential for a happy retirement: much to live on and much to live for.

Let's look at what an extra five years can do to a portfolio. If you had $50,000 invested and you were able to get a 9 percent return, it would grow to $77,000. And if you were able to save and invest $4,000 each year as well, that would add another $24,000 to your nest egg, which would now be worth $101,000.

Of course, if you run out of money, you can always go and live with one of the kids. Gotcha, didn't I? None of us wants to do that, especially if we love our kids. And if you don't love 'em, go live with them and make them miserable.

Getting Your Money Out

So how do you get your money out of the retirement plans? You know you have to wait until at least age 59 ½ with most of these plans; otherwise you will be required to pay a 10 percent penalty. That's what I've been telling you. But do you?

Getting at your IRA money before you reach 59 ½ is possible. If you want to retire early and most of your money is in your IRA account, there is a way around the 10 percent penalty but not the taxes. You can use the rule of 72t, which allows you to take the money in substantial equal periodic payments. Under this rule, you must take the payments for a period of at least five years or until you have reached age 59 ½. You don't want to mess this up for you will be assessed the additional 10 percent penalty by the IRS. These payments are based on the IRS tables you find on their website or in IRS publication 590.

This method can also be used with 403(b) plans. With a 401(k) plan, the rules are different. If you retire and leave your job at age 55 or older, you are allowed access to your 401(k) account without the 10 percent penalty, but you still owe the taxes. Here you can take out as much as you want or need.

The best thing about the future is that it comes only one day at a time.
—Abraham Lincoln

Minimum Required Distributions

Minimum required distributions (MRDs) must begin at age 70 ½ for almost all retirement plans except the Roth IRA and some old 403(b) plans. You are required by law to start minimum distributions by April 1st of the year after you turn 70 ½ but you will need to take your second distribution that year also. Receiving both payments in one year could bump you into a higher tax bracket. Consider taking the first payment by December 31 of the previous year instead. Got all that?

The distributions are based on your life expectancy using an IRS table, the Uniform Lifetime Table. You may be sure you're going to make it to 100, but the IRS has other ideas. Don't mess with the minimum required distribution because, if you are late in taking that first distribution, there is a 50 percent penalty on the amount of the required minimum distribution. That'll hurt worse than paying an early distribution penalty! The IRS wants to begin to collect taxes from you that you were able to defer all those years. If you are married and your spouse is more than ten years younger than you are and he is the beneficiary on your IRA you should use the Joint Life Expectancy Table to calculate your distribution. Your required distributions using this table will be smaller for the IRS takes into consideration that the younger spouse will outlive you. Now if you married a man ten years your junior that was smart planning for women usually outlive their spouses by an average of seven years. So now you will have someone to take care of you in your old age!

If you have multiple IRAs, you must use the combined value to determine the minimum distribution. You need only use one account to withdraw funds from though. If you have not rolled over all of your qualified retirement plans into an IRA, you must make minimum distribution calculations for each plan.

This can be complicated stuff! The custodian of your IRA or retirement plans should be there to help and to remind you that you are getting close to age 70 and need to make some decisions. That's the reason they ask you for your birth date on the application.

Failure is a detour, not a dead-end street.

If you need help in making your decision a trusted advisor is the only way to go. You may need to seek out a certified financial planner or a CPA to help. Check out Chapter 18.

So what if you have a pot of money that is not in a retirement plan? How long will it last? Here's a very simple calculation: If every year you only take out 4 to 5 percent and it is earning at least 6 percent, you'll always have money left in your pot. If your portfolio is returning over 10 percent a year, you can withdraw 8 percent year. There are many calculators online as well as software available to help you make your money last, and if you have a financial planner they can run annual calculations for you as well.

The Bottom Line

This is a very important chapter. IRAs will become more important as you continue to do your retirement planning. If you are using an employer sponsored plan such as a 401(k) for your retirement planning you will eventually transfer your 401(k) plan into an IRA. The Chicks from Dixie showed you how important savings for retirement is.

Notes:

ette had come to a book signing wanting some money questions answered and some help with her husband, Rob. I explained to Bette that help with her husband was out of my domain. I like to think that money questions are what I handle best, not marriage questions. Her concerns did revolve around money she told me; how to get her husband to start saving for retirement. He's never saved for retirement, figuring he would die at a young age and leave Bette a widow with life insurance and Social Security. At 50 he believes he's on borrowed time right now for his father died at age 48.

A year ago Rob lost his job and to add to their problems he suffered a heart attack and had bypass surgery. He has been working part time for the last couple of months and is hoping to find something full time. His fear is that no one will want to hire a 50 year old with his health history.

Bette's wake up call came when she received a benefits statement from the Social Security Administration. She realized that with her current savings and her projected Social Security benefits it was not going to be enough to maintain her current life style in retirement. She started to increase her contributions to her 401(k) plan and her husband began to complain about not having enough money available right now to do the things he wants to do.

One of their favorite past times is trying new restaurants. They enjoy eating out and Rob wants to continue, but Bette thinks the money would be better spent contributing to their 401(k) plans. She figures if the doctors are correct and Rob takes care of himself he could be around for another 20 to 30 years. But right now they are living paycheck to paycheck. They haven't gone over board so they are not spending more than they are earning, but Bette has been working overtime to keep up with the credit card bills and she is beginning to resent it she said.

Like a lot of people, Bette and Rob counted on Social Security to fund a larger portion of their retirement expenses than it ultimately will. Bette may have to reconsider her standard of living if something should happen to Rob for she would not be eligible for widow's benefits until she was age 60. And despite Rob's protests Bette needs to be diligently funding her 401(k) plan.

Chapter 9

Social Security and You

* * *

In This Chapter

This chapter is all about Social Security and some things you need to know because you are a woman. Social Security will always have a role in retirement and benefits planning. For some it may be a major source of retirement income and for others it will supplement your own retirement savings.

* * *

Why include a chapter on Social Security? Because, for many of you, it will be a significant portion of your retirement income. According to the Older Women's League (no, they're not retired women baseball players, but a nonprofit group dedicated to making older women's lives better), women represent 60 percent of all Social Security beneficiaries at age 65, and that number rises to 72 percent at age 85. Social Security represents 90 percent of the income of 41 percent of older women, with 25 percent of older women having no other source of income in retirement. Social Security will be part of your overall financial planning.

In 1999 the Social Security Administration (SSA) began mailing to all workers age 25 and older an individualized Social Security statement that shows their earnings history and gives estimates of retirement, survivor, and disability benefits. This statement should help you with your planning.

Those rainy days, for which a man saves, usually come during his vacation.

If you did not receive one or inadvertently tossed it out without looking at it, you can request another. The SSA sends these statements out on an annual basis, and you can expect yours a couple of months before your birthday. Contact Social Security online at www.social security.gov or call them at 800-772-1213 if you did not receive one.

A Brief History

The Social Security Administration celebrated its sixty-eight anniversary this year. The Social Security Act was passed by Congress and signed into law by President Roosevelt on August 14, 1935. This new act created a social insurance program designed to pay retired workers age 65 or older a continuing income after they retired. Early on, benefits were only paid to the primary worker. A 1939 change in the law added survivor benefits and benefits for the retiree's spouse and children. In 1956, disability benefits were added. In 1972, the Supplemental Security Income (SSI) program was added. This program provides a minimum income for poor individuals whether or not they are collecting Social Security benefits.

A major change came about in April 2000. President Clinton signed into law the "Senior Citizens' Freedom to Work Act of 2000," eliminating the earnings test for those beneficiaries at or above normal retirement age.

In the past, Social Security benefits had always been conditional on the requirement that the beneficiary be substantially retired, meaning you could earn only a limited amount of money while receiving Social Security benefits. If you exceeded that amount, you would lose some of your Social Security benefits. With the new Freedom to Work Act, however, this is no longer the case.

The Medicare program was created in 1965. Medicare is a health insurance program for the retired population over the age of 65, persons of any age with permanent kidney failure, and certain disabled individuals. This program is now administered by the Centers for Medicare and Medicaid Services (CMS) in the Department of Health

---

Money may still talk, but every year it makes less cents.

and Human Services. The Social Security tie with Medicare is the fact that applications for and general information about Medicare can be found at Social Security Administration offices around the country.

Is Social Security Going to Hell in a Handbasket?

No, it is not going to hell in a handbasket. But certainly there is much turmoil whirling around the system right now. Social Security will be there in the future, and it will be there for you today if you need it. It will look different in the future, but it will continue to be there and will evolve into what's needed for American workers and their families. You may have to contribute more, and you may be taxed on all of your benefits, but there will still be benefits.

Social Security and Medicare make up the largest part of our national budget. Social Security provides a minimum foundation of protection for retired workers and for workers who face a loss of income due to a disability or the death of a family wage earner. Social Security was never meant to be the sole source of retirement income for retirees.

The baby boomers, 76 million of them, will begin to retire in 2011, and as with everything else this group has done, it will have a big impact on the Social Security system and will put a strain on it. At that time, there will be more retirees and fewer workers paying into the system. Social Security is a pay-as-you-go system with most of the taxes being paid today going to fund current benefits. Excess funds are credited to the Social Security trust fund.

There is about $1.4 trillion currently in the trust fund, but benefit payments are projected to exceed taxes in 2018, and the trust fund will be exhausted in 2042. If this does happen, the SSA will only be able to pay about 73 percent of benefits owed, using dollars that are coming in from workers paying into the system. Now, this is if nothing is done about the situation. Some of the trustees want congress to raise the Social Security tax, some others want the retirement age to increase to 70 and still others want benefits to be decreased, while others want to

---

We got to get some other kind of distribution of money. The rich never had as much, and the poor as little. —Will Rogers

privatize Social Security. The judges are still out on which approach will solve the problem, but there is time to fix the problem.

Your Benefits

In order to get benefits from Social Security, you must work and pay taxes into the system. An exception would be an at-home spouse or a child of a worker, who would collect benefits as a dependent or a survivor. You earn Social Security "credits" that count toward eligibility for future Social Security benefits. You can earn a maximum of four credits each year. In 2003, you need to earn $890 for each credit. The amount of money needed to earn one credit increases every year.

Most individuals need 40 credits (10 years of work) to qualify for retirement benefits. Younger people need fewer credits to be eligible for disability benefits or for their family members to be eligible for survivor benefits if they die.

During your working lifetime, you hopefully will earn more credits than you need for eligibility. These extra credits do not increase your final benefit. However, the income you earn will increase your benefit because the more you earn and the longer you work, the larger your benefit will be because of the way the benefit formula is set up.

In 2003, you and your employer each will pay 6.2 percent of your gross salary, up to $87,000, to Social Security. Self-employed individuals will pay 12.4 percent of their taxable income into Social Security (again, up to the annual limit). Self-employed individuals are allowed a deduction when filing taxes for one half of the amount paid. The limit on the taxable income goes up every year. So the more you make, the more you'll pay.

Medicare needs to be dealt with here under this tax-bite section because it gets a piece of your paycheck each week also. There is no income limit on the amount you pay into Medicare. You contribute 1.45 percent, as does your employer; if you're self-employed, you contribute 2.9 percent. So if you get a $2 million bonus like Erin Brockovich did, you'll owe a 1.45 percent Medicare tax on all of it,

Money often costs too much. —Ralph Waldo Emerson

and her boss, Ed Masry, had to match it as well. For those of you who don't do math real fast, she paid $29,000 in Medicare taxes on her bonus.

Your benefit is based on your earnings averaged over your working lifetime, your date of birth, and the type of benefit for which you are applying. You want to be sure you have been credited for all of your earnings.

The key here for you is to keep good employment records. Hang on to those W-2s you receive from your employer. That W-2 may be the only proof you have of former employment. The Social Security Administration records your earnings information on an annual basis. It receives the information from your employer in order to credit your account. If your name or Social Security number is incorrect, someone else may be credited with your earnings.

Employers only have to keep employment records for four years, but the larger corporations keep them much longer. It is your responsibility to keep track of your Social Security earnings. When you receive your Social Security statement, check it against your old W-2s for any errors. If there are errors, correct them as soon as possible with the SSA. It is important to note that, as long as proof of earnings is presented, the SSA will make the correction, no matter how far in the past the error occurred. With women, errors may occur more often because we are in and out of the job market, and we may change our names more than once during our working careers. These opportunities are all ripe for errors.

Full Retirement Benefits

For 2003 full benefits are currently payable at age 65 and 2 months, with reduced benefits as early as age 62 to anyone with enough Social Security credits. Beginning this year, the age at which full benefits will be payable will increase gradually until it reaches age 67 (see chart below).

Experience teaches slowly and at the cost of mistakes. —J.A. Froude

Full Social Security Benefits

Year of Birth	Full Retirement Age
1937 or earlier	65
1938	65 and 2 months
1939	65 and 4 months
1940	65 and 6 months
1941	65 and 8 months
1942	65 and 10 months
1943- to 1954	66
1955	66 and 2 months
1956	66 and 4 months
1957	66 and 6 months
1958	66 and 8 months
1959	66 and 10 months
1960 and later	67

You can also retire at any time between age 62 and full retirement age. However, if you start at one of these early ages, your benefits are reduced a fraction of a percent for each month before your full retirement age. Your benefit amount will be lower if you begin your benefits before your full retirement age. They are reduced five ninths of one percent for each month. Ugh, I know, more math. But now you see why I recommend setting up a meeting with the people at the SSA to find out just what you are eligible for.

For example, if your full retirement age is 65 and 4 months, the reduction for starting your Social Security at age 62 is about 22 percent. If your birth year is between 1943 and 1954, the reduction factor is about 25 percent. If your birth year is after 1960, your full retirement age will be 67; if you take early benefits at age 62, your benefits will be permanently reduced by 30 percent. This is one of

---

It used to be that a fool and her money were soon parted, but now it happens to everybody.

those everlastingly decisions because you can't go back and change your mind once you start collecting benefits. The positive side of this is that you can still collect benefits at age 62.

Reduced Social Security Benefits

Year of Birth*	Full Retire-ment Age	Age 62 Reduction Months	Monthly % Reduction	Total % Reduction
1937 or earlier	65	36	.555	20.00
1938	65 and 2 months	38	.548	20.83
1939	65 and 4 months	40	.541	21.67
1940	65 and 6 months	42	.535	22.50
1941	65 and 8 months	44	.530	23.33
1942	65 and 10 months	46	.525	24.17
1943–1954	66	48	.520	25.00
1955	66 and 2 months	50	.516	25.84
1956	66 and 4 months	52	.512	26.66
1957	66 and 6 months	54	.509	27.50
1958	66 and 8 months	56	.505	28.33
1959	66 and 10 months	58	.502	29.17
1060 and later	67	60	.500	30.00

* Note: Persons born on January 1 of any year should refer to the previous year

After the government takes enough to balance the budget, the taxpayer has the job of budgeting the balance.

As a general rule, early retirement will give you about the same total Social Security benefits over your lifetime, but in smaller amounts to take into account the longer period you will receive them.

There are disadvantages and advantages to taking your benefit before your full retirement age. The advantage is that you collect benefits for a longer period of time. The disadvantage is that your benefit is permanently reduced. Each person's situation is different; so make sure you contact Social Security before you decide to retire.

The SSA does not require you to start your benefits just because you have reached your full retirement age. If you delay your retirement beyond full retirement age, you will receive an increase in your benefits when you do retire. I would recommend that you not wait beyond your full retirement age. With the Senior Citizens' Freedom to Work Act of 2000 eliminating the earnings test for those beneficiaries at or above normal retirement age, you can still work full time and collect your full Social Security benefits. My grandmother would have called it double dipping.

Disability Benefits

The SSA has very strict requirements before you can collect disability benefits. The requirements are based on your ability to work. You will be considered disabled if you cannot do work you did before, and then you must meet the strict requirement that you cannot adjust to other work because of your medical conditions. The disability must be expected to last for at least a year or result in death. This is not intended for a temporary or short-term disability, nor are benefits paid because of a partial disability. This is only for catastrophic stuff.

The average monthly benefit for a disabled worker with a spouse and one or more children in the year 2003 is $1,395. That's not enough to survive on much less pay essentials like a mortgage and buy groceries, but it does provide a base of protection you can count on each month.

Disability benefits are available for children as well. It is part of your benefit as a worker, and it provides for children who may suffer from mental retardation or other childhood afflictions. Always ask if

If it's such a small world, why does it take so much of our money to run it?

you are eligible for a benefit, the Social Security Administration does want you to get all that you're entitled to.

When you start collecting disability or retirement benefits, other members of your family may be eligible for benefits also:

✔ Your spouse if he or she is at least 62 or older

✔ Your spouse if he or she is under 62 and but is taking care of your child who is under age 16 or is disabled and receiving Social Security benefits

✔ Your child if she or he is not married and is under 18, or is under 19 and is a full-time student in a secondary school

✔ Your child over 18 if she or he became severely disabled prior to age 22

What Women Need to Know

When it comes to retirement benefits, you're entitled to your own benefits or one-half of your spouse's, which ever is larger. As always, there is an exception to every government rule. If you begin to collect benefits before full retirement age (currently age 65 and 2 months), your benefit will be less than the one-half. In that case, the amount of the spousal benefit is permanently reduced by a percentage based on the number of months before you reach full retirement age that you begin to collect. For example, if you begin collecting benefits early, the benefit would be about 46 percent of his at age 64; at age 63, it would be about 42 percent; and at age 62, it would go down to about 37 percent.

If your husband decides to continue to work past full retirement age and you have earned your own Social Security credits, you can retire and receive benefits based on your own record. Then when he retires, you can get benefits on his record if they would be higher.

You can take reduced benefits on your wage record before full retirement age. If you do, your benefits will always be reduced, even if

Always put off until tomorrow what you should not do at all.

you begin to take the wife's benefit once your husband retires. However, it still may be a good deal for you to do so. Upon the death of your spouse, you will begin to collect his benefit and lose yours.

You can collect benefits on a former spouse's Social Security record if:

✔ He is at least 62 or is deceased.

✔ Your marriage lasted at least 10 years.

✔ You are presently unmarried.

✔ You are age 62 or older. If he is deceased, you can collect benefits at age 60 (or age 50 if you become disabled).

If you have been divorced for at least two years and your ex-spouse is at least age 62, you can apply for Social Security at age 62 even if your former spouse has not retired (if you meet the preceding criteria). The amount of benefits that a divorced spouse receives has no effect on the amount of benefits a current spouse can get.

As a former spouse, if your ex dies, you could be eligible for a widow's benefit on his Social Security record even though you were not married to him for 10 years if:

✔ You are caring for his child who is also your child.

✔ You are unmarried.

Once you reach age 62, even if you have never been employed outside the home, you will be eligible for Social Security benefits when your spouse retires, becomes disabled, or dies. You will also be eligible for Medicare coverage at age 65.

Here are two more rules you need to be aware of:

✔ If you remarry before reaching age 60, you cannot receive widow's benefits as long as the marriage remains in effect.

✔ If you remarry after age 60, you will continue to receive benefits on your deceased husband's Social Security record.

Inflation is when half your salary goes for food and shelter and the other half does, too.

Household Workers

You need to be thinking about paying Social Security and Medicare taxes when you employ someone to work in your home, such as a cleaning person, a cook, a gardener, or a baby-sitter.

If you are a household worker, seriously consider asking your employer to pay these taxes for you. It may seem great at first to be paid "under the table," and there is a whole underground cash economy going on out there, but the problems come as you age because you are not building any retirement benefits or disability benefits. Consider going into business for yourself. Not only will you be able to build Social Security benefits, you will be eligible to contribute to a self-employed retirement plan or an IRA with earned income.

The rest of this section will be geared toward the employer. If you pay a household worker $1,400 or more in cash wages during the year, you are required to deduct Social Security and Medicare taxes and report the wages on an annual basis. Failing to do this in a timely manner may mean that you'll have to pay a penalty in addition to overdue taxes.

As always, there are special rules to work with. If you run a rooming house or a boarding house, all wages you pay must be reported even if they are less than $1,400. Earnings for household help under age 18 are exempt from Social Security taxes unless the household employment is the worker's primary occupation. If the kids next door work for you all summer baby-sitting and working in your garden, there are no taxes due.

You will be required to keep records of your employees: their names, addresses, Social Security numbers, and the amount of wages paid. You are required to withhold from their wages their share of Social Security and Medicare taxes and are required to match those withholdings. The Social Security rate is 6.2 percent of wages, and the Medicare rate is 1.45 percent.

It's easy to file your report because it gets filed with your income tax return (1040), and you pay the taxes with your return. You must

Lack of money is the root of all evil. —George Bernard Shaw

also give your household employee the IRS form W-2 by January 31 after the year in which the wages were paid. You'll need to also submit copy A of the W-2 to the Social Security Administration by the end of February. I know it appears to be a pain in the neck, but remember Zoe Baird and the "nannygate affair." President Clinton nominated her for Attorney General, and it was discovered she had not paid taxes for her household help. She never made it past the nomination process. Contact the IRS for the forms you need at 800-829-3676 or www.irs.gov.

Medicare

Medicare is a health insurance plan run by the Centers for Medicare and Medicaid Services (CMS) for people who are 65 or older. Individuals who are disabled and have received Social Security benefits for 24 months or have permanent kidney failure can get Medicare at any age. Medicare has two parts: Part A, which is hospital insurance, and Part B, which is medical insurance.

Medicare has been around since 1965 and has seen better days. According to the Hospital Insurance Trustee Report of 2003, income for the program will exceed expenditures through 2013 and then will begin to fall short (remember those baby boomers?) and will need to draw upon the trust fund, which they estimate will be depleted in 2026. So Medicare is in trouble!

Expect some changes down the road to Medicare. They have already been introducing HMOs, which have not worked out well for many of our seniors because some of them have gone bankrupt or have stopped servicing the seniors. I believe that, eventually, the eligibility age of 65 to receive Medicare benefits will be raised to 67. There may also be increased taxes and fewer services offered by Medicare in the future. The closer you are to retirement, the more attention you should pay to what Congress is doing that will affect your future Medicare benefits.

Bills travel through the mail at twice the speed of checks.

Medicare has two parts, hospital insurance and medical insurance. Hospital insurance, sometimes referred to as Part A, covers inpatient hospital care and certain follow-up care. You have already paid for Part A through your Medicare taxes.

Medical insurance, referred to as Part B, pays for physicians' services and some services not covered by Part A. Medical insurance is optional, and you must pay a premium that will be deducted from your Social Security check. If you are not collecting Social Security payments, you will be billed quarterly for the Medicare Part B premium.

If you're already getting Social Security benefits when you turn 65, your Medicare (Part A) starts automatically. If you're not getting Social Security, you should sign up for Medicare close to your 65th birthday, even if you are not ready to retire. For more information on Medicare, request the "Medicare and You" publication from:

Centers for Medicare and Medicaid Service (CMS)
800-MEDICARE (800-633-4227)
www.medicare.gov

Signing Up For Benefits

Signing up for benefits is not hard, but you do need to produce certain documents so that you have proof you're who you claim to be. You can also sign up for Medicare at your Social Security office. Call the Social Security Administration at 800-772-1213 to get the phone number and address of your local Social Security office. When you are making the appointment, ask what documentation you will need to bring with you. Depending on your circumstances and what benefits you are applying for, you'll need some or all of the following documents. You will need original documents or certified copies of all documentation the SSA requires. Do not mail these documents to Social Security! Always take them in personally, allow the employees to copy the documents, and then keep the originals. Do not leave them there; things

Just when you think you can make both ends meet someone moves the ends.

have a way of innocently disappearing. Social Security will now allow you to apply for benefits online (www.socialsecurity.gov).

You may need the following documents when applying for benefits:

✔ Social Security card

✔ Birth certificate

✔ Spouse's Social Security number

✔ Ex-spouse's Social Security number

✔ Divorce documents

✔ Spouse's birth certificate

✔ Spouse's death certificate

✔ Marriage certificate

✔ Children's birth certificates

✔ Children's Social Security numbers

✔ Most recent W-2 form

✔ Most recent tax return if you are self-employed

✔ Military discharge papers

✔ Proof of U.S. citizenship or lawful alien status if you were not born in the United States

✔ The name of your bank and account number (so your benefits can be directly deposited into your account)

You can work while receiving Social Security benefits. Earnings in or after the month you reach your full retirement age won't affect your Social Security benefits. In 2003, if you choose to begin early benefits (before your full retirement age), for any amount you earn over $11,520 ($960 a month), $1 in benefits will be withheld for every $2 in earnings. The limit has not been mandated by law, so it could very

A journey of a thousand miles begins with a cash advance.

well change for the future. This limit applies only to earned income that is wages or net income from self-employment (alimony is not considered earned income by the Social Security Administration). Things like pensions, interest, dividends, and capital gains do not count toward the dollar limit.

The Bottom Line

Social Security has some complicated rules and regulations. If you are unsure of when you can collect a benefit check it out with them. Keep the documents you will need to apply for benefits in the future in a safe place.

Early to bed and early to rise, makes a man healthy, wealthy, and wise. —Ben Franklin

andy told me she has paralysis by analysis and all of her family's savings are in just that, a savings account. Sandy and her husband analyze everything thoroughly before they take any action. But the more they learn about investing the more frightened they become about putting their hard earned money into stocks. So they have done nothing, they are paralyzed. She has wanted to venture into the stock market but figured it was too late to start now. The great bull market was over, but she did miss the great bear market for which she was thankful.

Sandy and Frank are a young couple in their mid thirties who have been married since they were both 22 years old. They were highschool and college sweethearts. They have the American dream, two children (a set of two-year-old twins), needing childcare when Sandy is working, a house in the suburbs, two cars in the garage and a new puppy. Sandy hopes to work full time when the children are older, but for now she works 25 hours a week, just enough time to qualify for the 401(k) plan and get the company match of three percent.

Sandy and Frank want to develop an investment portfolio that is more aggressive than what they are presently doing. They have a savings plan and not an investment plan. They understand that they need to take more risk with their investments but risk of any kind has proven to be very difficult for them.

Frank has his 403(b) plan invested in the fixed income portfolio. Sandy has her 401(k) money in the money market account, which is earning about one percent. Their personal savings amounts to their checking account, which is paying less than 1 percent, and their savings bonds program through work. They hope to use the savings bonds to help with college for their kids. They have been educating themselves about financial planning and they have got as far as goal setting. "But we get hung up on the investment planning" Sandy said. It is Sandy's mother-in-law that is pushing for them both to learn more about investing so they will be comfortable with investing their money and no longer suffer from paralysis by analysis.

Chapter 10

Achieving Your Goals Using Investments

In This Chapter

This chapter is about stocks, bonds and mutual funds. Learning about investing will help you successfully reach your goals. Our financial lives are more complicated than our mothers or grandmothers were for we need to know about this investing stuff and we need to be able to teach our daughters and sons.

So you'd like to be a millionaire, but you don't think you could survive one of those reality shows where you end up on an island eating anything that doesn't wiggle too much! And the lottery tickets you've been buying produce just enough winnings to buy more lottery tickets. So what's a girl to do?

More millionaires have been created by simply spending less than they earn and learning to invest the rest. Any time you have a dollar in your pocket, you have a choice: spend it or save it.

The first rule [of becoming wealthy] is not to lose money. The second rule is not to forget the first. —Warren Buffet

Debt or Equity

There are only two kinds of investments available for you: debt or equity. Everything else is a derivative of these two. When you purchase a CD from your local bank or a Treasury Bill from the U.S. Treasury, you are in essence loaning your money to the bank or the U.S. Treasury for them to use. The bank may make the money available for someone else to buy a car or a house; the Treasury may use it to pay down debt or buy a Hummer for the troops to use.

They promise you that they will pay you a fixed rate of return (interest) and tell you when you will be repaid in the future. They will also guarantee you the return of your entire principal. It sounds like a sweet deal: Your money earns interest, and you are guaranteed to get it back. But because it so safe, the bank and the Feds know that they can pay you the going interest rate, and you'll be very happy because you are looking for safety here.

When you participate in the equity market, you choose to buy something with your money. Equity is ownership, and you hope that whatever you buy will appreciate in value over time so you will be able to sell it for a profit. No one will guarantee a rate of return for your money, and no one will guarantee that you will get your money back. You have an equity position when you purchase stocks, real estate, mutual funds, or collectibles.

Equity investments may also produce income such as dividends or rental income, but investors look to them primarily for growth. Because there is no guarantee here, investors expect to be rewarded for the risk they are willing to take. That reward they hope is a higher return than they would get if they bought a CD.

What's a Stock?

A share of common stock equals a share of the ownership, or equity, in a corporation. The corporation sells shares of ownership to the public to raise money. With an IPO, an initial public offering, a privately

---

An investor should be more interested in the return of her money than in the return on her money.

held company will decide to sell shares in the company to raise money. That money may be reinvested in the company, or the owners may want a way to get some of their money out of the company.

Once it is a public company, it will be traded on one of exchanges in the stock market. The stock market represents a secondary market where sellers and buyers can get together, although you never ever see whom you are buying your stocks from.

Stocks usually sell in round lots of 100. You no longer get certificates when you buy stocks, but your purchase is registered with your brokerage firm and is held in "street name." You can buy stocks through a brokerage firm, and depending on your sophistication level, you can set up online trading through many discount brokers out there.

The price of a stock reflects its value in the market, what a buyer is willing to pay a seller. Prices are also affected by supply and demand. A stock may be undervalued due to a problem with earnings or sales. It may be overvalued because the market is expecting great things from it. Many experts today think that many of the technology stocks are still overvalued (that they are priced too high).

Stocks reward you in two ways. You may get a dividend, which is the way a company shares its profit with its shareholders, or the price of a stock may appreciate, and you can sell it for a profit. If you hold the stock for a year or longer, it is considered a long-term capital gain and is taxed at a maximum of 15 percent. If held for under a year, when you sell, it is taxed as ordinary income.

For help in evaluating stocks, head to www.morningstar.com. To hear all the news and some of the gossip, check out CNBC on cable TV. CNBC has teamed with MSN to bring you up to date information on their website: www.moneycentral.msn.com. Also CNN now has a cable station dedicated to money, CNNfn. There are several good shows featuring women anchors and reporters. CNN has teamed up with Money magazine to create another website dedicated to money, www.cnnmoney. com. CBS also has a very good website, www.cbsmarketwatch.com. Also check out the mutual fund

---

The patient woman realizes a profit on her investment whereas the only thing the impatient woman realizes is her mistake.

companies and the brokerage companies' web sites, were you can find helpful information as well. But beware of what can happen to you with all this information at your fingertips: the dreaded disease *paralysis by analysis*. You'll have so much information that you won't know which stock or mutual fund to buy or sell.

What's a Bond?

Bonds are used to raise money for corporations, municipalities, and governments. It's an IOU: You loan them the money, and they promise to pay you back at the end of a specified time period (the maturity). They also promise to pay you a set interest rate over that time period.

Bonds are usually considered safer than stocks because, if a company goes bankrupt, it will pay back its bondholders before it ever gets to its shareholders. All state and federal bonds are usually backed by the taxing power of the government.

Bond prices do fluctuate. A bond selling at a discount is selling below its maturity value, and a bond selling at a premium has a price above the maturity value. Why? Because interest rates go up and down. If you buy a five-year $1,000 bond with a coupon rate (interest rate) of 6 percent, you expect to be paid $60 a year or $30 semiannually over five years and then your $1,000 is returned.

If you have to sell the bond after three years because you need the cash, you may get more or less than your $1,000 depending on the prevailing interest rate in the bond market. If interest rates are higher than 6 percent, you will get less. This is because whoever buys your "old" bond could buy a new bond with an 8 percent interest rate and receive $80 in annual interest instead of the $60 your bond is currently paying. Your bond will sell for less so that the new owner will receive the equivalent of the 8 percent rate. If you hold on to your bond no matter what happens to interest rates over that five-year time period, you will get back your $1,000.

Bonds are rated by some of the same firms that rate insurance companies. Bonds with the highest quality and lowest risks are rated

Investing is not as tough as being a top-notch bridge player. All it takes is the ability to see things as they really are. —Warren Buffet

"AAA." Check with Standard and Poor's (www.standardpoor.com) or Moody's Investors Services (www.moodys.com). To learn more about investing in bonds, try www.investinginbonds.com. For US Treasuries go to www.publicdebt.treas.gov.

What's a Mutual Fund?

A mutual fund is pooled money provided by individual investors and the money is invested by a professional money manager. Mutual funds may have a load (commission) in which you are charged a fee to buy into the fund. They may have a back-end load, meaning you are charged a fee when you sell your shares, or they may be a no-load mutual fund, meaning there is no fee to buy into the fund.

All mutual funds do have fees; the mutual fund company is not managing your money out of the goodness of its heart. The fees for managing and running the fund come out of the fund before any profits are shared with you. If you are buying your fund through a planner or broker, you may end up paying a trailing commission each year to the planner through the 12b-1 fees charged by the mutual fund.

Mutual funds offer instant diversification because they are by their very nature diversified; they own more than one stock or one bond in a fund. They offer you the ability to get into the stock market with very little money, as little as $100 a month. To be really diversified in the stock market when you own individual stocks, you will need to own at least 10 stocks, and you might not have the money available or the time to learn about 10 companies. Mutual funds offer you a money manager who is diligent in keeping track of the portfolio every day. Mutual funds have individual objectives and investment philosophies. You'll need to get the fund's prospectus to see if it matches up with your needs. Mutual funds are categorized by their style of investing and their overall objectives.

Mutual funds can own stocks, bonds, CDs, and even real estate. A money market mutual fund owns debt investments that mature in

You only have to do a few things right in your life so long as you don't do too many things wrong. —Warren Buffet

under a year and that can include very large CDs. To understand what you are buying, you should read the prospectus. The prospectus is a document that describes the operations of the mutual fund. It divulges financial data about the company, the background of its officers and other information needed by investors to make an informed decision. The SEC requires that you get a copy, but it can't send someone to your house to be sure you read it! There is no Prospectus Police!

I can recommend this until I am 88, but most of you will not pick up a prospectus and read it. It is like reading the phone book in some ways because the legal department of the mutual fund company got hold of it. But it truly does hold valuable information.

Check out the finance books at your local library as well as the bookstores. I love sending people to the library, it is such an underused resource. Some libraries may even have computers for you to use if you don't have one at home, and many of them have a hard copy of the Morningstar report. Morningstar (www.morningstar.com) is a good tool to learn how to use because it will help you evaluate your mutual funds (as well as stocks) and find ones that meet your investment needs. Also check out the financial magazines on the newsstands (the library has copies as well). *Kiplinger's, Money, Fortune* and *Forbes* magazines all have titillating articles about mutual funds, stocks, bonds, taxes, investing, and almost anything else that has to do with your money. There is some good information there. Check the magazines' web sites as well. Then there are several good newspapers you can use as well. *Barrons,* the *Wall Street Journal,* and *Investor's Business Daily* and they all have good websites. If you don't have access to a computer at home do learn to use the ones at your local library.

Risks and Rewards

Every investment you make has some type of risk involved. If you decide to stash your cash in your mattress, keep it in a savings account, or buy the hottest biotechnology stock, you are putting your money at risk. Each simply has a different kind of risk.

Don't gamble: buy some good stock, hold it till it goes up and then sell it—if it doesn't go up, don't buy it! —Will Rogers

For accepting risk, you expect to be rewarded in some way. The more risk, the more reward, right? But you need to reach a balance with risk and reward.

The two major risks your have when investing are:

✔ **Loss of principal.** The risk here is that you will lose your original dollar amount invested.

✔ **Loss of purchasing power (also known as inflation risk).** The risk here is that you get a return on your investment dollars, but the return isn't enough to beat the inflation rate. Your dollars are intact; they just won't buy as much as they once did.

Here are some other risks you incur when investing and saving that you have no control over:

✔ **Market risk.** The stock market fluctuates, and oftentimes there is what is known as a herd mentality. If some things are down, everything goes down.

✔ **Interest rate risk.** This risk occurs when interest rates change. If you lock in a 6 percent return on your bond and then interest rates go up to 8 percent, you're not happy. The same is true if you locked in a mortgage at 8 percent, and then rates drop to 6 percent.

✔ **Currency risk.** When you invest overseas, dollars are converted to the foreign currency and need to be converted back again. Your gain or loss is reduced or increased by the change in the currency exchange rate.

There are many risks you face when investing. Learn what the risks are before you invest, and then decide whether the reward is worth the risk. The following investment pyramid illustrates the risk-reward relationship.

At the top of the pyramid are investments offering an extremely high return for your dollars and an extremely high risk of losing some of those dollars. These are speculative investments such as options,

It's not the bulls or the bears you need to avoid—it's the bum steers.

futures, limited partnerships, and commodities. These are the Maalox moments of investing, not for the average investor.

At the bottom of the pyramid are investments offering you security that your dollars will be returned, but they also have relatively low rates of return. The risk you face with these investments is loss of purchasing power. These include bank saving accounts, certificates of deposit, and federal securities.

Investment Vehicle Pyramid

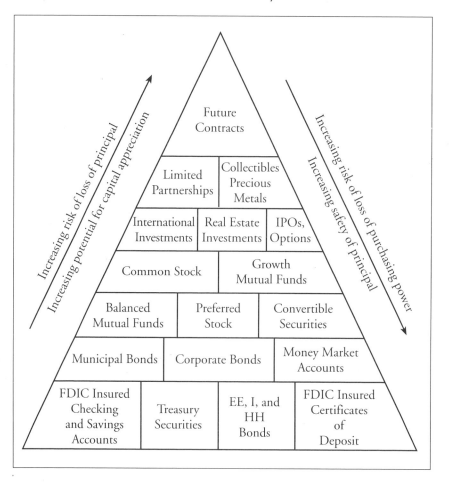

Investments from the base of the pyramid should make up the base of your personal investment pyramid. Then you will need to fill in the rest of the pyramid, staying away from the top 2 tiers.

Time Horizon Determines Risk Tolerance

So how much risk should you take on? Just enough to reach your goals and not lose any sleep while doing it. It's a tricky balance!

Your time horizon actually dictates how much risk you can take. If your goal is to accumulate $10,000 for a down payment on a home that you would like to purchase in one to two years, your time horizon is very short. With a short-term time horizon, you want to use investments at the bottom of the pyramid; you don't want to assume much if any risk. You want to be sure that, if you find just the right house, your down payment is sitting there waiting for you. Using a money market account to hold your money while accumulating the down payment would be a good choice here. I know its not paying very interest right now, but its safety you are after here.

If the goal is a comfortable retirement and you're 30 years old right now, your time horizon is very long. You have a long time to invest, but more importantly, you have time on your side. Time to ride out the ups and downs of the stock market. So with 30 years or more before you will need the money to reach your goal, you can assume a lot more risk with it. Here, you venture into the middle of the pyramid and look at growth mutual funds and stocks for your retirement portfolio.

If the goal is to put the baby through college and the baby has just started middle school, you have about six years before you need the cash to make the first tuition payment. You can take on more risk than you would with the down payment for a house, investing in stocks and growth mutual funds, but as you get within a year or two of that first tuition payment, you want to be sure you have tempered some of the risk by putting the first year's expenses into a money market account. This way, the money is available no matter what happens in the stock market.

The principal interest of an investor should be the principal and not the interest.

Diversification: The Key To Successful Investing

I've already got you thinking about risks, rewards, and time horizons. Next is diversification. Big word! When you invest, you make choices; in determining those choices, you consider what your goals are for the investment, your time horizon, and your risk tolerance. But putting all of your money into one investment isn't wise. If that investment goes up, you're happy, but if it goes down, you're not happy—and worse, you could be broke.

My grandmother always told us not to put all of our eggs in one basket when we went to the hen house. Grandma would have made a great financial planner. Don't put all of your money into one investment. You want to spread your money around, and by doing so, you spread out your risk of loss.

Spreading your investment dollars among different asset classes is referred to as "asset allocation." You are allocating your assets. The asset classes are stocks, bonds, cash, and real estate. You can break these down even further. For stocks, you can break it down to domestic (U.S.) and international, and then you can look to include large company stocks, mid-size companies, and small companies to further diversify the equity portion of your portfolio. Bonds, well, you might want some corporate and government bonds. Corporate bonds usually pay a higher interest rate. Real estate could be the home you live in or a rental property or a mutual fund invested in real estate properties.

Stocks and bonds usually have an inverse relation. If stocks are up, bonds are down. Real estate values are usually up when stocks are up and interest rates are down. So if you have your money spread around, part of your portfolio will always be doing well. You want to create a balance between asset classes. A balanced portfolio consists of stocks and bonds and cash.

> *Investing has a vocabulary all its own. In Appendix B there is a list of 5 good web sites to check out. A good book is* Decoding Wall Street *by David Caruso and Robert Powell.*

When someone tries to get you to invest money in a good buy, make him spell out the term.

Over long periods of time, stocks have outperformed bonds. If we take into consideration taxes and inflation, stocks are the only investment that has beaten them both. The real return on large company stocks if we were to factor in taxes would be 7.7 percent and then add inflation and your *real* return would be down to 4.5 percent . Check out the following chart. Over the last 77 years since 1925, inflation has averaged 3.1 percent.

Rate of Return for The Last 77 Years (1925 thru 2002)

Investment	Rate of Return (%)	After Taxes (%)	Factor in Inflation (%)
Large Company Stocks	10.2	7.7	4.5
Government Bonds	5.5	4.3	1.2
Treasury Bills	3.8	2.2	-0.8

The Inflation Police

What is this scary thing called inflation? Inflation has been described as "too much money chasing too few goods." When this happens, the prices of goods will go up. Supply and demand. If prices go up too much, this could cause inflation to increase too much. There will always be some inflation around because you and I want our wages to increase. If you work for a bakery and want a raise, the bakery then must charge a higher price for bread to be able to pay the employees a higher wage.

I, on the other hand, as a consumer of bread products, see bread prices going up along with everything else, so I go to my employer and ask for higher wages so that I can afford the higher price of bread. My employer sells cars so in order to pay for an increase in my wages he raises the prices of the cars on the lot. As a baker you need a good car to get to work at 3:00 AM and your car just broke down so you are on

Inflation is being broke with a pocketful of money.

our sales lot looking for a replacement and remarking that the prices have gone up. It's a cycle. Can you remember when ice cream cones cost 50 cents? I bet there are a few of you who can remember 10 cents cones! Too much inflation, however, leads to economic problems.

The inflation police is the Federal Open Market Committee, which consists of 12 members: the seven members of the Board of Governors of the Federal Reserve System, the president of the Federal Reserve Bank of New York, and for the remaining four memberships, which carry a one-year term, a rotating selection of the presidents of the 11 other reserve banks. This committee, led by current Federal Reserve Chairman Alan Greenspan, has an affect on every one of us. The committee meets every six weeks to evaluate how the economy is doing. This committee has been charged by Congress with keeping inflation at bay; doing so supposedly prevents recessions in our economy.

This committee controls inflation in the economy by raising or lowering the discount rate. The discount rate is the interest rate that the Federal Reserve charges its member banks when it loans them money (yes, even banks borrow money). If the discount rate is high, it discourages borrowing; if it's low, it encourages borrowing. This controls the money supply in the market. The banks make money by borrowing money from the Feds and then loaning it you, charging you a higher interest rate than they are paying. If it's too expensive to borrow, you won't buy that house or finance that car. This, in turn, slows down the economy and slows down inflation.

Higher interest rates are not bad for all consumers. Many retirees are delighted when rates increase because their CDs will pay them a higher return. On the other hand, a young couple will put off buying a house, or a startup business may not be able to afford the new equipment it needs. This is what slows down growth in the economy.

Two other interest rates affect you. The federal funds rate is the rate that banks charge each other for the use of the fed funds. The rate the banks charge their most credit worthy customers is the prime rate. Many other interest rates are tied to the prime rate such as a home equity line of credit.

Inflation is when your nest egg is no longer anything to crow about.
—Jimmy W. Marsh

How to Measure Success

Measuring financial success is nebulous at best. If you have enough money to finance a great retirement with some left over for the kids to inherit, this is a good thing. If your nest egg didn't reach the $1 million goal you set, is this a bad thing?

Some goals are easier to measure than others. If you need to save $75,000 to put the twins through college and you only come up with $50,000, you didn't make it. But you can do other things to get them through college like borrowing—both you and them. And they could get jobs. In the end, they would receive their college degrees, and your goal of getting them through college would be met.

Using Benchmarks

The way money managers measure their success in the stock market is to compare their results against a benchmark to see if they outperformed the benchmark. If you were an athlete, you would do the same thing—look for something to compare your performance against.

You must, however, compare apples with apples. When listening to the evening news on the way home from work, you hear that the market was up for the day. The DOW was up, NASDAQ was down, and the S&P was up. What does that mean to you? They are all indexes that give us an indication of what is happening in the stock market. Indexes are a collection of stocks or bonds, and when you hear the results of the day, it is an average—sometimes a weighted average—of what happened within the indexes. If you own an individual stock, it may be up or down for the day compared to the index.

You'll want to use an index to measure how well your mutual fund or stock has done, but doing this daily will drive you to the funny farm. Do it annually, semi-annually.. You'll also want to measure your mutual fund against other mutual funds in the same category. For instance, if you have a balanced mutual fund that owns stocks and bonds, you don't want to measure it against just a stock index because

The wise investor in stocks or mutual funds always seeks outcome rather than income.

it will come up short. Use a mutual fund rating service like Morningstar to help you here (www.morningstar.com).

Here is a list of the most popular indexes and what's in them. The DOW, which you hear the most about, has only 30 stocks in it. In my opinion, it's not the best barometer of the stock market. Look at what the S&P is doing to get a broader perspective or even the Russell 5000.

- ✔ **Dow Jones Industrial Average (DJIA).** Price-weighted average of 30 actively traded blue-chip stocks. Prepared and published by Dow Jones & Company (*The Wall Street Journal*), it is the oldest and most widely quoted of all the market indicators. The average is quoted in points, not in dollars. It is often referred to as "The Market."

- ✔ **Morgan Stanley International World Index.** This index is compiled by Morgan Stanley, a large brokerage and financial services corporation. The index measures global markets, including the United States, and is weighted both by country and by industry.

- ✔ **Morgan Stanley EAFE Index.** This is Morgan Stanley's international index. It measures market performance in Europe, Australia, and the Far East (EAFE) that includes 21 countries and is widely used to measure international performance.

- ✔ **NASDAQ Combined Composite Index.** This index is based on the National Association of Securities Dealers Automated Quotations (NASDAQ). It is a market value—weighted index of all the stocks listed on the NASDAQ. Is a good mid-cap index.

- ✔ **The Russell 3000.** The Russell 3000 is compiled by the Frank Russell Company and is an index of the 3,000 largest U.S. stocks.

- ✔ **The Russell 2000 Index.** This index measures the performance of smaller companies—it is a weighted index of the 2,000 smallest companies in the Russell 3000.

The best time to buy stocks and bonds is always in the past.

✔ **The Russell 1000.** An index of the 1,000 largest companies in the Russell 3,000, representing about 92 percent of the total market capitalization of the Russell 3000.

✔ **Standard & Poor's 500 Composite Stock Price Index.** This index is compiled by Standard & Poor's Corporation, a large financial services company that also publishes credit ratings. The stocks in the S&P 500 represent approximately 70 percent of the total market value of all publicly traded U.S. corporations. The S&P 500 is a popular indicator of overall stock market performance because it measures such a broad segment of the equity market. There are 400 industrial stocks, 20 transportation stocks, 40 utility stocks and 40 financial stocks.

✔ **Wilshire 5000 Equity Index.** The broadest of all the averages and indexes, the Wilshire Index is market value—weighted and represents the value, in billions of dollars, of all companies with headquarters in the U.S. There are over 7,000.

✔ **Lehman Brothers Government/Corporate Bond Index.** This index is compiled by Lehman Brothers, a large brokerage and financial services company, to measure the broad bond market. The index contains more than 4,000 government and corporate bonds.

For more help with investing think about starting an investment club. All-women clubs have historically done better than any other groups. The National Association of Investors Corporations (NAIC) is a good place to start. They will send you everything you need to organize an investment club. Call 877-275-6242 or write to them at P.O. Box 220, Royal Oak, MI 48068. Their web site is www.better-investing.org.

Another organization you should consider joining is the American Association of Individual Investors (AAII), 625 N Michigan Ave., Chicago, IL 60611. You can contact them at 800-428-2244 or www.aaii.com. They have a monthly journal that is worth the price of the membership fee. They also put together an annual list of the top investment web sites.

Our problem is not what is the dollar worth in London, Rome, or Paris, or what even it is worth at home. It's how to get hold of it, whatever it's worth. —Will Rogers

The Bottom Line

Investments come in two flavors, debt or equity. Debt provides us with financing for our short-term goals for we are usually guaranteed a rate of return and we use equity to finance our longer-term goals. Both have a place in your portfolio. The key to successful investing is to be an informed investor.

Inflation has made it possible for only the rich to afford a recession.

Notes:

"I'm a busy young retiree," Lois explained. And she truly is a young retiree. She retired two years ago at 53 and has not looked back since. Widowed at a young age with two small boys, Lois learned what she should have done about estate planning very quickly. They had no will and although they owned many things jointly the house was in her husband's name as well as all of their securities. Getting through the emotional turmoil and the endless paperwork was difficult. And worse she found that the state law did not allow her to inherit her husband's possessions entirely. She received 50 percent and the children received 50 percent, making her future planning more complicated.

One of the first things Lois did after the death of her husband was to get her affairs in order so her children would be protected if something should happen to her.

Lois worked for one company for 25 years and was burned out. So when an early retirement package was offered to her she jumped at the chance. She took the pension and ran, but left her retirement money in the company's 401(k) plan. Lois knew she could not live on her pension alone especially when she couldn't collect Social Security until she was at least age 60.

There were two major concerns for Lois when she retired—her two kids. The oldest is in college and youngest a senior in high school. The oldest is living at home and going to school. So that means feeding and clothing him. The boys are four years apart, (great college planning) so when one finishes up the second child will start college.

Lois found a part time job with a lot less stress and pressure and she is using that income stream to pay for the education costs of the kids. Lois has told the kids that she will come up with $10,000 annually for school and they will have to figure out a way to manage any extra costs above that. With those parameters, the state college system became very appealing to the kids.

Lois updates her will and estate plan every five years unless there is a major life change like one of the boys reaching age 21.

Chapter 11

The Last Big Planning Hurdle: Estate Planning

In This Chapter

We're all going to die, we just don't know when and if we did know we could plan very well. This is the last taboo subject. Being prepared helps those we leave behind.

Discussing death is the last taboo in American society. That's why most individuals put off doing anything about estate planning. "Why, estate planning is too expensive," they tell me. "Why it's only for the wealthy or for very old people or maybe if you're sick. Why it's only for married folks, and I am single." Did you hear yourself in those excuses? These are just a few of the excuses I have heard when I ask members of an audience if they have done their estate planning. Some of the excuses have been quite creative!

Dealing with your own mortality and morbidity does take a certain amount of fortitude. Statistically, I know that 30 percent of you have dealt with it, but the other 70 percent have your heads in the sand. Elderly parents find it easier to talk to their adult children about sex than about death, dying, and estate planning. But by not doing proper estate planning, the burden of financial and legal confusion is added to a time already fraught with emotional turmoil.

Money may not be everything, but it keeps you in touch with your children.

What do J.P. Morgan and Elvis Presley have in common? They actually do have something in common. They did not do proper estate planning. They did some but not enough! J.P. Morgan, who had enough money to bail out the banking crisis at the turn of the twentieth century, lost almost $12 million of his $17 million estate to taxes. Elvis, well, his heirs lost $7 million to taxes of his $10 million estate. His ex-wife Priscilla was behind the phenomenal growth that took place at the Elvis Presley Enterprises after his death for the estate was left in trust for his only daughter, Lisa Marie. Okay, so you're not J.P. or Elvis, but you do have an estate, and you do need to protect it. Elvis wisely chose his ex-wife to handle the estate if he were to die.

Everyone Needs Estate Planning

"Estate planning" is a broad term that encompasses many important issues. Most of you think it is just about dying, but it's not. Estate planning is planning that you do for yourself as well as for your heirs. Your estate plan is used while you are alive and upon your death. It is all about arranging your affairs so that things will be easier for both you and your heirs. It allows you to do the following:

✔ Name a guardian if you have dependent children

✔ Name the executrix/executor of your choice for your estate

✔ Reduce or eliminate estate taxes

✔ Identify your assets and liabilities in order to plan for your family's protection in the event of an untimely death

✔ Distribution of your belongings according to your wishes at the time of your death

✔ Help your heirs settle your affairs

✔ Protect yourself during a period of possible physical or mental incapacity

Money is a commodity that is constantly changing hands—and people.

✔ Provide direction to loved ones if you are ever in a permanently unconscious state

✔ Possibly avoid probate

Now, if you have done nothing to address the fact that you have an estate or need to care for minor children, the state where you reside will step in. Through its laws of intestacy (a term meaning that you have died without a will), the state will designate who your heirs will be and what property they will receive. The state will also appoint a guardian for your minor children. Whether your estate is large or small, I can guarantee that there will be family feuds over who gets what and who cares for the kids unless you have spelled it out. It's not a pretty sight!

What It Could Cost

Your estate is the total value of all your possessions: all you own (like your home, car, pension plans, plus what may be owed to you) minus all that you owe. It sounds like your net worth, doesn't it? A word of caution: When reviewing all that you own, it is just the assets that are held in your name that get included in your estate. If you own your home with your spouse/child/partner, only part of the value of the home is yours, and only that portion would be included in the value of your estate.

What you do need to include here that you did not include in your net worth is the proceeds from your life insurance policies if you should die. So pull out your net worth worksheet and add in the life insurance proceeds to see what the value of your estate might look like. This will give you some numbers to work with when doing estate tax planning.

The estate and gift tax is a transfer charge assessed on property you give away either during your lifetime or upon your death. The estate and gift taxes are called "unified" because the same tax rates, deductions, and rules apply to both. You can, during your lifetime or upon

The world is full of willing people; some willing to work and the rest willing to let them. —Robert Frost

your death, give away $1 million of assets in 2003 without incurring a federal estate tax. This is your "exemption." If you have not given away assets while you were alive, the federal estate and gift taxes would apply to your estate only if it was valued at more than $1 million for 2003. Now that limit will increase to $1.5 million in 2004 and eventually reach $3.5 million by the year 2009 and for the year 2010 the estate tax is repealed just for that one year. Then in 2011 it sunsets, reverts back to 2001 limit of $675,000 unless Congress changes the tax laws again, and I can assure you they will for they mess with them every year!

If your estate exceeds that amount of the exemption, your estate is subject to marginal estate tax rates starting at 49 percent. This too will change and as the exemption increases through 2009, the tax rate will decline. The chart below provides more specifics.

Tax Planning

Year	Estate and Gift Exemption	Top Estate and Gift Tax Rate
2003	$1 million	49%
2004	$1.5 million	48%
2005	$1.5 million	47%
2006	$2 million	46%
2007	$2 million	45%
2008	$2 million	45%
2009	$3.5 million	45%
2010	N/A Taxes repealed, top individual rate, 35% (gift tax only)	N/A
2011	$ 675,000	45%

She made money the old fashion way—she inherited it.

A look at your net worth will let you know if you need to do some complicated estate planning. If you are married, you may leave everything to your spouse free of federal estate taxes. This is the unlimited marital deduction. If your combined estates are over $1 million for 2003, you may want to do some fancy estate planning using trusts or gifting so that each of you can take advantage of your $1 million exemption. If you do no planning and leave everything to your spouse, upon his death, he is only entitled to use his own exemption amount in his planning—yours, if not used, is lost forever.

Let's look at an example. Suppose that you finally surrender to my not so subtle hints that you fill out a net worth statement. You discover that your family's net worth is $2 million. Many of your assets are owned jointly and each of you is named as beneficiaries on the retirement plans and the life insurance policies.

Upon the death of the first spouse, everything will go to the surviving spouse. There will be no federal estate taxes owed because of the marital deduction. But what happens when the surviving spouse dies? She now has an estate worth over $2 million and if she does not deplete the assets before she dies, she'll be able to use her $1 million exemption for 2003 to shelter some of the taxes. But her estate will still owe taxes on $1 million. At the marginal rate of 49 percent that amounts to $490,000. With some planning, though, you can disinherit Uncle Sam and give the $1 million to your heirs free of estate taxes.

Both spouses need to take advantage of their unified credit exemptions and you'll need to set up a trust. Rather than owning most of the assets jointly, you should try to equalize your estates. (That may not be easy if one spouse has a large retirement plan.)

For example, let's give the husband $1.4 million and the wife $600,000. When the husband dies (wives usually outlive husbands), his will leaves his assets to a family trust (also called a bypass or a credit shelter trust) designed to take advantage of his unified credit exemption. What does not go into the trust the wife can receive free of federal estate taxes. His widow can receive all of the income from the family trust and will be able to control it. When she dies, the assets in

Money is relative, the more money the more relatives.

the trust pass to their children free of estate taxes. Her assets will also pass to the children free of federal estate taxes, because of her unified credit exemption. That planning results in a savings of $490,000. Now if we could plan exactly when they would die and if it would in the year 2010 we would have no need for planning at all would we?

> *If you are not a United States citizen, you will not qualify for the unlimited marital deduction unless the assets pass to a qualified domestic trust (QDOT). The rules require at least one trustee of the trust be a U.S. citizen because the government does not want you leaving the states with the inherited assets.*

The Economic Growth and Tax Relief Reconciliation Act of 2001 was the tax law that gave us the increases in the estate tax exemption, which indeed will bring some people relief from federal estate taxes. But as always there are side effects to tax law changes.

If your estate was large enough to require paying taxes on the federal estate tax form, there was a credit allowed to the state you resided in. Most states just "sponged" the credit from the Feds and were happy to get the extra revenue. In essence the Feds shared the taxes. But with the tax law changes the Feds began to reduce the credit by 50 percent in 2003, 75 percent in 2004 and then repealing the credit entirely for 2005.

Many states have taken action and changed their laws accordingly. Most states are in fiscal distress and many will be looking to get some relief by adding new estate taxes. There are 50 states with 50 different sets of laws. So you may not owe the Feds anything but there may still be estate taxes due.

Where There's a Will There's a Way

Everyone needs a will. Do I need to say more? None of us is getting out of this world alive! We are all going to die; we just don't know when, so you need to prepare as if you were going to die tomorrow. Not a pleasant thought, but for planning very practical!

Borrowing is the American way. How else did the national debt get so big?

A will allows you to rule from the grave. You can't take it with you, but you can decide where it goes. A will is simply a document that expresses your wishes as to how you want your assets distributed after your death. In addition to distributing your estate according to your wishes, a will can do many other things. A will can allow you to choose a guardian for minor children and an executrix (executor if it is a man) to distribute your assets to those named in the will.

If you do not have a will when you die, you are "intestate," which simply means you have died without a will, the state where you reside will distribute, according to state law, your assets. If there are minor children involved, the state will decide who will become their legal guardian. The legal lines of succession vary from state to state. Your assets will go to your next of kin in proportions and in sequences mandated by state law.

If you own anything jointly with right of survivorship, that asset will automatically pass to the joint owner. If you have named a beneficiary on your IRA, 401(k) plan, pension plan, or life insurance policy, the money will pass automatically to the named beneficiary.

There are some states where you cannot disinherit a spouse or child. Some states allow a spouse to take more than was allotted in the will. For most states, you can disinherit anyone but your spouse.

A will is legal document, and to be valid, it usually must be signed in front of two witnesses and be notarized. Additionally, you should initial each page. You can change a will either by executing a new will or by adding a codicil. A codicil is just an amendment to the original will. The codicil must be witnessed and notarized.

There is lots of do-it-yourself estate planning out there. You can use this information to learn about estate planning, but my preference is for you to interact with an attorney because it is too easy to have some small detail mess up the do-it-yourself estate plan. I know some of you would rather have a tooth pulled than go to an attorney but go!

There are many web sites that can help. Check out the sites and buy the books, but in the end, head to an attorney for the final document. Make one mistake, even a small one, and it could possibly mess

---

Old bankers never die—they just lose their balance.

up the very lives of the people you are trying to protect. Check out www.nolo.com, a resource for do-it-yourself books and software. Because situations change throughout life, you should be sure to review your will periodically:

✔ Every five years at a minimum

✔ When there are major life changes caused by a marriage, divorce, birth, death, job change or a disability

✔ When the needs or circumstances of your beneficiaries change

✔ When the size of your estate increases or decreases

✔ When you move or retire to a different state

✔ When the estate tax laws change

Probate

Probate is the process by which your will is proved to be valid. The named executrix must present the will in court before being allowed to carry out the deceased's wishes as stated in the will. Probate validates the will, approves inventories, determines the value of property, pays creditors, and distributes assets.

State laws govern the probate process, and each state has a different set of laws. The proceedings take place in the probate court of the county where the deceased person resided. The process can take a few weeks to many months, depending on the complexity of the estate. Charges incurred in probate are generally regulated by state law and can be based on the value of the estate. The fees may include court costs, appraisers' fees, the executrix's fees, CPA fees, and attorney's fees.

The probate court will appoint someone to administer your estate. In most cases, the court will name the person you have chosen as executrix in your will. The executrix supervises the cataloging, the appraisal, and the distribution of your assets. She is charged with managing the estate until it is settled, arranging for your family's immediate needs, and preserving any business interests you may have.

Money—you can't take it with you, but where on earth can you go without it?

Some of the obligations of the executrix are to:

✔ Handle funeral and burial arrangements.

✔ Probate your will.

✔ Collect and take an inventory of your assets.

✔ Collect all your financial records.

✔ Collect and pay your debts.

✔ Distribute your assets.

✔ File final federal and state income tax returns for the year in which you died.

✔ File estate tax returns, even if there is no tax due.

Your Executrix

So who should be your executrix? It can be a thankless job, especially if the beneficiaries create problems. A candidate could be a child (name only one), your spouse, friends, siblings, or professionals such as attorneys and bank and trust companies.

Those closest to you may have the advantage of knowing and understanding your final wishes, but they may be at a disadvantage in dealing with beneficiaries. This may be especially true if you choose one child over the others. A professional may be helpful if you have a complicated estate or a business you would like to continue. Or you can choose a family member as the executrix and have her look to your attorney for guidance and to file all the proper paperwork. Many attorneys will charge an hourly fee for this service. Executrixes are allowed to charge a fee for their services as well.

You should keep in mind that it is difficult to settle an estate long distance. If you name a child who lives far away, he or she will have to travel or hire someone locally to help. Also, it will be the child who lived near you who will do all the running around for the estate. Make sure you give whoever will have the responsibility the authority.

Our only solution of relief seems to be to fix it so people who are in a hole through borrowing can borrow some more. —Will Rogers

Tell 'Em What You Want to Tell 'Em

Not all of your wishes and instructions regarding your estate and assets need to be detailed in your will—especially those instructions that may change over time. Directions for the distribution of some of your personal property can be included in a letter of instruction. If you want your jewelry to be given to your granddaughters and your walking stick to go to your nephew, these can all be addressed in a letter of instruction.

Funeral instructions can also be part of this letter. A word of caution: If you have planned your funeral and want it carried out as planned, be sure your family and friends know about it and know where your letter is kept. Many a family has found the letter of instruction of a loved one well after the funeral. It is much easier to alter or create a letter of instruction than it is to deal with a new will.

While not legally binding, a letter of instruction can be a helpful guide to your family and executrix. You can include such things as:

✔ Names and addresses of people to be notified of your death.

✔ Instructions for your funeral or memorial service and information on preparations already made.

✔ Your obituary if you would like to write your own.

✔ Location of important papers (use the inventory worksheet located in Appendix A which was discussed in Chapter 3).

✔ Disposition of personal property such as jewelry and furniture.

✔ Life insurance information and beneficiaries.

Trusting Your Assets to Trusts

Trusts are legal arrangements in which a grantor transfers assets to a trustee, who holds and manages them for the benefit of the named beneficiary. The *grantor* is the person who establishes the trust. The

---

Old bank tellers never die—they just yield to maturity.

trustee is the person to whom the property is entrusted for safekeeping. The *beneficiary* is the person receiving the benefit of the assets. With some trusts, such as a living trust, you may be wearing all three of these hats at the same time.

For example Elvis set up the trust so he was the *grantor* and Priscilla was the *trustee* for she managed the trust until the *beneficiary*, Lisa Marie reached 30. This trust was set up for Lisa Marie who was a minor when her father died.

Here are some of the reasons for establishing a trust:

✔ Avoiding probate

✔ Providing privacy

✔ Protecting assets from creditors

✔ Managing money for minor children

✔ Managing assets if you are unable or unwilling

✔ Providing for a child with special needs

✔ Utilizing your unified credit and marital deduction

Trusts are very complicated estate planning tools. A word to the wise: Don't try this at home. Get help but be sure your help is competent. Scam artists are selling living trusts door to door to the elderly.

Trusts can be set up while you are alive or be created by your will upon your death. These are referred to as testamentary trusts. I will briefly outline some of the more common trusts here. The more complicated your life and finances, the more likely you will be a candidate for using trusts in your estate planning.

✔ **Revocable living trust.** This is created while the grantor is alive, and it may continue after her death. Revocable means that, as long as you are alive and competent, you can change any or all parts of the trust at any time. You can even tear it up! The assets in a living trust are not subject to probate, and beneficiaries can be given immediate access to them upon death. If you should

One reason you can't take it with you is that it goes before you do.

become incapacitated and cannot handle your own affairs, naming a successor trustee when you set up the trust will allow someone to manage your affairs for you. A living trust does not avoid estate taxes.

✔ **Insurance trust.** Established while you are living, this typically holds or acquires insurance policies on your life. The trust receives the life insurance proceeds upon your death. These trusts are usually irrevocable to keep the insurance proceeds from being taxed upon your death. Irrevocable means that these trusts cannot be changed once set up. With the proceeds of your life insurance in trust, funds are guaranteed to be available to the executrix to settle the estate and give immediate income to the family.

The following trusts are examples of testamentary trusts, trusts that are set up through your will and become effective upon your death.

✔ **Credit shelter trust.** Sometimes referred to as an AB trust, this is used to protect your ability to use your unified credit exemption and unlimited marital deduction when joint assets are over the unified credit amount. On the death of the first spouse, assets valued up to the exemption amount are placed in the trust. The surviving spouse has an automatic right to all the income from the trust but may only have use of the principal at the trustee's discretion. If the surviving spouse is the trustee, it is critical to use specific language approved by the IRS for the use of the principal. Done incorrectly, the language can invalidate the trust. This is another reason to use a good attorney. Upon the death of the second spouse, the assets of the trust, including any growth, pass to the children free of federal estate taxes.

✔ **Qualified terminable interest property trust (QTIP).** This provides the surviving spouse with income from the assets in the trust, but you have control as to the ultimate disposition of the assets in the trust. Usually, the principal passes to your children upon the spouse's death. The trust qualifies for the marital

---

Experience is not what happens to a man. It's what a man does with what happens to him. —Aldous Huxley

deduction and is a very popular tool to use in second marriages, ensuring that children from a first marriage eventually receive your assets.

✔ **Special needs trust.** This is set up for dependents with special needs. If properly set up, the trust can benefit your dependent child by protecting their access to government benefits as well as by creating a management system to support the dependent when you are no longer around. These trusts must be carefully drafted so as not to disqualify a child for government benefits.

Estate Planning Tools You Need While Here on Earth

There are two more documents that should become part of your estate-planning tool kit. Both allow you to choose individuals who will be able to make decisions for you and act on your behalf should you become incapacitated. These may entail medical, legal, or financial decisions. These documents are not just for elderly parents; they are for anyone over 18. They are a durable power of attorney and a health-care directive.

Durable Power of Attorney

A durable power of attorney allows you to name someone to act as your attorney-in-fact, sometimes referred to as your agent, if you are unable to do so. This person is then authorized to manage your affairs if you are absent, ill, or become incompetent. Carefully choose your attorney-in-fact. You should trust the person completely.

If you should become incapacitated and do not have a durable power of attorney, a guardian would need to be appointed by the courts to handle your affairs. This applies even if you are married. The healthy spouse would have to ask the courts for the authority to manage your affairs. The decision as to who will be named is the judge's. The judge may or may not appoint the spouse. The healthy spouse

Money may not buy happiness, but it surely helps one look for it in more interesting places.

cannot sell, mortgage, or transfer your interest of any property if you are incapacitated. A guardian is limited in power and must report to the courts at least annually. Guardianship is also costly; in most states, it costs an average of $3,000. Durable powers of attorneys are powerful legal instruments that allow someone access to your money and assets. Choose carefully here! The person you give the power to will be managing your money for you. Can you trust this person, and just as important, is he or she capable of handling your affairs?

Healthcare Directives

Bill and Judith Moyers put together a series for PBS about dying in America called *Dying on Our Own Terms* in 2000. What they encountered is the high and oftentimes unnecessary cost of dying. According to a *Time* magazine poll, 7 out of 10 Americans say they want to die at home; instead, three fourths of them die in medical institutions. More than a third of dying people spend at least 10 days in an intensive care unit, enduring attempts at a cure, hooked up to life-support machines. That's not where they want to be. They want someone to help them control their pain, and they want to be home with people who care for them.

One of the best ways to ensure that you will receive the care you want is to plan ahead. You are looking for two documents here. The first is sometimes referred to as a healthcare directive, an advanced directive, a medical directive, or a living will. It details your wishes as to what you want for medical treatment and, more importantly, what you don't want for treatment. Your doctor and the medical institutions where you may be a patient are duty bound to honor your instructions.

The second document is a durable power of attorney for healthcare, sometimes referred to as a healthcare proxy. This document allows you to choose another person as your agent, your proxy, to act on your behalf to make medical decisions for you if you are incapacitated. Your proxy should be willing to be an advocate for you, lobbying on your behalf to carry out your wishes, not his or her own. Too often, relatives have trouble saying goodbye and don't want to let go

Being of sound mind, I spent all my money before I died.

of the dying. Remember that you want someone who will carry out your wishes!

Your durable power of attorney for healthcare should evoke a conversation, no matter how difficult, with the person you name as your proxy. He or she should know how you feel about the issues surrounding dying, pain, and heroic measures.

The two documents should work together and, in some states, are actually covered in one document. These documents, for most states, should be available for free from your local hospital, hospice, or nursing home if you are admitted as a patient.

We have 50 states, and we have 50 different laws regarding healthcare directives. If you spend time in two states, you may want to complete documents for both states. Your estate-planning attorney can help you with these, or you can check out the following sites: www.hospiceinfo.org, www.aarp.org, www.agingwithdignity.org, www.nolo.com, www.partnershipforcaring.org, and www.lastacts.org.

How to Give It Away

Giving it away only becomes an option if you have more of it than you need. If we only knew exactly when we were going to die, I could help you do some exceptional planning. You could give it all away, and your heirs would have to sell your car to pay for the funeral.

Certainly, after completing your net worth and adding in your insurance proceeds, if you find that your estate is $1.1 million, you may want to consider gifting as a way to pare down your estate—but only if you can tell me you aren't going to need the money. Aging and dying can bankrupt an individual, and I believe you should hang on to your money if you think you may need it.

The unified credit allows us to give away the exempt amount during our lifetime or upon our death without incurring a gift/estate tax on it. Gifting this away when you are alive gives you the ability to see just where the money goes and the good it can do. If it is in the form

---

Save a little money each month and at the end of the year you'll be surprised at how little you have. —Ernest Haskins

of a contribution, it becomes a deduction, and you don't need to worry about using your unified credit exemption.

You also have the ability to use the $11,000 annual exclusion for gifting. This number will be indexed in the future. You can make a number of unlimited annual gifts of $11,000 maximum in the form of cash or property, free of the gift tax to as many recipients as you wish or have funds to provide for. These gifts are free of taxes to the recipients upon receipt of the gift, but if the asset creates income, there could be income taxes due. If you are married and your spouse joins in, you could give away $22,000 to each recipient.

For example, you would like to help your children buy a house, and they are short of the money for the 20 percent down payment. You and your husband could join together and give the kids $44,000–$22,000 to your daughter and $22,000 to your son-in-law for the down payment. Now, if they buy the house in December and need to do repairs and buy furniture, a snow blower, and a washer and dryer, you could help them out again in January with another $44,000. Of course, all this sounds wonderful, but be sure you have it before you promise it or give it away.

If your grandson is going off to college this year, you can slip $11,000 into his bank account. If you are really feeling generous, you could actually pay his tuition bill and his medical insurance as well. The check would need to be paid directly to the school and should not pass through his hands. Because of financial aid considerations, you would want to slip him his $11,000 after he was accepted into the school of his choice and got his first tuition bill. Paying someone's medical bills or tuition bills directly is permitted under gifting and is not considered part of the $11,000 annual exclusion.

Giving away cash is the simplest thing to do, but you don't always have cash available. You may have to sell your stocks or mutual funds to get the cash, and then there is a tax liability to consider. Consider giving the stocks or mutual funds directly. You can still give $11,000, but it is the value of the stock at the day of the gift, not when you originally bought it. By doing this, you may get appreciating assets

---

If you can count your money, you don't have a billion dollars.
—J Paul Getty

out of your estate. But if your grandson has to sell the stock to pay for college, then he will owe capital gains taxes on the difference between the value when he sold it and the value at which you bought it. He does use your basis of the stock, but he uses his tax bracket, which could be as low as 5 percent.

Consider giving a charity your appreciated stock or mutual fund. Your deduction is for the amount of the stock on the day you gift it, but when the charity sells it, it will owe no tax on it. Kind of like having your cake and eating it, too.

Go First Class or Your Heirs Will

I first saw this saying "Go first class or your heirs will" on a plaque on the desk of my travel agent. She tells her retired clients to go first class; otherwise, their heirs will after they are gone. How right she is! It's funny but oh so true.

I have met retirees who are saving it for the kids. Why? Most kids have the ability to make it on their own. We struggle to educate them and make their life free of hassle. Again, why? Do we really do them a favor by giving them everything? I'm not so sure. Live your life to its fullest, and if there is anything left over, sure, the kids should get it. But my plans are to have my kids have to sell my car to pay for the funeral!

The Bottom Line

Where there is a will there is a way. Estate planning is essential in completing your financial plan. Estate planning protects your assets and allows you to decide how those assets should be distributed upon your death.

Money can't buy friends, but it can get you a better class of enemy.
—*Spike Milligan*

Notes:

PART TWO

The Roles You Take on As Women

The second half of the book is dedicated to helping you understand the financial component of the different roles we as women take on in life. They include wife, ex-wife, widow, mother, daughter and partner. Most of us will experience many of these roles during our lifetimes.

Each chapter covers one of the roles. And the chapters are filled with specific advice for that role. The section "Applying What You've Learned" in each chapter will walk you through what you need to review in the first part of the book. Helping you strategize a financial plan for your life stage. Helping you figure out what specifically will work for you. The rest of the chapter will help you manage this role.

ara is in her early thirties and has been married for four years and has an exceptional and adorable five month old (her description of her daughter, Rebecca). Cara has been on maternity leave and will need to report back to work within a month. Here in lies the problem. Cara would like to be a stay at home mom for a while, but is concerned about the financial loss and opportunity loss to her career. Her husband tells her they can manage for he figured it out she told me. But she is feeling stupid about this money stuff for he has always handled the finances and she has handled paying the bills.

She was earning $40,000 before she stopped work and has been on an unpaid maternity leave. Cara and her husband, Brian, have actually been doing okay living on one salary since the baby was born. They had paid off all of their credit card debt and finished off the car payments knowing they would be down to one paycheck for a while.

They have been looking into childcare and it is so expensive. They ruled out having an au pair or a nanny for they don't physically have the room for someone to live with them right now and a licensed day care can run as high as $10,000 a year.

They are living in a four-room apartment, which in reality they told me is a three-room apartment with a very large closet, which is now converted into a nursery for Rebecca. Owning a home sooner rather than later is their primary goal and increasing retirement savings comes in second. They have been reviewing their budget and Cara has been keeping a tight rein on their expenditures, so much so that Brian has nicknamed her, "Scroogette."

But it is working she assured me and they are actually ahead of schedule with their savings estimation. So the big question was could they make it on one salary, still buy a house and save for their retirement without jeopardizing their present life style too dramatically?

Chapter 12

What You Need to Know as Somebody's Wife

In This Chapter

This is a chapter about being someone's wife and the things you'll need to know. As a wife you are often to busy with family, work and a household to run to take the time to add finances to your schedule. This chapter is about why it's important to add finances.

When you are somebody's wife, it's easy to lose your identity. Most women find that they begin to look at things like a couple and then as a family with children. They often depress their individuality to make things easier. Marriage is a partnership, true partners try to share equally in this adventure.

Oftentimes as a couple, one of you sort of falls into managing the money and handling the checkbook. More often than not, it is the man because he believes it is his job, and you as a new wife may have been more interested in getting your home together or caring for the babies. But the money plays a big part of the partnership.

As a woman, understanding the family finances is essential because 90 percent of women end up managing their own finances at some point during their lifetime. According to the AARP, the average age of widowhood is 56. And with one in two marriages failing, you need to

---

One should never marry for money; it's cheaper to borrow it.

know all about the family's finances. As you apply what you've learned in the past 11 chapters, I will be noting what you need to be doing or at least what you should be thinking about because you are somebody's wife.

Applying What You've Learned

Financial Goals

Have you and your husband established long and short-term financial goals together? Do you know when he would like to retire? Where he might want the kids to go to college? Setting goals together is important because it opens up the lines of communication that keep you both working toward the same goals.

Net Worth

In Chapter 3, "Figuring Out Your Starting Point," I mentioned that, if you are coupled, you should struggle through the net worth worksheet together. It's like dancing the tango—not so easy to do alone. Completing the net worth worksheet will give you a broad overview of what your family has as assets. If you already got your husband to fill it out, you need now to go over it with him. What do you have? Where is it? Find out where you husband keeps everything. If its on the computer, you need to be able to access it, and there should be paper backups for you to review.

Okay, where does your money go each week? Do you understand the whole of your family's budget, or are you just dealing with household bills? How much are you saving with each paycheck? Look at the pay stubs from the paychecks, yours and your husband's. What is being taken out? How much is going into savings? Where does your money go?

> *Always be sure there is money in your own name. If your husband should die unexpectedly, you will have money to work with while the estate is being settled.*

Two ways to get rich—spend less than you make or make more than you spend.

The inventory worksheet in Appendix A lists the important stuff in most people's lives. Take the time to fill the worksheet out and organize your stuff. You should do this so you know where things are. Set up your filing system so you know where everything is.

Debt and Credit

Even if you and your husband have your own credit cards and pay your own bills, you still need to know about each other's cards. You need to know what cards each of your carry, and somewhere in a file, the card numbers should be in a safe place. This is important if cards are ever lost or stolen. If your husband is in Europe and his wallet is stolen, you should know where a copy of these numbers are so you can notify the credit card companies here in the States.

Check your credit history. Be sure, as a wife, that you have credit in your own name. If something should happen to your husband, you may not be able to use the credit cards that are in his name. Having a card that reads Mrs. James Smith may sound prestigious, but you really need something that says Mary Jane Smith. If you did not change your name when you got married, be sure the credit history on file for you is correct.

Insurance

Is your family properly insured? If your husband is the main bread-winner, is he adequately insured? Could your family survive without his income? You need to be sure you are protected if something should happen to him. How much life insurance does he have and where is it? Who owns it? If he owns it and dies, it becomes part of his taxable estate. If you own the policy, it is not part of his estate upon his death.

Could your family survive without your income? Is there enough life insurance on you? If you are currently not employed outside the home, is there enough insurance on you to cover the services you provide to your family? Think about that for a moment. Who would care for the kids? Clean the house? Mow the lawn? (Hey, I mow the lawn at my house!)

The woman who saves money nowadays isn't a miser—she's a wizard.

With life insurance policies, it is important to check the beneficiary designation on all policies. With marriages and divorces, life insurance policies previously owned before these events often don't get the designations changed. This could be a real problem if your husband put his brother down as the beneficiary on his life insurance policy at work when he first started his job 10 years ago. Even if the two of you have been married for seven years and have two wee ones, if he dies in a car accident, his brother is the beneficiary of the $250,000 life insurance policy. Even if a will indicates that your husband meant for you to have all of his worldly possessions, the beneficiary designation has your brother-in-law's name on it, and by law the money is his.

If you and your husband each have health insurance through your employment, learn about each other's policies. Why? Play the "what if" game with me again for a moment. Your husband wakes you up in the middle of night with terrible chest pains. You're not fooling with this, so you take him to the emergency room. Do you know if the emergency-room visits are covered? Do you have to call his primary care physician to get an okay? Do you know his policy number and where he keeps his medical card? Should you know these things?

How much this ER visit is going to cost is not even on your radar screen right now; you just want him taken care of because you love him. Well, after several hours in the ER, he is feeling much better. The diagnosis is gas due to too much beer and the chilidogs he had at the ball game that night with his buddies. You are relieved that its nothing more serious (although perhaps you're a bit put out for having spent most of the night in the ER). You take him home, counting your blessings until the bill comes for $500. An unauthorized visit to the emergency room could cost you hundreds of dollars. You know, my grandmother used to say that an ounce of prevention is worth a pound of cure. She was smart, my grandmother! She'd probably make him give up the chilidogs!

If you have kids, whose health insurance policy covers them? If your husband is at a soccer game with your 10-year-old goalie and the kid makes a terrific save, only to bang her head against the goal post

---

If you want to keep out of debt, you must earn more than you yearn.

and need stitches, does your husband know where the card is and which doctor to call? What if you are away on a business trip? Get my drift here?

Taxes

Taxes are everyone's favorite subject. So, what do you need to know about taxes? Here's another "what if." It's April 14, and your husband just did the tax return. He sticks it under your nose and says, "Honey, sign this. I need to get it in the mail tomorrow." You dutifully sign it because you trust him, and you really don't really want to look at it. Why, he would think you didn't trust him! And you hated math in school, so where would you begin anyway?

Two years later, there is a letter waiting from the IRS one day when you get home from work. They're looking for money! It seems your husband forgot to include some income on that long-ago-forgotten tax return, and that's considered fraud. Well, you are now divorced, so you're thinking that it's his problem. Wrong! You signed it, and it has your Social Security number on it. You are also responsible here. To top it all off, he's not working at the moment, so they're coming after you because you are. I realize that this scenario is not going to happen to many women, but it happens often enough that it is definitely worth mentioning.

The IRS does have some new rules regarding the innocent spouse, but you must prove that you were the innocent spouse. It's better to be the smart spouse and learn about the taxes. Don't sign anything you don't understand! A bit of stubbornness at that moment can prevent all kinds of future problems. It's probably a good idea to have your taxes done by a tax preparer and go together for the meetings. Pick up one of the many tax books that come out each spring to familiarize yourself with the new tax laws and how they affect your family.

> *Never sign anything without reading it, no matter how much pressure is being put on you. There are tales of women who have signed over their homes without realizing it to a controlling husband. Knowledge gives you power.*

By the time you have saved for a nest egg, inflation turns it into chicken feed.

Two that are readily available; *J.K. Lasser's Tax Guide* and the *Ernst & Young Tax Guide* are easy to read and informative and they are sold on line as well as in bookstores.

The Golden Years or The Golden Arches

Do you know what kind of retirement plans your husband has at work? Is he eligible for a pension? Does he have a 401(k)? Who is the designated beneficiary on the 401(k)? That's right, if it's not you and something happens to him, it goes to the designated beneficiary. By law, with a 401(k) plan, you are the beneficiary. But if he started his job before you were married and put his brother down as the beneficiary, you are out of luck! This happens often enough that I need to warn you about it.

You want to check the beneficiaries on his plans and on yours. Get out that net worth worksheet. What's there? Begin to play detective. How many IRAs do the two of you have? Check them all. Does he have an annuity? Who is the beneficiary?

Now that all of this is done, are you saving enough for retirement? Are you making use of the plans you have available at work? Are you both at least contributing enough to get the match from your employers? Lets put things in reverse. Does he know what is available for you from your employer? Where you keep all of your paperwork? Have you updated your beneficiary designations?

Social Security

Is your husband eligible for Social Security benefits? There are some states that do not require state employees to pay into the Social Security system. If he has worked for one of them, he will get a state pension and probably not a Social Security benefit unless he has also acquired 40 quarters of Social Security earnings. Have you seen his current statement from Social Security? Do you know what his benefits will be? You are eligible for one half of his benefits or your own, whichever is larger. He is also eligible for one half of your benefits or his own which ever is larger.

Most couples need two incomes these days; one for the principal and one for the interest.

Investments

Does you husband make all of the investment decisions in your household? Why? Do you know where all of the account information is? Have you seen a recent statement? Is it a joint account? Is it in his name alone? Do you live in one of the 40 states that allows payable-upon-death accounts so that, if something did happen to him, you would have immediate access to the account if it was in his name?

Do you understand your investments? Has your husband or your advisor told you not to worry about it, that they are handling it just fine? That sends a big red flag up the pole for me. *Family Money,* a magazine targeting women and money, published an article several years ago titled "Married to a Day Trader." The husband lost all of the woman's inheritance, and to make it up, he borrowed from his 401(k) and invested that in the market as well—only to lose that also. Day trading is akin to gambling. Knowing what is happening with your finances is just as important as knowing where the kids are after 10:00 P.M. and do you know where the kids are?

His Will

Have you seen your husband's will? Do you know who gets his stuff? This is especially problematic if either of you has been married before and already had a will when you got married. It's important to update wills when major life events happen.

Again, here's a "what if" story. It's your first marriage, and for him it's his second. You married an older more mature fellow. You start a family, never thinking about the hereafter with little kids running around. He tells you they are what's keeping him so young. He's financially astute and takes care of all of the finances and you are happy about that for you like being taken care of.

When he dies suddenly of a heart attack at 62, his lawyer contacts you and explains that your husband never updated his will. He left all his worldly possessions to his two adult children from his first marriage, including the house you are presently living in. Can you contest

---

An accountant is a man hired to explain that you didn't make the money you did.

the will? Depending on where you live and which state laws apply, you may have a chance. Remember what grandma said and do something about it now. Go through those important documents listed in Chapter 3 and understand what your husband has. This is not espionage; this is just being pragmatic!

Durable powers of attorney are needed even if you own everything jointly. Easy to get, these documents can save you time and money if one of you should become incapacitated. There are some financial institutions that may prefer to use their standard power of attorney forms, so check with your brokerage firm or bank to see if they will accept the forms your lawyer prepared for you. If something should happen to your husband and he becomes incapacitated and you need to sell your jointly owned home you may not be able to. By law you may not be able to sell or mortgage his half of the jointly held assets unless you become his guardian. To become his guardian you will have to petition the probate or family court. That process could take months and $3,000. A Durable Power of Attorney is a whole lot cheaper!

Estate-planning documents are part of an overall financial plan. You should be discussing what your wishes are for disposition of your assets with your husband. Each of you should have a letter of instruction so that, if something should happen to him, you do not become engrossed in a major battle for his belongings with the kids from his first marriage.

Where Do We Keep Our Stuff?

At this point, I am sure you think I have been hammering on you, and I have been. My experience has taught me that women are often unprepared for the major stuff that comes their way. And it is not just women, most individuals are unprepared for the major stuff when it hits the fan.

I truly don't want to nag but I know it's important, and now you know it's important, but what are you going to do about it? I can only

Inflation is when the buck doesn't stop anywhere.

get you so far. But you can think of me as the guardian angel sitting on your shoulder, prodding you along. Even nagging a bit so I can rest while you take over.

You do need to get a handle on what you and your family have accumulated, and you need to know where it is and who owns it? Your husband may be relieved to share the job with you or happily turn it over to you completely. Many guys think its their job so they just do it. You need to ask about it. If he wants to keep the job because it's his thing, then you should be a part of the decision-making process.

If your family's stuff is scattered hither and yon, this is a good time for both of you to start organizing everything. Once it is organized, it will be easier for you to take the next step.

Taking a More Active Role

If you have never shown an interest in this stuff before, your husband may want to know the motivation behind it. Tell him that the average age of widowhood is 56, and you intend to be prepared just in case.

Ask him to teach you the ropes of the checking account and how he pays the bills. Does he do it online? How often does he balance the checkbook? Using software like Quicken is marvelous for people who hate to balance their checkbooks. If you have entered the checks and deposits correctly, it will just about balance itself.

Where is everything kept? Show him the inventory list. Where is all of this stuff? Don't give up! Remember that he may have been doing this stuff for years, and you only just started. It takes time to learn, and a math phobia is not an excuse any longer because there are great calculators available for everything you'll want to do.

Also, another excuse I hear quite often is that you will just hire someone to do it for you if something happens to your husband, like you hire someone to fix the washing machine. If the repairman messes up your washing machine, you can buy a new one. If your attorney or financial advisor mess up your finances, there may not be any money

---

Just when you think you can make both ends meet, someone moves the ends.

left to buy a new washing machine. You will need to know enough to keep tabs on your advisors.

Investing is next. Do you have a financial advisor? You'll want to engage someone's help to learn more. There are lots of good books on the subject as well as sites online. The financial magazines all have good web sites. Women's Financial Network at www.wfn.com is one of the few financial sites just for women. You just might decide you like this stuff. Money is a very powerful tool, and learning how to make it work for you can become seductive.

Understanding What He's Got

As a wife, you do need to understand what your husband has and where it is. With divorce rates being what they are (still at 50 percent) and the fact that most women outlive their spouses, it becomes crucial for your well-being and that of any children you may have. You should be helping your mother, aunts, and sisters do the very same thing. What do their husband have and where is it located?

If you worked through this chapter, you have a good idea where the stuff may be. If your husband keeps stuff in several places, ask him to consolidate it at home so that you both have access to it. Oftentimes when dealing with money, it becomes a control issue. I certainly don't want to advocate challenging your spouse so that it leads to confrontations, but if it does, there is a message in that. What I *am* advocating is that, as a woman, you are a partner in a relationship involving love and finances. You have a need and a right to know what's in the family's portfolio.

When a fellow says it ain't the money but the principle of the thing, it's the money! —Kin Hubbard

The Bottom Line

Here the bottom line is easy, if you are not already a full financial partner in this relationship you need to take a more active role so that you will be prepared if anything should happen to your spouse. What do you have as a family, where is it and how can you access it are all questions you need to get answered.

Too many people spend money they haven't earned, to buy things they don't want, to impress people they don't like. —Will Rogers

I met Grace recently at a money conference. Her parents had insisted she attend for they were concerned about her and her kids. Grace wanted to learn more about investing and money management in general she told me.

Grace is a divorcee supporting herself and her six kids ages 12 thru 22 with a lot of help from her parents. Grace will soon celebrate her 50th birthday and she is tired she told me. She is working two jobs right now to make ends meet and if it wasn't for her parents she doesn't know where she would be. She teaches during the day at a high-school and then four nights a week at a community college. Monday through Thursday she is gone from 7:30 in the morning until 10:30 at night. She then spends her weekends correcting papers and tests, watching soccer games, doing laundry and grocery shopping.

She moved in to her parent's home with the kids and was only going to stay a few months. That was three years ago she told me. Her parents converted the garage into an apartment for themselves and Grace and the kids now have the main house. January & February are tough for her because her parents are off to a warmer climate and not around to help with the kids. She must rely on the older kids to get the younger kids off to school in the morning and where they need to be during the after school hours. Her parents have also been helping with the education costs for there are three kids in college.

Her story is one of a trusting spouse that paid no attention to the family finances because she had no time. She was busy raising the six kids, running a busy household and teaching full time. She signed the tax return each year that her husband put in front of her, never questioning and never understanding the return. She thought her husband was saving for their retirement and he even showed her how much was in their accounts. So she never bothered to utilize her 403(b) plan at work for her husband explained he could do better for them. Grace had no idea that their home was mortgaged to the hilt to finance a business that went under and that there were no investments and savings for her husband had used that money to finance the business and a life style she knew nothing about.

She wonders how she could have missed all of the signs and clues that became so obvious to her after the fact!

Chapter 13

What You Need to Know as Somebody's Ex-Wife

● ●

In This Chapter

This chapter is about divorce planning and the steps you'll need to take so that you end up with a fair and equitable settlement. The problem is; everyone involved in a divorce, spouses, children, and the lawyers all have different ideas as to what is fair and equitable.

● ●

Consider these very sobering statistics:

✔ More than 50 percent of first marriages fail.

✔ More than 60 percent of second marriages fail.

✔ In 2002 there were 2.4 million marriages and 1.2 million divorces.

✔ The average duration of first marriages ending in divorce is eight years; the average duration of second marriages is six years.

✔ During the last decade, midlife divorce has tripled.

✔ The standard of living for divorced women age 50 and over declined 73 percent within the first year after divorce.

✔ Current studies indicate that children do suffer much more trauma than originally thought from a divorce.

Money may talk, but today's dollar doesn't have enough cents to say very much.

A divorce can be devastating emotionally and financially. It tears a family apart and can make friends and family members feel forced to choose sides. What may have been a loving relationship sometimes turns into an acrimonious one at best. If your marriage is rocky or you have already begun to discuss the big "D" word, there are some things you can do to be better prepared if you decide to go forward with a divorce. In this situation, money is very powerful and can be used as weapon. Divorce should not be used as an idle threat when arguing with a spouse. Children are ever so sensitive to the word "Divorce" because so many of their friends have gone through the experience.

The first thing you need to do is get some professional help. This does not mean asking your hairdresser about her divorce but asking her whom she used. Visit a divorce attorney and ask lots of questions. You want to know what your rights are in a divorce settlement and what you are entitled to. If there are young children involved, there will be custody issues and child support. If you are not working or are only working part time, you may need alimony.

Make a list of issues that are important to you and how are you going to share them. I have included a minimal list:

✔ Children

✔ Assets

✔ Real Estate

✔ Pension Plans

✔ Family Business

✔ Stock Options

✔ Pets

And who gets what of the property you have accumulated together? Understanding your rights is important because they could be different from state to state. You may need to enlist the help of a mediator and a financial advisor to help you and your spouse sort things out.

If a fool and his money are soon parted, how come they got together in the first place?

Applying What You've Learned

Friendly divorces? I've seen some that started out that way and but very few that ended that way. Each person who goes through this enters the process with very different ideas about what is fair and equitable. As we apply what we've learned, I will be noting what you need to be doing or at least what you should be thinking about.

Setting Goals Again

You are going to be in a rebuilding stage for some time to come as you reconstruct a new life for yourself (and if you have kids, for them as well). Revisit goal setting and begin thinking about what you need to do to reach those goals on your own.

Where does the divorce planning fit into the goal setting? Maybe the divorce was not your idea and you want no part of it. Do not bury your head in the sand while he continues to make plans without you. You need to be proactive here. You may be racked with the pain of rejection and filled with anger right now, but you can't wallow in it. You need to turn your energies into actions.

Was one of your original goals a comfortable retirement? If it is still part of your overall plan, you need to be very aware of that when negotiating your divorce settlement. Is providing an education for the kids still important? Who's going to pay for it now? Can you afford it on your own, or will you need help from your spouse? Will he be willing to help the kids? Again, this is a negotiating item.

> *Children are not entitled to a college education from their parents. It is a very generous gift. Many women get caught in the trap of letting their ex use college as a negotiating tool when discussing child support and alimony. He may want to lower child support or alimony if he has to pay for college. Be sure you have enough to live on and worry about college in the future.*

There are lots of new things to consider as you begin your new planning process. It is key here again, however, to write down your goals and dreams. You'll be more committed to them.

Everyone pays for their mistakes—Congress does it with our money.

Figuring Net Worth

If you have already done the worksheets discussed in Chapter 3, "Figuring Out Your Starting Point," you are a leg up here, but you'll need to review them.

The net worth statement is going to be very important for you. Be sure it is up-to-date and has all the family assets listed. If a divorce has been looming in the background for a while, you may need to play detective here to be sure your spouse has not begun hiding assets or income. You may be able to play detective on your own, but a new field called forensic accounting has popped up because spouses try to hides assets. Your attorney or accountant can help you find a forensic specialist who will be able to search for hidden assets.

Know what your husband owns in his name and what you have in your name. What assets did you bring to the marriage? What assets did he? What assets accumulated during your marriage? How much is in the retirement accounts? You may be eligible for some of his retirement account if you have very little or none in your own name. If you have the larger retirement account he may be entitled to part of that. Who owns the house? Stock options are often overlooked because a spouse may not be able to exercise them for several years, but they are still an asset and need to be included.

Is there a family business involved? This is always tricky because it may be the largest family asset. You want to obtain an accurate evaluation. If you plan to divorce and have been active in the business, how will this affect the business? Does he buy you out? Do you buy him out? Is there cash available to do that?

If you have a joint brokerage account, you may wish to notify the broker in writing that you and your husband have separated and that all transactions need two signatures. Check with your lawyer on this one as well.

What are your liabilities listed on the net worth worksheet? Car loans, 401(k) loans, a mortgage, credit cards? Do you have more debt than you have assets? Do you live in a community-property state, or have you ever lived in a community-property state while married?

Experience teaches you to recognize a mistake when you've made it again.

These states use the concept of community property, and each spouse has a 50 percent interest in assets acquired during a marriage. These states are Alaska, Arizona, California, Idaho, Louisiana, Nevada, New Mexico, Texas, Washington and Wisconsin.

Next on your to-do list is to evaluate the cash flow. What is coming in for income each month? Where does your money go each paycheck? How much income will you need to stay in your present home? What can be cut back or eliminated if you and the kids will only have your income for a while? Is there enough of an emergency fund to see you through some bumpy times? Do you know how much your husband earns? Does he get bonuses? Stock options? What's in his benefits package?

If you are not working right now, what will you use for living expenses if he's not as generous as you believe he should be? Can you start to look for a job and find childcare if necessary? If you currently have only a joint checking account, open one in your own name as well. You may need the joint account for household bills and so on, so don't close it just yet, but don't put any more money into it either.

Record the essential household expenses; you will need these numbers to negotiate for child support and alimony. Don't forget things like healthcare expenses or added insurance costs once you are divorced. Accuracy counts; neatness does not!

Have you filled out the inventory worksheet? The documents listed in this worksheet will be very important to you. Make copies of everything. With tax returns, go back three years or more (five is better). If your spouse is hiding assets, the tax returns may provide a paper trail. You not only want a copy of the list, you want to get your hands on everything on the list and make copies of the most recent statements for all of your financial accounts. Make

> *Do you have household pets? Pets are considered property and are not subject to shared custody, visitation rights or shared financial support. Work with a mediator to create any special resolution needed to be included in the divorce decree.*

Experience is the name everyone gives to his mistakes. —Woodrow Wilson

copies of pay stubs, benefits statements, and pension and retirement accounts. Make sure you have easy access to these documents during this crisis period.

Credit and Debt

If you and your husband will be negotiating debt, you need to document whose debt it was. Take a look at what debt you are carrying that you can eliminate so your cash flow is manageable. If he gets his car, then he gets the car loan that goes with it!

You want to review your credit history, so send out requests to the credit-rating services for copies of your credit history. You'll want to see what the three major agencies have on file for you. What happens to the mortgage if it is currently in both your names but only one of you will live there and make the payments? What's the liability involved? You will want to have a credit card in your own name. Get that established as soon as possible. Then you'll want to cancel the joint credit card accounts you have with your husband. As a word of caution, creditors won't cancel an account until the balance is paid off, but they will close off the ability to post additional charges to the account.

Insurance

Health insurance could be a major issue for you. Who will provide the insurance for the kids? And for you if you are not working? You should be able to get at least 18 months of health insurance through your husband's employer, but it could be costly. You are protected under the Consolidated Omnibus Reconciliation Act known as COBRA. But COBRA is only a temporary solution. You'll have to come up with a permanent solution at least for yourself and possibly the kids also. If your husband is going to pay alimony and child support, you'll want to be sure he is properly insured with both disability and life insurance. Part of the settlement could be that he carry life insurance until the children are finished with college or the alimony payments cease.

Every path has some puddles

Don't forget yourself. You'll need both disability and life insurance as well. Remember that the kids are also relying on you and your income for survival.

Beneficiary designations are important here. If you own your current life insurance policy, consider changing the beneficiary on the policy if it is your spouse. If your husband owns a policy on your life, only he can change the beneficiary designation. The same would hold true for you if you owned a policy on his life. What was a good estate-tax-planning tool becomes a potential divorce-planning problem. It's one more item to negotiate. You also will want proof of insurance. Trusts can be an important planning tool here. A properly drafted life insurance trust can provide that his life insurance policy is owned by the trust and the kids are the beneficiaries.

Once the divorce is final, be sure you insure what is now yours. If you purchased your auto, homeowners, or any other insurance through your husband's employer, be sure to get new policies as soon as possible—even before the divorce is final. If he stops payment on the policies, you could lose your coverage in 30 days, and you may not be aware that you are uninsured. Also be sure to change the registration for your car when you get your new auto insurance.

Taxes

If you are in the process of a divorce, you will probably be filing a joint tax return. Caution prevails here. Don't just sign it; you will want to know what's in it. You will also want to talk to the preparer. Your Social Security number and signature will be on it so you are liable as well. If there's a problem, consider filing as married, filing separately. You can file as a single taxpayer or head of household if you have the kids in the year the divorce is final.

Alimony is income to you and a deduction for your spouse on his 1040. Child support is not a deductible item nor is it considered income to you because it is a foregone responsibility of a parent to provide support for his or her children. Check out the tax credits in Chapter 6, "Pay Only What's Due Uncle Sam, No More!" They are

---

Money isn't everything, but it's mighty handy if you don't have a credit card.

only available for the parent who has custody of the kids and, in some cases, like the Hope Scholarship, the parent who is paying the college expenses and has custody. There are income limits for all of the credits.

When you begin to divide up assets, the bottom line is always important—what something is really worth. The bottom line will work for the retirement plans, but there is the also tax side when you eventually have to sell an asset that is not in a qualified retirement plan. Let's say there are two stocks worth $25,000 each, and your spouse says he'll take one and you take the other. Sounds fair. Is it?

The ABC stock was bought for $20,000 and the other, XYZ, for $5,000. If they are both sold the day after the divorce, XYZ will have taxes owed on the $20,000 of capital gain, which would be $3,000; with ABC, taxes will be due on the $5,000 gain and that would be $750. This may be fair in value, but it's not an equitable deal. The proceeds for ABC stock would be $24,250. The proceeds of XYZ will be $22,000.

A better way is to divide everything down the middle, with each of you getting half of the shares of XYZ and half of ABC. Check with your accountant or financial advisor on the future tax consequences of property you receive in a divorce settlement. What appears to be fair is not always equitable.

Often a woman feels that she must get the house because she and the kids need to live somewhere. If there are lots of assets to divide, this may be a good idea. If you currently own your home jointly, your spouse can sign over his half at the time of the divorce. When you do go to sell the house, however, you will be subject to capital gains based on the original cost of the house.

Currently, when selling a primary residence you have lived in for two of the last five years, you may exclude $250,000 from capital gain as a single taxpayer and $500,000 if you are married, filing jointly. If you do decide the house is what you want, be sure you can afford to make the full house payments from your income in case your ex falls behind on child support or alimony. Another thing to think about is the maintenance of a house. With a full-time job and two kids to drive to soccer on the weekends, are you going to have time to maintain the

Money is not the root of all evil—no money is.

house? And if you can't, are you going to have the cash flow to hire someone to maintain what may be your largest asset?

The Golden Years or Golden Arches

A divorce can really mess with your retirement planning, and here's more bad news: divorces among women over 50 are increasing. If you have been out of the job market for a while because you stayed home to raise the kids, you probably don't have very much in your own retirement nest egg but he may in his. Over the years, you may have assumed he was saving for your retirement as well as his. And he was!

But now you may have to battle for your share of the retirement assets. A house worth $200,000 and a 401(k) plan worth $200,000 do have the same bottom line, but they are not equitable. Don't settle for the house and let him walk away with the retirement assets. It is better to split assets down the middle including the retirement plans and the pensions. If your husband will be eligible for a pension from his employer, you have a right to part of the pension, and you will want to be sure there is a survivor benefit for you if something should happen to him. Remember that the average age of widowhood is 56, so you will probably outlive him, married or not. Be sure your attorney understands the particular pensions your husband is eligible for.

According to the Women's Institute for a Secure Retirement (WISER) (www.wiser.heinz.org), you want your attorney to build a court order right into the divorce settlement. If your husband has more than one pension, the settlement must refer to each one in order to get benefits from them all. Again, you'll need to play detective here. You may need to check with his previous employers to see if he is eligible for a pension from them. Employees can become eligible (vest) for pensions after as little as

> *The Women's Institute for a Secure Retirement at www.wiser.heinz.org has several booklets on divorce planning around a pension. The first is "Divorce, a Time For Caution: An Introduction to the 12 Worst Mistakes lawyers make in Preparing Pension Orders," the second is "Key Questions You Need to Ask Before Your Divorce is Finalized."*

Frogs have it easy; they can eat what bugs them!

three years of employment. It is not unusual over a lifetime career that someone may be eligible for two or three pensions, have a 401(k) plan, and have an IRA. If these were acquired during your marriage, you are entitled to part of them.

You'll want to be sure your attorney obtains a court order to present to the pension plan administrator. This is a qualified domestic relations order, a QDRO. Each retirement plan has its own set of rules regarding QDROs, so it would be a good idea to have the attorney check with the plan administrator about what is needed for that particular plan so that the QDRO is valid.

> The U.S. Department of Labor offers a publication explaining QDROs called "QDROs: The Division of Pensions Through Qualified Domestic Relations Orders." You can receive this by calling 800-998-7542.

QDROs are expensive. If you are just dividing defined contribution plans such as IRAs or 401(k) plans and not a pension plan, you may want to take your share from a single account, saving money and time.

Social Security

As an ex-wife, if you were married for at least 10 years, you will be eligible for Social Security benefits based on your ex's Social Security earnings record. If you are about to get a divorce and have been married 9 years and 11 months, postpone it a bit so you come in over the 10 years. If you haven't remarried, you can qualify for Social Security benefits at age 62 as long as your ex has reached 62 and the divorce must have been finalized at least two years ago.

You will be eligible for either one half of his benefits or all of your own benefits based on your earnings record, whichever is higher. Now remember the reveres is true, he can collect on your Social Security earnings record as well. Collecting benefits on your ex's work record does not affect his collecting his full benefits and if he were to collect on your earnings record it would not impact the amount you are scheduled to receive. If your ex is deceased, you will be entitled to 100 percent of his benefit amount. When you show up at Social Security,

---

No one can make you feel inferior without your consent.
—Eleanor Roosevelt

you'll need his Social Security number, your old wedding certificate, the divorce decree, and your birth certificate.

A Will

While you are still married, you will not be able to change the beneficiary on your 401(k) without your spouse's consent and neither will he. You can change the beneficiary on your life insurance if you own the policy, however, and on your IRAs unless you are living in a community-property state.

Getting a new will done as soon as possible after the divorce is a good idea. In some states, you cannot disinherit a spouse during the divorce process. You will want a new durable power of attorney and a durable power of attorney for healthcare if you had named your spouse as your attorney-in-fact on these documents. Take care of these changes before the divorce.

When drafting a new will, pay attention to who you wish to be the guardian for the children and, if you are leaving them assets, who will manage the assets for them.

Alimony

Alimony sounds great on the surface, but only 15 percent of women are awarded alimony. Even then, only about two thirds of them ever collect what is due. You might want to consider a larger share of the assets in exchange for future alimony or, if your state allows it, a lump sum in lieu of a future stream of alimony payments. Alimony ties you to your ex-spouse forever or until the payments stop. You may not want to be tied to him financially for years after the divorce.

If you think you deserve alimony, begin to build a case for it from the start:

✔ Did you put him through school?

✔ Did you forego your own education to be sure he had one?

You learn from successful failures.

✔ Did you help him with his business but were never on the payroll?

✔ Did you quit work to stay home and raise the children or care for elderly parents? His elderly parents?

✔ Have you been out of the job market for the last 10 years or more?

✔ Is he expecting to receive a large inheritance?

✔ Is your current income significantly lower than his?

✔ Will your lifestyle change dramatically without the added income from alimony?

Alimony will probably not last forever. The judge may award it to you while you are in school to acquire more job skills, until you return to work full time, until you reach the age at which you are eligible to receive full Social Security benefits, or until you remarry or move in (shack up) with someone. Very often, there are cohabitation clauses in alimony agreements, meaning that, if you have lived 30 consecutive days with a new partner, you could have your alimony discontinued. Alimony may also end if your spouse loses his job or suffers a financial setback. It will definitely end when your ex-spouse dies or you die.

If you are one of the lucky ones that actually get your alimony, it is considered earned income to you, and you will owe taxes on it. If this is your only source of income, you are eligible to make contributions to a deductible IRA or a Roth IRA because it is considered earned income. Taxes will not be withheld by your ex, so you will be responsible for making estimated quarterly tax payments to the IRS.

Child Support

Child support is regulated by state laws. You will need to get a copy of the state's formula from your attorney to figure out what you may get to help you raise the kids if you have custody. If you don't have custody, it will let you know what you'll be paying.

Old accountants never die—they just lose their figures.

You'll need to document what it costs to raise the kids. Do you need to send them to camp in the summer because you are working? If you have a child prodigy or a budding musician, how much do the extras cost? As kids grow, so does the cost of raising them. Keeping them in diapers is a snap compared to keeping them in clothes as teenagers. Don't forget healthcare expenses. Who is going to be responsible for them? If you are carrying them on your insurance from work, what happens if you change jobs? And here's the big question: Who is responsible for college expenses? You want this all taken care of up front and in the divorce settlement. A handshake or a "Don't worry about it, you know I'm good for it" is not enough here. Circumstances change, and no one knows what the future will hold so get it in writing.

Okay, so you've been awarded child support. Now the key is to get it. There are news stories weekly about deadbeat dads who run away from their responsibilities. More states are cracking down on deadbeat dads and are garnishing wages. Child support can actually be withheld from your ex's paycheck, his pension, and his Social Security benefits. The IRS is also on your side here and will deduct overdue support payments from any tax refunds due to your ex as well.

Even with all of this help, only two thirds of families receive any of the support awarded them by the courts, and only one third ever receive the full amount due. Collecting child support from an ex may become a never-ending battle. For help and to find out what your rights are, contact the National Child Support Enforcement Association at www.ncsea.org or 202-624-8180.

The Team

The divorce process is an overwhelming one and you will need to assemble a team to help you with the different aspects of the process. Divorce is very stressful and you go into a survival mode of flight or fight. There will be lots of emotions tangled up here. Guilt, pain, rejection, abandonment, anger, loss, hurt, fear even envy. And dealing with them on your own is not easy.

One day at a time.

A Counselor

At the top of your list of professionals ought to be a counselor for you and the kids. You may need someone to talk to, and the kids will definitely need someone to talk to. More often than not, they believe it is their fault that the family is coming apart at the seams. Seek referrals from the kids' counselors at school, friends, family, or your pediatrician or use the referral source at the American Association for Marriage and Family Therapy, www.aamft.org or 703-838-9808.

An Attorney

You need a good attorney on your team. Ask your friends and family for a referral, and they'll probably figure out its for you. That's ok. Ask them to keep it under wraps if that makes you feel better. You can contact the American Academy of Matrimonial Lawyers at www.aaml.org or 312-263-6477 for a referral. But do look for an attorney whose area of expertise is divorce. You want to know if he or she has handled cases like yours before. Using your brother-in-law because he'll be cheap could cost you in the end.

A Mediator

A mediator may save you and your spouse from putting on the boxing gloves and going at it! Hiring a mediator will probably save you big bucks in attorney fees as well. After all, much of the work is done by you and your spouse with the help of the mediator rather than lawyers going back forth to each of you—and then back again and then back again For help in finding a mediator, ask the professionals you are working with or contact the Association for Conflict Resolution at www.acresolutions.org or 202-464-9700.

A Certified Financial Planner

A Certified Financial Planner (CFP) may be needed as well to help you. He or she will be able to help you develop a new financial plan and put it into action. They should be able to help in deciding how to

If you find yourself in a hole, quit digging! —Will Rogers

divide the assets. A good planner on your team is an asset, pun intended. Check out Chapter 18, "The Hired Help," for information on what to look for in a planner and use the Financial Planning Association's web site to find one at www.fpanet.org or 800-322-4237.

An Accountant

Next you may need an accountant to sort through tax stuff. You may have a relationship with the gal who prepares your taxes and want to use her. A word of caution; don't if your spouse is also using her. It is so hard for any professional to serve two masters. A forensic accountant may also be a key player on your team if you think your husband is hiding assets. Ask your accountant for a reference. This is a new field, and there are a couple of organizations that will be able to help: the Forensic Accountants Society of North America (www.fasna.org or 402-397-9433) and the Association of Certified Fraud Examiners at www.cfenet.com or 800-245-3321.

The Bottom Line

This is not easy is it? Your world as you know it is coming apart at the seams and I'm advising you that you have some things you must deal with. And you must deal with them. Realizing that things are not fair six months after the divorce is final does not give you any leverage. This is not easy but try to get the most equitable settlement for both you and your spouse.

The best way for a person to have happy thoughts is to count her blessings; not her cash.

oanie needed advice. She explained that she had received an insurance settlement and wanted to know if she should pay off her mortgage or invest the money for her daughter's future education expenses.

Recently widowed Joanie had a lot of questions relating to money. She lamented that when life hits you below the belt with the loss of a spouse the worst of it is dealing with the financial decisions and the paperwork. Joanie's husband of six years passed away unexpectedly leaving her struggling with a huge loss. They had just begun to acquire the American dream. They had bought a house in the suburbs and had spent months fixing it up. They had a daughter two years ago and Joanie decided to work only part time until she was in school. Usually the days Joanie works her mother-in-law baby-sits. So life was good and was going along as planned and then the unexpected happened at age 34 she became a widow. Widowhood at 34 is a foreign concept she told me.

Joanie has been poring her energy into painting the house and caring for her daughter but she knows she needs to make the hard financial decisions soon. The paperwork involved with the death of a spouse keeps pricking her conscious forcing her back to reality and the problems at hand.

She has been looking at her budget and knows it is tight with no margin for error. She would like to continue working part time if she could survive on her Social Security benefits and the interest from the insurance settlement. But she is getting conflicting advice from family and friends about what she should do with the insurance settlement. The insurance salesman, the one who sold her husband the life insurance policy wants her to purchase an annuity and more life insurance. Her father thinks she should pay off the mortgage so she won't have to worry about house payments. Her father-in-law thinks she should keep the money safe and buy a CD and use the income to help support her. All conflicting advice!

Chapter 14

What You Need to Know as Somebody's Widow

In This Chapter

You need to be prepared for widowhood. According to the AARP, women on average outlive their spouses by as many as seven years and the average age of widowhood is age 56

There are things you can do to prepare yourself for the possibility of going it alone, things that will make it easier if you outlive your spouse. Chapter 12, "What You Need to Know as Somebody's Wife," is full of advice on getting organized and understanding what you and your spouse own together.

What you will find in this chapter is what you need to do should you go from spouse to widow. It's also about you being able to help a friend, your mom, or a sister who may be caught up in the immediacy of losing a spouse. Maybe she is still in the "I can't believe this has happened!" stage. She might be numb to everything and everyone. She needs to get past this stumbling block and take some action, one foot in front of the other. That's all we're going to do in this chapter—plod along together to get a new widow through those excruciating first few months.

Life is not measured by the number of breaths we take, but by the moments that take our breath away.

Applying What You've Learned

"There's this hole in my heart, and nothing seems to fill the emptiness I feel right now." This was how widowhood was described to me recently. The pain a surviving spouse feels can only be known by another person who has lost a spouse.

Right now, you would like to make the world disappear, but it won't. There may be others relying on you for direction, so you will need to take charge or find someone you can trust to take charge of things like the funeral and burial arrangements. Get someone to make the phone calls for you to relatives, friends, and your husband's co-workers.

If you and your husband had done estate planning, do you know where those documents are? Is there a letter of instruction? This may help in planning the service. Did the two of you ever talk about what each of you might like for a service? Special music? Readings? Get someone to accompany you to make the funeral arrangements, someone you know who is very practical. This is such a tumultuous time that it can be very difficult to make good decisions regarding things like caskets and flowers. Now I will be very practical. Look at all of the caskets in the catalog or showroom. Too often you are offered caskets that cost as much as a car. There are less expensive ones in the back room!

Setting Goals

The dreams and goals you shared with your spouse may be shattered now. You will need to shape new goals and dreams for yourself and for your family if you have dependent children. These goals should fit your budget and your lifestyle.

Many of the goals you shared with your spouse may need to be altered now that you are alone. Retirement in an exotic climate may not seem as important as being near your family for support. Take your time when modifying your goals; don't leap into anything right away that you could regret later.

Dance like no one is watching.

A private college education for the kids may be out of reach now because there won't be enough dollars to cover this goal with the loss of your husband's income. You will need to rethink what your goals are for educating the kids. Trying to make up for the loss of their father by telling them nothing is going to change won't work here. Reality will set in, and they won't trust you. There are still options open for them (and you) regarding education. Maybe it's not Notre Dame, maybe it's a state university.

Don't sell your house because your brother-in-law says it's too big and costly to maintain or buy a condo near your sister in Phoenix. Take the time to grieve and reevaluate your needs, and then slowly create new goals for yourself.

As you slowly see the fog lifting, you need to set up some sort of an action plan. Making lists will help you get through the necessary things that need your immediate attention even if you are still numb with pain. Then make out a to-do list for the next month and the next six months. The rest of this chapter will help you with what should be on your list.

Figuring Net Worth

Your net worth may change after the death of a spouse. If your spouse had life insurance and you are the beneficiary that will increase your net worth. If he named someone other than you as the beneficiary on retirement plans, your net worth may actually decrease. After things have settled down, review your net worth. Things that you held jointly with your spouse with right of survivorship will pass to you automatically, but "automatically" only means that the asset will not be probated. You will still need to contact the institution that holds the asset and change the actual title of ownership. They will ask for a copy of the death certificate.

Who owned what will be important to you. If your spouse left you everything, you will need to change the title on such things as the car, the house, and the stock portfolio. This does not have to be done immediately but should be tended to in the months following his death.

The road to success it always under construction.

The cash flow will definitely change upon the death of a spouse. According to the Women's Institute For a Secure Retirement (WISER) www.wiser.heinz.org, for a woman in retirement when her spouse dies, expenses are likely to be 80 percent of what they were before the death of the spouse, but the widow's income may only be two thirds of what it was prior to the spouse's death. Pension benefits from the husband's work generally are reduced by 50 percent, and Social Security benefits could be reduced by a third or more.

For a younger widow, things may be worse because there may be nothing available to replace the loss of your husband's income stream if there was no life insurance policy. If there are minor children, you and the children will be eligible for Social Security benefits if your husband paid into Social Security.

Do not think that you can allow your bills to slide during your mourning period. The mortgage company and telephone company want to be paid. Get someone to go through the bills and help you write out the checks so that your immediate bills are paid. Do you have an emergency fund to fall back on for the next few weeks until you get the finances in order? Are there savings bonds, a savings account, a money market account, or a short-term loan from a relative available to help you over this bumpy time? When getting it together for the future, be sure you have an emergency fund set aside.

If you need immediate cash, call the benefits department of your husband's employer to be sure it will send you his paycheck, any back pay, and unused-vacation or sick-time pay as well. Most employers provide life insurance for their employees as part of the benefits package. Let them know your spouse has died and ask what paperwork they will need from you. Some companies also have a death benefit they pay to the employee's survivors. If your spouse

> *If you don't know whether your spouse was eligible for a pension or if a company has gone out of business or you can't locate it, write to the Pension Benefit Guaranty Corporation (PBGC) at 1200 K St. NW, Washington, DC 20005. You also can contact the corporation at 800-400-7242 or www.pbgc.gov.*

What you do speaks so loud that I can't hear what you say.
—R.W. Emerson

belonged to a union, check with the union to see if it provides any death benefits.

Take some time to review the Inventory and Location of Important Documents worksheet discussed in Chapter 3. This document is shown in Appendix A. This will give you an idea of where all your important papers are located. Hopefully, you took the time to find your important papers before they were needed, and someone else can now get at them for you. If you haven't filled this out, the documents listed will give you an idea of what you will eventually need to locate.

The following is a list of documents that may have belonged to your husband that you may need immediately:

✔ Letter of instruction

✔ Will

✔ Social Security card

✔ Military discharge papers

✔ Birth certificate

✔ Insurance policies

✔ Title to cemetery plot

If your husband managed the family finances, start to search for the important papers you'll need. Where might he have put things? Does he have a safety deposit box? Did he have a filing system at home? Did he pay the bills at work? Did he use a computer to pay the bills? At home? At work? You may need to get permission to go into his office to pack up his things. And as long as you are there, you should check out his computer. Did he keep things on his office laptop computer? Where is it right now? These are hard things to do right now, but you do need to do them before your husband's employer just packs up things, sends them home, and wipes his computer clean for someone else to use.

The cure for anything is salt water—sweat, tears or the sea.
—Isak Dinesen

Credit and Debt

You've looked at your net worth, you've done your cash flow, and maybe you've opened some the bills. Are you in debt? Did you know about it? This is not an opportune time to find out that what was left to you was debt. If the debt is in your husband's name alone, you may not be liable for it, but if he refinanced a house that was owned jointly or ran up the family's credit card to its max, you will be liable. Did he borrow against his life insurance to finance a business?

You may need to get some help from a financial planner or contact the National Foundation for Consumer Credit. This is a national network of nonprofit organizations that provide consumer credit education, debt counseling, and debt-repayment programs. Many of its members are locally managed, nonprofit agencies operating under the name Consumer Credit Counseling Service (CCCS). Contact them at 800-388-2227 or visit their web site at www.nfcc.org. Getting out of debt may be a slow and laborious process.

Whose name were the credit cards in? If you don't have a card in your own name, apply for one. You will need to notify the credit card company of your spouse's death if the cards are in his name. Check your credit history and correct any mistakes you find on it.

While you are digging through stuff, check to see if your spouse ever bought mortgage or credit card life insurance. This type of insurance is offered through the mortgage company or bank and from the credit card company. If he did have this type of life insurance, the debt will be considered paid upon his death. The debt could be the mortgage, a car loan, or the credit card balance.

Insurance

Have you found all of the important papers? Life insurance policies that are paid up could be filed just about anywhere. Check with your husband's employer as to what he had at work. Also, if his parents took out a policy on him as a youngster, there could be a small policy floating around somewhere as well.

Life is a canvas; you fill in the picture.

When you are up to it, take the time to wade through old documents your husband may have kept. Was he a veteran? He may have a paid-up veteran's life insurance policy. Check his fraternal and professional organizations as well; often, they offer low-cost term insurance for members. Did he belong to a union? Check with the union as well to see if there's a policy they offer members as part of the membership.

> *Don't rush to pay off your mortgage with the life insurance proceeds until you are sure you won't need those dollars to produce an income. Wait at least six months before you make any major financial decisions. You want to be sure you have some cash available for an emergency fund.*

If you are entitled to life insurance proceeds, you will be asked to make a decision as to how you want those proceeds paid to you, either in a lump sum or in installment payments over your lifetime. Be careful here. Many widows have inadvertently purchased an annuity that will not allow them to access the money without a penalty until they are age 59 ½. That may feel good if you are already retired, but if you are 34-year-old widow with kids to feed and educate like Joanie in our story, you want your money in a lump sum.

All widows should take the payout in a lump sum. If an annuity is such a good deal, it will still be a good deal in six months from now when you can devote yourself to making that sort of long-term decision. Put the money in a mutual fund money market account with check-writing privileges so that you can get at it easily. This is not a permanent solution but a holding pattern until you are ready to make decisions again. Health insurance will need to be dealt with if your husband's employer provided it. If you are working, can you and the kids easily transfer to your employer's plan? If not, speak to your husband's employer about continuing the present coverage through COBRA. You are protected under the Consolidated Omnibus Reconciliation Act, known as COBRA. COBRA is only a temporary solution. You should be able to get at least 18 months, possibly 36 months, of health insurance through your husband's employer, but it

---

"In three words, I can sum up everything I've learned about life. It goes on." —Robert Frost

could be costly. It will buy you time, however, until you can find something on your own.

On that to-do list, add changing the name on your homeowners insurance and your automobile coverage, especially if you re-register the car in your name.

It's time to review your disability and life insurance needs. As the sole breadwinner in the family, you need to be adequately insured. Oftentimes, with both spouses working, they considered the other spouse's income as their backup if they should become disabled. You will not have the comfort of that second income coming in, and should you become disabled and can't work for a while, you will need some sort of coverage. Check with your employer to see what is offered through work.

Are you carrying enough life insurance? Take the time to review your policies at this time. If your spouse was listed as the beneficiary you'll want to add a new beneficiary. How much more will you need? If you have no one depending on you for their support, you may not need any life insurance, but if there are children and you want to educate them, then you may need more life insurance. Term insurance will work well for you if have a specific time need (for example, until the youngest child reaches 22).

Long-term care insurance is always a tough decision. Do you need it? As an older widow, if you were the caregiver for your spouse and there is no one available to care for you, perhaps you should be considering long-term care insurance, but if you have to struggle financially to make the premium payments then forego the insurance for you would probably be eligible for Medicaid. If the kids are worried that you might lose the house to pay for your nursing home care, let them buy the insurance for you.

Taxes

You're going to need to find copies of the last three years of tax returns. If you have someone prepare your taxes for you, he or she should be able to help if you can't find them at home. Tax returns can

You can't run your life on empty.

also provide a paper trail to assets you may not know about. If there were dividends paid or capital gains, the assets would be listed on Schedule D of the return.

If you and your husband filed joint tax returns, you will not be required to file a separate return for his income taxes unless you remarry during the tax year. You may also need to file an estate income tax return for income that his estate earned after his death. These things get tricky, so get some professional help if things are complicated. The following year, you can file as a qualifying widow, and if you have dependents, you can file as head of household the following year.

You will not owe any income tax on any insurance proceeds you receive. If you deposit the money into a money market account or a CD and there is interest earned, you will owe income taxes on the earnings though.

Next there may be federal estate taxes due as well as a state inheritance tax on your husband's estate. Your husband can leave everything to you (assuming you are a U.S. citizen), and the estate will not incur any federal estate tax. This is the unlimited marital deduction. Your spouse also has the ability to give away to other family members or friends at death up to $1 million (personal exemption) in 2003 (check out chapter 11) without incurring any federal estate tax as well.

The Golden Years or The Golden Arches

The death of your spouse can be catastrophic to your future. If you're a young widow and your spouse's income was larger than yours, you may feel that you just don't have anything extra to contribute to your retirement plan right now. If not much was saved for retirement, you will need to begin to do it on your own. It is never too late to start saving! Check out Chapter 8, "Providing the Glitter for the Golden Years," to learn more about how much you should be saving.

If you have inherited your spouse's retirement plans, there will be decisions you'll need to make about them. You'll be able to roll his 401(k), 403(b), Keogh, SEP-IRA, or IRA into your own IRA. If you roll them into your own IRA, you won't be able make withdrawals

The most important things in life are not the things.

until you reach age 59 ½ without paying a 10 percent penalty. You don't have to begin mandatory distributions until you reach age 70 ½. With the IRA in your name, you will be able to name a new beneficiary, and you do have the ability to convert the IRA to a Roth IRA if you meet the income limitations.

If you roll your husband's retirement accounts into an IRA in his name with you as the beneficiary, you will be able to access the money in the account before reaching age 59 ½ without incurring the 10 percent penalty. You will still owe income taxes on the withdrawals, and you must begin withdrawals the year he would have turned age 70 ½. So it's a trade-off.

If you inherited his IRA and he had already begun mandatory withdrawals, then you will need to continue withdrawals on the same schedule. Taking money out of retirement plans is much more complicated than putting money in. Get yourself competent help here. Reread Chapter 8 for more help on making the money last as long as you do.

You may need to become a detective here to find out if you are eligible for any pensions you husband may have been eligible for from previous employers. Put together a list of his previous employers, and if he worked at any one place longer than three years, contact their benefits departments to see if you might be eligible for a pension.

Social Security

Social Security benefits will be different depending on your age and whether you have dependent children. A young widow with minor children will be eligible for Social Security survivor benefits for herself and the children. You will be eligible for benefits if the children are under age 16. The children will be eligible for benefits until they reach 18 (or are under age 19 and still in highschool).

If you are 60 or older as a widow, you can begin to collect Social Security survivor benefits as well. If you are disabled, you are eligible to start those benefits at age 50.

Life is filled with shadows, but it's the sunshine that makes them all.

If you and your husband were already collecting Social Security, you will need to notify Social Security of your husband's death. If you receive any checks for him, you will need to return them. If you use the direct deposit method, notify the bank to return any funds received in the month of his death. It is a bit complicated.

You will also need to notify Social Security because your benefits status will also change. As a surviving spouse, you may be eligible to collect a higher benefit based on your husband's earnings.

If your husband worked for the federal government or for a state or county government, you may not be eligible for Social Security survivor

> *As a widow, if you remarry before age 60, your Social Security spousal benefits will be based on your new husband's earnings record. This could have an affect on the amount of your benefit. It might be worth a phone call to the Social Security Administration at 800-772-1213.*

benefits if he never paid into the Social Security system. If he worked in both private industry and the public sector, you may be eligible to receive reduced benefits from Social Security. You will need to head to the Social Security office to see what you are eligible for.

A special one-time death benefit payment of $255 is payable to the surviving spouse if you were living with your husband at the time of his death. If you were living apart and were receiving benefits based on his earnings record, you are eligible to receive the death benefit.

Investing

When you catch your breath, take the time to review your portfolio. Sit down with your financial planner and review your goals for your investments and your risk tolerance. Both may be different now that you are on your own.

If you have inherited retirement plans, you may need to make some immediate investment choices. If you have inherited your husband's 401(k) plan, when you roll the account into an IRA, the trustee of the 401(k) plan will liquidate the assets in the plan and send it along to the trustee of the new IRA. When you fill out the paperwork

---

Life is a series of accomplishments and failures that begin with learning to walk.

for the transfer, you will need to indicate your new investment choices to the new trustee. You can buy time by rolling the retirement plan money into a money market account at a brokerage house and then decide later where you want to invest the money.

With the inherited IRAs, if you leave them with the same company where they are currently, you can easily transfer them into your own name and continue with the same investments. But do consider consolidating all of the IRAs at one financial institution. You can receive one monthly statement, cutting down on the multiple statements you would receive if the IRAs were scattered. It also will be much easier when it comes time to begin mandatory withdrawals from the IRAs to only have one plan trustee to deal with.

A Will

This is important stuff! Review what you have in place for yourself. If your husband died without a will, you now know from experience why this is important for those you leave behind. A will is a very simple document that will (pun intended) allow you to direct how your assets are to be distributed upon your death.

A current will can easily be updated with a codicil, a simple amendment to your present document. When you are coupled, your wills are often intertwined by naming each other as the executor. You may need to update and make changes to your durable power of attorney (DPOA) as well as the medical directive you have previously executed.

If you have more than one child do not and I repeat do not name more than one child to be in charge. Certainly name the second or third child as an alternate or back-up if the first child cannot serve in that capacity. If they fought over the size of the cake slices when they were little they will fight over the estate.

This is easy enough to do. Make an appointment to see your attorney and get this done as soon as possible. If the kids are grown, you may want one of them to serve as the executor of your will. If they live nearby, you may wish to name one of them on both your DPOA and

Life is either what you make of it, or what it makes of you.

medical directive. Here's a word of caution: Ask them if they think they would be able to serve in these capacities for you.

A young widow with children will have more choices to make: a guardian for minor children, a trust for any assets the children might inherit, who to choose as executor, and choices for the DPOA and medical directive. A good friend, siblings, or even a parent will serve you well, but always list a successor so that, if your first choice cannot serve, there is a backup in place. Again, before putting anyone's name on these documents, talk to them about the responsibility first. Will they be willing to accept the responsibility? Your single sister may not be able to care for your two kids if her job requires her to travel two weeks every month.

The letter of instruction is an evolving composition. This can easily be updated on your own and should be looked at annually for any changes you may wish to make. After the death of the spouse, you may have even more specific thoughts about your own service and where you would like to be buried.

What to Do First

The following list is meant to prompt some forward thinking if you do become a widow or if someone you love has been recently widowed. This list can help you get through the first few days of the emotional turmoil by offering practical advice. The likelihood of someone becoming a widow and immediately getting this book for help is preposterous. I know that. But it may prepare some women and give others the ability to offer advice and comfort to their sisters, mother, nieces, daughters or friends.

I have interviewed several recent widows, and they all wished someone had been there with them, walking them through their decisions. Many of the decisions that need to be made revolve around your finances. Each of the women interviewed admitted to making mistakes, usually because they were overwhelmed and physically worn out from the grief. Allow yourself time to mourn. That is not a luxury!

Never be afraid to try something new. Remember, amateurs built the ark and professionals built the Titanic.

Two web sites that can offer some help when you are feeling up to an evening on the computer are www.widownet.org and www.aarp.org/griefandloss.

The most immediate needs are help in making funeral arrangements, children's care, and food for the family. For the most part, any major financial decision can be postponed until you are feeling in control again. And for the most part, these decisions *should* be postponed until you are in control.

1. Call your minister, priest, or rabbi, someone who can bring comfort to the family and you. Many hospitals have a chaplain available as well.

2. Notify family, friends, and co-workers. If you are planning for the future, I suggest you put together a list to be used in an emergency. If you are helping elderly relatives plan ahead, ask them who should be called. While you have their attention, ask them about what kind of service they might like as well. The more planning that is done, the easier it will be for the survivors.

3. Call your husband's employer and let them know that he has passed away.

4. Locate the estate-planning documents. Did your husband create a letter of instruction, or did he preplan his funeral? Or pre-pay his funeral? These documents will help you through the next few days.

5. Make the funeral arrangements. Depending on where the death occurred, a funeral home may already have come for the body. Take a friend or family member with you when you go to the funeral home for the first time. You want a companion who is practical and can help you make decisions. Funeral directors are very knowledge about cemetery arrangements and local churches and synagogues.

Courage is grace under pressure.

If your husband was a veteran, he can be buried in one of the national cemeteries. The funeral director should be able to help you make the arrangements if this is what you would like. You may also be eligible for some of the funeral expenses to be covered by the Veteran's Administration. You will need to find your husband's discharge papers to move this process along. Visit www.va.gov for information on benefits.

Speak to your clergyman about what you actually want for a service: music, flowers, time, place, and so on. If he or she didn't know your husband well, you will probably need to answer some questions about him. Let others help by putting together a reception after the service. People have a need to do something for you right now, so allow them to help.

6. Have some cash available for the many incidentals that will crop up. Credit cards will work for many things, but you will need some cash as well.

7. Ask a neighbor or friend to housesit on the day of the funeral or notify the local police to keep a watch. It's a sad piece of advice, but it's necessary because would-be thieves read the obituary columns regularly.

8. Ask the funeral director to get you 15 to 20 copies of the death certificate. You want them to be certified copies. Once you begin the paperwork involved, you will find that "original" copies are required. The more complicated the financial life of the decedent, the more copies you will need.

What's Needed Next

I have another list for you, a list of things to begin once the activity quiets down. Having a list helps you set goals and offers some satisfaction when crossing off the completed item. This list is to prompt you into action. Some of these can wait, and others will need to be done

We can't all be heroes because someone has to sit on the curb and clap as they go by. —Will Rogers

soon. This is as complete a list as I could devise. There may be things you need to add to your own list as you begin this next phase.

1. Take the time to answer the cards and letters from family and friends if that is what you want to do now. No one is expecting an immediate response, so when you are ready, begin.

2. Try to arrange for an organized space to work. It may simply be the dining room table, but it should be a place where you can leave everything spread out and come back to it when you have the energy. You may want it to be in a room where you can shut the door and make it go away for a day.

3. Locate the important papers you'll need: the will, trust documents, deeds, insurance policies, retirement plans, and contents of the safety deposit box if there is one. Begin to take inventory of the assets your spouse owned in his name and jointly with you. It's not necessary to list all the tools in the garage, but you will need to come up with a list of all that was his. Then you will need to do some reasonable calculations so you know what his estate is worth. Also list all of his liabilities, everything he owes.

4. Start the probate process. Make an appointment with your attorney for help. If you don't have an attorney, ask friends and family or other professionals you have dealt with for a referral. You'll want to see your tax advisor and your financial planner or stockbroker if you have one. You may need a team to help you wade through the financial maze of probate.

   If you decide to tackle this process on your own, call the county court house and ask what you need to do first.

5. Check in with the benefits department of your husband's employer. You may need permission to clean out his workspace. You'll also want to know about back pay, vacation pay, sick pay, bonuses, a pension plan, and retirement plans such a 401(k) or a profit-sharing plan and health insurance coverage.

We are shaped and fashioned by what we love. —Goethe

If your husband had a job in the public sector, such as working for the state or a county job in which he never paid into the Social Security system, there will be additional death benefits offered by his employer for you and minor children.

6. Contact the Social Security Administration (800-772-1213) and make an appointment to go and see them.

   Allow yourself some breathing space. You're on autopilot right about now. Try getting through one thing a day. As I mentioned at the beginning of the chapter, just put one foot in front of the other. Take a breather because all of this stuff will still be here later. I know this list appears endless but it's not.

7. Notify the Veteran's Administration if your husband was a veteran. You may be eligible for benefits.

8. File the life insurance claims if your husband had insurance. The sooner they are in, the sooner you will have the proceeds.

9. Contact the bank, credit card companies, brokerage houses, and financial institutions. If you had joint accounts, you will need to change the name on the accounts.

10. Get a credit card in your own name if your cards were all in your husband's name.

11. Contact the union if your husband was a member to see what benefits you may be entitled to. Some unions provide a pension for their members and survivors.

12. Pay your bills! Don't let this slide. If you have never paid the family bills, you may want some help at first. Learn how to balance the checkbook. If money is tight until the estate is settled, call and let your creditors know.

13. Change the car registration and insurance if they were in your husband's name. If you were a two-car family, consider selling one of the cars, especially if there are car payments due each month.

Happiness is not a destination; it is a manner of traveling.

14. Check with the state's inheritance division if you live in one of the states that impose an inheritance tax.

15. Contact service providers such as the electric company that may have your account listed in your husband's name and arrange to have your name put on the account. With the telephone company, you may want to consider using just an initial for your first name in the phone book listing or consider an unlisted phone number.

16. Research health insurance for you and the kids.

17. Update the beneficiary designations on your own life insurance policies.

18. Update your estate planning including your will, trusts, durable power of attorney, and medical directive. If you have not done any planning, it is time to do something to get your affairs in order. Meet with your attorney for help with this.

19. Update the beneficiary designations on your retirement plans and IRAs.

20. Open a checking account for the estate to pay your husband's bills.

21. Set up a new budget that reflects your new cash flow and get help revising your financial plan.

22. Go out to dinner and to the movies with a friend. Often!

Probate and Taxes

The probate process is a court-monitored process in which the will is proved to be valid and the assets of the decedent are distributed according to the will. This is done in probate court, which may also be referred to as surrogate court.

The executor or executrix carries out the wishes of the decedent as stated in the will as to who gets what and when. This can be very simple

You have to have darkness . . . for the dawn to come.

or complicated and can be drawn out depending on the complexity of the will and the amount of the estate.

If your husband has died without a will, he has died intestate. You would then need to go through a process of administration in which someone is appointed the administrator to settle the estate. You can petition the courts to be appointed or to have your attorney be appointed.

If your husband had a living trust, the beneficiaries listed in the trust will receive their inheritance without those assets having to go through the probate process. Anything that was not owned by the trust, however, such as his car or boat, may have to go through the probate process. IRAs and retirement plans with designated beneficiaries will also bypass the probate process.

What Not to Do

I have spent most of this chapter giving you advice as to what needs to be done; now you need to know what you shouldn't do. This is such a tough time in your life, and you are so vulnerable. I don't want anyone taking advantage of your vulnerability.

This is the best advice I can give you. Read my lips: Do not make any major decisions for at least six months and, if you can, stall for a year. Why? Because your head will not be making the decision, your emotions will. I have seen many widows and widowers regret decisions that were made in haste.

Major decisions such as selling your home and moving should be postponed if they can be. So often, relatives and friends give you advice, and they are well meaning and loving. Indeed, the house may be too big for you to maintain, but selling it and moving in with the kids could be a catastrophe as well.

You need to test the waters. Find a house sitter and go visit the kids for eight weeks. It is easier to leave if you have a home to return to.

Be wary of anyone wanting to borrow money from you, and that includes your kids and your church! The insurance proceeds look like

If you're going thru hell, keep going. —Winston Churchill

a big pot of money to everyone, and they have expectations on how you can share it. Don't! No matter how noble the cause is or how much it hurts to say no, no it is. You need to figure out where you are financially and what you need to do for yourself before you can share with anyone.

The weeks right after a spouse's death are also froth with phone calls from people wanting to sell you life insurance or annuities. They may want you to invest the insurance proceeds with their firm, offering to come to your home to help you set up an account with them. Politely hang up the phone. If you don't want to be polite, that's okay, too. Just don't give them an opportunity, or they will be in your kitchen trying to sell you something.

Another scam often used is a workman will show up and claim that your spouse wanted the house washed or painted or some other work done. You would have known if the house needed to be painted. Send them away quickly and don't give them any money even if they start a job.

You will also be overwhelmed with phone calls from people offering you their services, from lawn mowing to gutter cleaning and tarot card readings. They may offer to buy your husband's car or clean out his closets for you. Again, say no thank you and hang up. Do not let strangers into your home! This may be a good time to get an answering machine and begin to screen your phone calls.

Another common scam is that someone will deliver an item and tell you that your husband ordered it. The person will want a cash payment for it. Tell him or her to send the item to your attorney, who will take care of it. Send the person away without giving him or her any money or your credit card number.

Review your bills carefully. Check credit card statements against the receipts. Be sure you are paying for a service that you or your husband ordered and that has been completed satisfactorily.

Another con game to look out for is the building inspector, plumbing inspector, or electrical inspector wanting to come in and check things out. Someone flashes what looks like an official badge

---

Life is not about how fast you run, or how high you climb, but how well you bounce.

and you open the door. What happens from there is that the person usually will find something wrong and will tell you that, for a bit of cash, he or she can fix it and never have to report it. Don't open the door until you call the city inspector and see if this is for real. You can make the person go away just by telling him or her to go away. If the person is for real, he or she can come back.

It's a sad world when humans prey on the vulnerable, but they do and you need to be forewarned. If any of these things happen to you, report them to the police. What's worse, people are embarrassed that they were so naive and that they allowed themselves to be taken advantage of, and they don't tell anyone about it.

Don't allow anyone into your home you don't know. Just don't open the door. You may think it is not polite, but I know it is not safe.

The Bottom Line

This is a tumultuous time burdened with both sadness and sense of urgency to get so many things taken care of. It's okay to take your time in both the grieving process and the paperwork required of you. In our fast paced society it is expected that within a couple of weeks things are back to normal for the widow. That's not so! Don't make any major decisions until you have had time to weigh your options and that can be six months, a year, or more.

When one door of happiness closes, another opens; but often we look so long at the closed door that we do not see the one opened.

Bella, a lively 75 year old, had lived in the country all of her life until recently when she reluctantly moved to Boston to be closer to her daughter and grandchildren.

Bella could no longer afford to live in her own home after her husband died. He had taken his pension as a 100 percent benefit with no survivor benefit for her. She soon discovered that her Social Security benefit check wasn't enough to buy groceries, medicine and heating oil. She quickly eroded her meager savings and had decided to take in a boarder when she told her children of her plans.

Her kids were appalled when they learned how little she had tucked away for retirement. Both her son and daughter immediately offered her housing in their homes. The son is in San Francisco and the daughter in Boston. Nowhere near what was home to her in Minnesota.

"Everyone is happy I came to live here," she told me, but she is missing her friends in Minnesota. Bella had an active social life playing cards with friends twice a week and sewing with her church group a couple of times a week. Now most of her evenings are spent alone with her TV. She has an in-law apartment in her daughter's home with her own entrance and a parking space right outside her door. Her car is ready when she is but she doesn't go much further than the local shopping center for she's not yet comfortable with the traffic, the lights. and the noise of the city. Bella's feeling much like an outsider in her new surroundings.

Chapter 15

What You Need to Know as Somebody's Daughter

●　●　●　●　●　●　●　●　●　●　●　●　●　●　●　●　●　●　●　●

In This Chapter

Reversing roles with your parent and becoming the caregiver will not be easy. There is always an emotional price you pay when this happens. The role reversal is equally difficult for your parent.

●　●　●　●　●　●　●　●　●　●　●　●　●　●　●　●　●　●　●

Consider the following:

✔ More than 22 million Americans who are caregivers are working full or part time.

✔ In 2002, there were an estimated 35 million persons age 65 or older in the United States, and about 1.5 million of them resided in a nursing home.

✔ The average American woman can expect to spend 17 years caring for a child and 18 years caring for an elderly parent.

✔ Women comprise more than 80 percent of the family caregivers.

You were a daughter before you acquired any of life's other titles such as somebody's steady, somebody's wife, or somebody's mother. You would think it would be a snap to help your parents now that

---

The worst thing about growing old is having to listen to a lot of advice from one's children.

they are getting on in years. It's not going to be that easy to do a role reversal with the most domineering forces in your life.

They don't want to give up being your parents. They still want control of their lives and all that is theirs, and that may include you. To go from the grand matriarch of a family to the ailing granny does not have much appeal to any of us; so if it happens to your mom, allow her some slack.

This chapter is about dealing with aging parents who may or may not want your help. Plus, wanting your help and accepting your help are two different things. Remember how stubborn you were as a teenager when your parents wanted things done their way and only their way would work. Ultimatums are just empty threats; they never worked on you growing up, and they won't work with the elders in your life now.

I am going to address dealing with your mother primarily because most women will outlive their spouses and will be the major caregiver for that spouse. For most adult children, it is our mother whom we must help in her declining years, but the lessons are not lost on our fathers.

Applying What You've Learned

There are things you can do to help your parents plan for old age, and they actually are the very things you need to do to plan for your old age. If you have your "stuff" in order, it will be so much easier to advise your parents going forth.

Setting Goals

No matter what age we are, we have hopes and dreams. When we are very young, it may be as simple as hoping our mother made apple pie for dessert. As we age, our world enlarges and so do our hopes and dreams. Have you asked your mother what she wants? That's a good place to start. It also is a great way to begin to know who she is.

Some people think they are worth a lot of money simply because they have it.

Don't put words in her mouth. Let her tell you what her dreams are, and nothing is silly. Remember that you once wanted to be a princess! Just think of Rosie O'Donnell here for a minute; she would love to be in your shoes right about now because she grew up without a mother around to nag her. Okay, so I couldn't resist a little guilt trip here.

Now help your mother put some corners on those dreams. For example, if she would like to stay in her own home after your father dies, what will it take to accomplish that? What does your father do that she is not physically capable of doing? It may mean she has to hire someone to mow the lawn and shovel the snow in the winter. Maybe she has to cut back on the size of her vegetable garden next spring. Maybe you have to come home and put the storm windows up for her or hire someone to do it. You want to find ways to help her control her environment and live in it comfortably.

Net Worth

Now here's where I really can do the guilt trip thing. Have you figured out your own net worth? Done a cash flow analysis to see where your money goes each month? Tackle yours first and then approach the subject gingerly with mom. At first, she may think you are being nosey and a bit presumptuous. She also may actually be embarrassed about how little she has.

I met Evelyn at conference a few years back, and she asked me for help. She had gone back to work after her husband died at age 69 and was tired of working at 74 and wanted to quit. So, in my most amiable manner, I told her to do just that. Quit, I said. She couldn't she said. Her husband had died and with him his pension. She was living on her meager savings, which were dwindling, her Social Security, and her paycheck from working at the local library. She had not changed her lifestyle since his death and continued to live in the family home, helping her children, and spoiling her grandchildren.

> Videotape the contents of mom's house and ask her to make comments as you walk around. The camera will give you a pictorial inventory of the contents of her house.

People are funny—everyone wants to live a long life but no one wants to get old.

She needed to call a timeout with her family and come clean, but she was feeling very foolish and didn't know how to do this. Her kids thought she was working to keep herself busy after the loss of their dad. When she did speak to them, they were embarrassed because they never thought to ask how she was getting on. And, of course, they wanted to help, and more importantly, they wanted her to stop helping them so she could have a life in retirement. Communication is key when dealing with anyone we love.

Tell your mom about having done your own net worth statement and why this is an important first step in strategizing a financial plan. Also, after the death of your father, it will help to get things organized, and that in itself could make things easier for mom. You know the drill if you have been through it. Tell her Evelyn's story. You're not looking for control here; you just want to know that she is in control.

Does mom have enough income to support her lifestyle? Again, her expenses may be minimal, but sit and review the cash flow worksheet with her. Is she afraid to use her principal to pay bills? What are her monthly bills? Is she paying for something she doesn't really need? How much is she giving to charity each month? Does she answer every one of the solicitations that come in the mail for help? Has she given them her credit card number, and is she automatically making a monthly gift to one of these TV evangelists?

If the two of you are on a roll, tackle organizing the paperwork. Get out the Inventory and Location of Important Documents worksheet (in Appendix A) and help her put things in order. This truly is a gift that you will give her and yourself, especially if ever you need to find something in the future. Set up a filing system that makes life easy. There are probably lots of things you can throw out, but if she wants to save them, let it go. It's probably not worth arguing about as long as she has the space to store them.

Now, if mom is living in a three-room apartment and it is cluttered with stuff, I'm on your side. But give everything you toss out a thorough going through before it gets the pitch. Why? While helping a family go through rooms of stuff their father had left, we found over

Most folks like the old days better—they were younger then.

$100,000 in savings bonds. Some had been used as bookmarkers, others were in drawers, and still others were in a pile of old mail.

Credit and Debt

You've done the cash flow; how does it look? Is mom able to afford what she is spending? Is she spending her time in front of the TV, watching the shopping channels? Those stations prey on the lonely. Why, just buy this and you'll feel so much better, is their message. Check out her credit card bills. She's a grownup so you can't ground her like you can your teenager, but hopefully you can reason with her. Is she paying only the minimum on the bills each month because she doesn't have enough income to pay it off in full?

If she can't get out to shop, her credit cards can bring her almost anything she wants. Catalogs, TV and online shopping are all right there at her fingertips. Check around the house. Is she using the stuff she is buying? So often, once it arrives, it's so much effort to return the item that people just keep it. The rationale often is that it didn't cost very much. Shopping may be her recreation if she can't get out. Talk about why she is doing this, and if she truly likes the shopping channel, ask her to hide her credit card or put it away so that it's not tempting to use. This may be a good time to suggest that she find some interests outside her four walls.

Insurance

As you're going through the paperwork, consolidate all of the insurance paperwork into one pile and spend some time reviewing the policies. What's mom got?

✔ **Homeowners.** Does mom have this up-to-date? Has she forgotten to pay the bill and the insurance has lapsed? Is she covered for at least 80 percent of the value of the house? What about her silver and her antiques? Does she have a special rider to cover them?

Inflation is when you never had anything and now even that's gone.

✔ **Health insurance.** Medicare is for everyone over age 65 who paid into the system or is receiving benefits on someone else's record. Medigap insurance is needed to cover what Medicare parts A and B do not cover. Oftentimes, there is paperwork to fill out, and it may be easier for mom just to pay the bill rather than hassle with the insurance forms. You could offer to help by filling them out for her, or there are firms you can hire that will fill out the forms for you and follow up with the insurance company. Mom only needs one Medigap policy. Log onto www.medicare.gov for help.

✔ **Auto insurance.** How much driving does mom do? If it's less than 7,500 miles, she may be eligible for a discount. Check the policy to be sure it is up-to-date. Also, if the car needs an annual inspection, check to be sure mom is driving around with a current inspection sticker on her car.

✔ **Life insurance.** Check to see what mom has and who is the designated beneficiary. Go through that mound of papers because there are often paid-up small policies that people forget about because they have been paid up for years. If you do find policies, catalog them, file them, and keep a list of them in a safe place.

✔ **Long-term care insurance.** Mother may need it. The younger she is when she purchases it, the cheaper it will be. And usually, you need to be healthy to qualify for it. If she has a pre-existing condition such as diabetes, the rules may be so strict, the terms so stringent, and the cost so high that it is not worth buying the policy.

Taxes

You'll need to keep copies of at least the last three years' worth of tax returns. Make sure mom is filing taxes. That's right, make sure she is filing her taxes. Lots of elderly women don't concern themselves with taxes because they've never filed; their husband's did.

If your father always did the taxes, hire someone to help mom. If mom's stuff is simple, the local tax preparer's office is a good place to

Money isn't everything—sometimes it isn't even enough.

start. You can help her by making up a tax file and telling her what she needs to keep in there: the 1099s that come the first of the year, her receipts for donations, medical expenses, and the real estate taxes.

Mom will be eligible to use a capital gains tax exclusion if she wants to sell her home and downsize. Individual taxpayers may exclude up to $250,000 from capital gains tax on the sale of their primary residence. She must have lived there for at least two of the last five years, but this period does not have to be consecutive. Married couples filing a joint tax return can exclude up to $500,000 of gain from the sale of their primary residence.

The Golden Years or The Golden Arches

Check on the distributions from the retirement plans. Be sure they are on schedule. If your dad was over 70 ½ and had started mandatory distributions, make sure mom stays on schedule. The IRS gets sticky about this and could whack her with a 50 percent penalty if she doesn't take out at least the amount she is supposed to. The IRA custodian should also be reminding her but don't count on it. A friendly tax preparer or a financial planner may be your best bet for help. Mom is not limited to the minimum distribution amount. She can take more out if she needs it.

Check to see that any pension money your mom is receiving is being directly deposited into her bank account. It's not uncommon for a woman to start receiving her survivor benefits from a pension in the form of a monthly check sent directly to her and then not depositing them. Open all the mail that has been sitting around in piles and say to yourself, "At least she saved all of this and didn't throw it away." There might be checks or other important documentation in there as well as bills that need to be paid.

If your mom is lucky enough to have a large portfolio that your father managed, get her some help if she does not want to manage it. Asking your husband or your brother to do it is not a good idea. Check out Chapter 18, "The Hired Help," which will help you find a financial planner for her. Be sure you find someone she is comfortable with.

Inflation is being broke with a pocket full of money.

Social Security

You might want to check to be sure mom is getting the benefit she is entitled to. After the death of a spouse, if she was receiving her benefit based on one half of his benefit, she will be entitled to a larger survivor benefit—but she must apply for it. The SSA won't automatically send it to her. Check out www.socialsecurity.gov or call 800-772-1213 to make an appointment at the office nearest you.

> *Elders should be cautioned never to give out their Social Security numbers and birth dates to anyone over the phone. The same is true with credit card numbers. Your Social Security number and credit card number should be treated like the formula for Coca-Cola—locked up and kept safe.*

Investing

Review mom's portfolio. Did dad pick out the stocks when the tech stocks were at the top of the market? Did he have everything in a CD? Is it valued at more than $100,000? If it is, FDIC insurance will only guarantee coverage for $100,000 if something should happen to the bank.

Having enough assets to cover mom's needs is great, but it needs to be managed properly. Find some help because, no matter how well intentioned you are, there are only so many hours in your day.

Mom's portfolio may need to be inflation proofed as well. Does she have some equity in her portfolio to beat inflation? She doesn't need to be holding a portfolio of 100 percent stocks, but she should have at least 40 percent of her portfolio in stocks no matter how old she is.

A Will

Has mom done any estate planning? Plow through the estate-planning documents if there are any. If not, you'll need to start from scratch. Mom needs a will, maybe a living trust, a durable power of attorney, and a medical directive.

It's good to have things that money can buy, but better to have things money can't buy.

The power of attorney allows someone she has appointed to act on her behalf legally and financially, and the power will not cease if she should become incapacitated. This power will allow you to pay bills for her, file her tax returns, and make changes to her portfolio.

If you are starting to plan from scratch, have the attorney give you at least six originals of the power of attorney; an original will have the notary seal on it. Many financial institutions will ask for an original rather than a copy, and many banks and brokerages houses may also want you to use their standard form. Check into that before you need to use the durable power of attorney.

A medical directive is controlled by state law and has many different names: a health care proxy, a medical power of attorney, a living will. This, again, allows mom to choose someone to act on her behalf for medical decisions if she should become incapacitated.

As an adult child, these last two documents will be most useful if you are to help an elder manage his or her affairs. If you live a distance from your mom and there is a closer sibling, you may want the sibling that lives closer to be named in these documents as your mother's attorney-in-fact.

If, during the planning process, your mom has begun to discuss plans for her funeral, don't shut her off. Listen to her. Write things down and ask her if this is what she wants. Tell her that you are going to put the information in a safe place, and if she wants to change any of it, you can do it together.

Compile a list of all your mother's advisors. Include her doctors, the fellow at the pharmacy, her lawyer, her clergy, financial advisors of any sort, her car mechanic and plumber, neighbors, friends, relatives, and anyone that you might need to contact if something happens to your mom.

If mom has a safety deposit box, ask her if you or a sibling could also have a key for the box. Keys do get lost, so it's important for there to be a backup. You and she may want to take inventory of what's in the box. People often forget what they tucked away in there.

Remember how comfortably you lived on what Uncle Sam now deducts from your paycheck?

Approaching Your Mom

If you were never been able to talk to your mom about difficult subjects while growing up, I can assure you that this won't have changed just because you are now a grownup. Most mothers still view their children as just that—children. You want to help your mom, but she may not be ready for that role reversal just yet. This will only work if she truly wants your help. Forcing this will be counterproductive, and she'll push you away.

Keep in mind that this will be a slow process. If your mom lives far away, do not expect to visit for a weekend and get everything taken care of. It may take up to a year to reach the point where your mom is comfortable discussing the taboo subjects with you, but don't give up. Remember how she helped you to learn to swim or drive a car. In the end, your mom will be grateful for your help.

If you have siblings, try to meet with them before you approach your mom so that you will have a united front when you begin this process. Your siblings may not share your concerns, but you will need to involve them in this process if it's to be successful. Choose a normal family gathering such as a birthday or holiday for a conference.

Bring up the fact that you just read this good book about women and their finances, and you realized how much you needed to organize your affairs. Talk about the general benefits such as knowing where things are, what estate-planning documents you need, and the need to start this process. Standing next to each other while washing the dishes is a great opportunity because she doesn't have to make eye contact with you.

Ask your mom if she has some concerns about outliving her money. Most women do! What are her healthcare concerns? Is she concerned about living alone? Falling? What about living in a nursing home? An assisted-living facility? Try to approach these questions casually. Do not sit down and go boom, boom, boom. She is not going to be able to answer if you are grilling her like she did when you missed curfew. When she does start to talk, listen. Do not belittle her fears.

Old age is a high price to pay for maturity.

LISTEN, LISTEN, LISTEN ... You may not be able to "fix" her concerns, but you can listen.

As this process goes on, hopefully she will realize that, if she is ever in a position in which she needs your help, you'll need to know where to begin. All you want to do is lay the groundwork now before a catastrophe occurs.

As you work through this process, remember that someday you may be in her shoes. Be sensitive to her concerns and to the fact that she is losing control over her life. Try to understand the anger and frustration that accompanies this loss of control. This process will truly be a lesson in patience.

Mom needs to be part of any of the decision-making that occurs on her behalf. Holding a family meeting without her to decide what you all are going to do about her will only alienate her. This is her life, and how and where she wants to spend her final years is ultimately her decision, not yours. Obviously, if she is in danger—whether from the neighborhood or from herself—then you must make the decisions. But think carefully before bulldozing ahead!

Eldercare

Eldercare is a very broad term, and it encompasses everything from reviewing mom's tax returns to providing her physical care in your home. What is needed depends on many factors.

What most elders want to do is stay in their own homes—not yours, theirs! And most can with some help. Whether you provide that help physically yourself or you manage the affair by getting others to help depends on distance, time, and money.

If you are living close to mom, you may be able to stop in on your way home from work to check on her or drop off dinner on your way to work in the morning. Certainly, the telephone links us to each other 24 hours a day. If mom needs more help than you can give, however, begin to do some research for assistance.

Parents should always remember that some day their children will follow their example instead of their advice.

Don't allow yourself to become so overwhelmed that you begin to resent the commitment you made to mom. There are resources available, and mom may be eligible for some assistance at no cost or on a sliding scale. Also consider getting some respite help if you need to get away. Try to keep a balance in your life. I know you are juggling a bunch of balls right now; there are the kids, your husband, mom, your job, and your sanity. Consider talking to a counselor about what's going on in your life. You are not just sandwiched between the two generations that need you; you have been stuffed into one of those fancy Monty Cristo sandwiches and then thrown into the deep fryer!

According to the AARP, 40 percent of working caregivers miss work on a regular basis due to the health needs of an elderly loved one.

For help, start with the Eldercare Locator at 800-677-1116. The Eldercare Locator is a public service of the Administration on Aging, and it has a friendly person on the other end of the phone to help you find needed services in the community where your mom lives. These services include meals, home care, transportation, housing, home repair, recreation, social activities, legal, and more. Check out the Administration on Aging's web site, www.aoa.dhhs.gov, for other resources as well.

Help on the Internet

While researching material for this section of the book, I was amazed at how much information is available on the Internet today. Assistance for mom can be found at Agenet (www.agenet.com), which operates a national eldercare network. Home Instead Senior Care (888-484-5759) is a national franchise and is a good source for non-medical companionship and home-care workers for your elder. These people can be hired for a couple of hours a day or a full day. They also offer respite service for caregivers as well. Learn more about them at www.homeinstead.com.

Another company worth mentioning is Senior Link, which is dedicated to keeping elders in their homes. They have a network of

Everybody is ignorant, only on different subjects.
—Will Rogers

geriatric care managers that can help you manage your mom's care from a distance. Visit their site at www.seniorlink.com or call them at 866-797-9697.

Two sites for Alzheimer caregivers are www.alz.org, the site for the Alzheimer's Association, and www.caregiving-solutions.com, a site dedicated to helping caregivers deal with the Alzheimer patient.

There are web sites that offer the caregiver help as well. The AARP (www.aarp.org) has a very comprehensive site on all aspects of aging. Another site worth logging onto is the Family Caregiver Alliance (www.caregiver.org), a good resource center with lots of practical information and helpful tips.

Assisted Living

Maybe mom needs more than you stopping by once a day and a caregiver coming in three times a week to help her bathe. There are assisted-living facilities that offer a homelike setting in which mom would have her own apartment and some supervision such as someone to help with bathing, meals, and reminding her of her medications. Assisted-living arrangements can cost between $1,000 to $3,000 a month depending on the services provided. Of the top 12 publicly held assisted-living chains about 65 percent were making a profit. So check the solvency of the facility before moving mom in. If it is having financial problems, that will affect mom's care because they may cut back on staff, activities, supplies, maintenance, and quality.

The Assisted Living Federation of America (www.alfa.org) has information on over 7,000 for-profit and nonprofit providers of assisted-living, continuing-care and retirement communities. Put the nonprofit facilities on the top of your list when considering an assisted-living facility for mom.

Taxes are the price we pay for all those government benefits we thought were free.

Long-Term Care Insurance

So, do you need to buy long-term care insurance for mom? It depends. If mom has very few assets and it would be a financial hardship for her to pay the premiums for the insurance, then she doesn't need it. She will be eligible for Medicaid should she need long-term care. Also, she will be eligible for community home-care services for very little cost because they charge a fee on a sliding scale.

Many advisors recommend long-term care insurance to protect assets from the cost of nursing home care. If mom has assets over $100,000 and a home, buy the insurance. It's really cheap protection. If her invested assets exceed $500,000, you may not need long-term care insurance because she can self-insure at that level. A good book to turn to for help is *The Complete Idiot's Guide to Long Term Insurance* by Marilee Driscoll.

Medicare

Many people believe they already have long-term-care coverage through Medicare. Not so! Medicare and most group medical plans for seniors over 65 offer only limited coverage for care given in a skilled nursing facility or at home, only for a relatively short period of time, and only for as long as skilled-nursing care is deemed necessary. This is the kind of care you might need to help you recover after major surgery or a fractured hip. Skilled-nursing care for a patient recovering from an illness or injury following a hospital stay is considered to be convalescent care as opposed to custodial care, which is provided to assist a person in the daily activities of living, such as bathing, dressing, or feeding. It is custodial care, for the most part, that one receives in a nursing home.

Medicaid

Medicaid and Medicare are often confused for one another, and many people think they are the same program. Medicaid is a jointly funded venture between the federal and state governments. It is

There is an advantage in being poor—the doctor will cure you faster.

designed primarily to help people with low income and little or no assets. Each state has its own rules about who is eligible and what is covered under Medicaid.

To qualify for Medicaid, applicants must have both income and assets below certain limits, which vary from state to state. Basically, you need to be poor with usually less than $2,000 in assets. Your home is not counted as an asset when applying for Medicaid. Within broad guidelines provided by the federal government, each state administers its own program, determining its own scope of eligibility requirements; the amount, duration, and scope of services provided; and the rate of reimbursement for services.

Nursing Home Care

According to the AARP, the national average annual cost of nursing home care is $50,000, with it costing closer to $72,000 on the East and West coasts. Many elderly people enter nursing homes and deplete their life savings very quickly. Once impoverished, they qualify for Medicaid coverage.

Three out of four nursing home residents are women.

Almost 70 percent of nursing home residents receive help from Medicaid, a few residents have long-term care-insurance, and the rest are private-pay residents.

Although the elder population is growing, nursing home occupancy is actually dropping, five of the top seven long-term-care chains filed for Chapter 11 bankruptcy in 2000, and many others are closing their doors. Yet assisted-living facilities have doubled in the last five years. Why? Our elders want to live on their own with their own stuff surrounding them and stay as independent as possible. Also, more communities are offering home-care services to allow elders to stay in their homes.

Taxes are the only things that grow without rain.

Buying Long-Term-Care Insurance

If you choose to buy long-term care insurance, the younger you are when you purchase it, the cheaper the premiums will be. The average stay in a nursing home is under two years. For a lifetime benefit your premium is almost double. The decision as to which policy is a personal choice. I have no magic formula to help you make that decision.

Long Term Care Premiums

Age	Benefit	Cost
40	3-year benefit	$562
	Lifetime benefit	$1,019
50	3-year benefit	$733
	Lifetime benefit	$1,362
60	3-year benefit	$1,120
	Lifetime benefit	$2,016
70	3-year benefit	$2,193
	Lifetime benefit	$3,782

Source: *The Complete Idiots' Guide to Long Term Care Insurance*

These are just general estimates. The premium for most policies remains the same each year that you age. This is referred to as a level premium. Many factors affect the premium price: where you live, your health, if you smoke, the type of policy you purchase, and the range of benefits.

Uncle Sam is encouraging you to purchase long-term care insurance. Part of the cost of the premium will be treated as a medical expense and will be deductible if you are over age 40. The benefits will be generally excluded from gross income. The government would like to get out of the business of funding long-term care through the Medicaid program.

The older I grow, the more I distrust the doctrine that age brings wisdom. —H. Mencken

For more information on long-term care, check out the AARP's web site at www.aarp.org. Get their publication, "Long-Term Care Insurance—To Buy Or Not To Buy" (D17186). Write to AARP Fulfillment at 601 E St. West, Washington, D.C. 20049.

You can find help at the Health Insurance Association of America's site at www.hiaa.org. They have a Guide to Long-Term Care Insurance that is worth downloading. The Centers for Medicare and Medicaid Services (CMS) is the federal agency that oversees Medicaid. Visit its site at www.cms.gov to learn about what your state requirements are for Medicaid eligibility and to help in your search for a nursing home.

The Bottom Line

Whoa! You didn't know there was so much you didn't know. Elder care is so much more than the physical care. That part may be the easiest for you to accomplish. Getting your mom to allow you to help is the first step. After that the rest does get easier. I promise!

Children seldom misquote you. In fact, they usually repeat word for word what you shouldn't have said.

manda is a 35-year-old single parent with an active four year old, two old tomcats and one three-legged gerbil all needing to be fed, usually just as she walks in the door after work she told me. She had her four year old in tow when I met her and after a few minutes I had a vivid picture of her existence.

Her life seems to consist of getting up in the morning and feeding her crew, dropping her son, Danny, off at childcare, going to work, picking up her son from childcare and feeding Danny, the cats and gerbil again and heading to bed. Then the routine starts all over again the next morning. This routine is so ingrained that the weekend we met she had gotten everyone ready on that Saturday morning and headed to daycare only to find it closed.

Recently divorced, Amanda is in serious debt. She wanted to keep the house so her son would have some stability after the divorce so she bought out her ex-husband's share with her savings, dipping into her IRAs and paying taxes. She then financed the divorce with her credit cards as well as some furniture purchases to fill the house when her husband moved out his belongings. And again wanting her son to have it all she financed a trip to Disney World recently.

Her dilemma is how can she afford to stay in her present home? Her father passed away this summer and her mother has made her an offer of sharing her parental home and the household expenses if that would help until she was out of debt. Her grandmother is also living with her mother and has offered to help with the babysitting.

She loves her own home but doesn't have the time to take care of the yard and the prospect of shoveling snow while her menagerie is inside alone is a scary thought. Last winter the gerbil lost his leg to one of the cats while she was outside shoveling snow. Her son opened the cage to play with him, the gerbil jumped out, and the cat ambushed him.

Chapter 16

What You Need to Know as Somebody's Mother

In This Chapter

Becoming a mom has been the hardest job I ever had. This chapter was written to guide you through all of the financial stuff you face as a mom. As for deciding what color hair is acceptable for your teenager, setting curfews, or the numbers of tattoos, you are on our own!

Being somebody's mom is an awesome responsibility! And what I found frustrating, the kid didn't come with an instruction manual. None! I checked!

As a new mother, I searched for an instruction manual because everyone in my life felt it was her or his duty to tell me how to raise my child. I wanted an instruction manual just so I could have a guaranteed outcome. If I did this, my child would be a great scholar. If I did that, my child would go to Harvard. If I did this, she would get a full scholarship to Harvard. If I did that, she would be an Olympic gold medal winner. I discovered that there's just no guarantee, no warranty, and no instruction manual. I was on my own!

When I held my child in my arms for the first time, I remember looking down into her tiny face, wrapping her little fingers around mine, and promising her the world. Now, her father and I didn't have

Never invest your money in anything that eats or needs repairing. —Billy Rose

the world, but we wanted to get it for her, and when her little brother came along, we wanted him to have it also.

And so it is with being a parent. We want so much more for our children. Your goals change when you become parent; a house in a good school district is more important than a new BMW. Funding a college education may supercede planning for retirement.

We make these mental promises to our children. It's an unwritten covenant. We don't want our kids to have to struggle the way we did. We want them to have an education. We want them to have a room of their own, nice clothes, books to read, a computer, their own telephone, their own TV, a car when they turn 16, and so on. Sound familiar?

As parents, we are overwhelmed with love and the need to protect and provide, but too often this gets out of hand. If we don't allow our kids to struggle, they won't acquire coping skills. If we never make them budget their allowance, they won't acquire money-management skills. If we never make them wait for a new video game or a new book, they will expect instant gratification and then abuse their credit card privileges as adults.

Applying What You've Learned

This chapter is definitely not an instruction manual for raising your kids, but your kids will learn their money smarts at your knee. They see how money affects your life and the power it has. This chapter is all about the need for you to view your financial plan differently now that you are a parent.

Finances

If you haven't done any planning and have taken a back seat, letting someone else take charge for you, reread the first section of this book—all 11 chapters! You need to be an equal partner in your finances, and you need to understand the financial-planning process.

Education will never become as expensive as ignorance.

It's important for you and for your kids. My grandmother, a very smart lady whom I mentioned earlier in the book, used to point out to me as I was growing up that good intentions paved the way to hell (or some other gruesome place). You're on a roll right now; you have gotten through 15 chapters, and we're rocking and rolling. So make some demands on yourself to learn as much as you can about your finances. This knowledge will protect you and your kids.

Setting Goals

Oh, how things change! Your home is cluttered with Fisher Price toys, your favorite TV show is *Sesame Street,* and you are in love with Ernie. Can you remember when your living room was not the baby's playroom? It never ceases to amaze me that something coming into this world weighing (usually) under 10 pounds can acquire so much stuff in such a short period of time and can manipulate all of the adults she encounters. And worse, can you remember looking at your sister-in-law's living room after her first baby and vowing that, when you had kids, it was going to be different? This would never happen to you. Our dreams change with the birth or adoption of a child. We are now somebody's mom and all that goes with it. Look at the changes motherhood has made in Rosie O'Donnell. This woman is ready to take on the NRA single handedly to protect her children and all children from guns.

This new little person in your life is now a dominating force. You may no longer dream of sailing around the world—who would care for your toddler while you were gone?

You have dreams for yourself, and you begin to formulate dreams for your child as well. Maybe it's college for the little one. Maybe it's a new house in a better neighborhood. Maybe it's a job closer to your family so the little one gets to know her grandparents. Write down these dreams. You know the drill. Discuss them with your spouse or partner. What will it take to achieve your new goals? What must you change in your current lifestyle to have the cash needed for a down payment on a house? Or to save for college?

College is wonderful because it takes children away from home just as they reach the arguing stage. —Will Rogers

Net Worth

I keep coming back to Chapter 3, don't I? That chapter does truly form the basis for your financial planning. You have got to know what you've got. You have got to know how and where you are spending your money and where everything is kept and filed. Knowledge is power.

That said, I'll leave it alone but do review Chapter 3. The experts tell me that you can expect increased costs of $6,000 to $12,000 a year for the first five years of a child's life. That's not including childcare! That's just cash you expend on incidentals. Your bundle of joy brings with her a bundle of bills for things like furniture, clothes, diapers, baby equipment, doctor visits, immunizations, and food. But that's the easy stuff, wait until she wants hockey equipment or a car!

So, where are those dollars going to come from? What will you need to adjust in your cash flow so you can afford formula? Of course, the first thing that happens is you don't go out as much.

Credit and Debt

It is so easy to put down your credit card to pay for something these days, and there are so many things you need once you have children.

Credit card debt will drown your dreams. Learn how to be a good shopper and spender. Of course the kid needs a snowsuit for the winter, but can you get it on sale? Hand-me-downs are fine as well, and thrift shops or church rummage sales can work wonders. From experience, I can honestly tell you that, to a 30-year-old, it really doesn't matter anymore if she had to wear her sister's old snowsuit when she was 3.

My son will tell you that his prowess in sports is due to the fact that he is ambidextrous. He will also tell you he is ambidextrous because he inherited his older sister's sports equipment. He was destined to be a lefty, but he and I didn't know he shouldn't be using the same baseball glove as his right-handed sister or be playing the same guitar that she used for lessons.

Money isn't everything, but without it college students would be out of touch with their parents.

Insurance

Insurance is a financial product you buy to protect yourself and all that you love. That seems simple enough. Health insurance is a must-have with kids. If you and your spouse are both working, who has the better coverage with the better choices? Consider family coverage using one plan because it may be less expensive. Look at the co-payments and deductibles because there will be lots of visits to doctors over the years and not just for checkups and shots. You'll have ER visits after your 3-year-old hits his sister with a bat or your little darling puts stones up her nose or falls from the garage roof while pretending to be Wonder Woman. Yes, kids do things like that!

With a dependent to feed and clothe, you want to be sure you have disability insurance. If you decide to stay at home for the first few years with the kids, what if something should happen to your husband? Disability insurance is not optional when you are a family with a single breadwinner. It becomes a necessity to protect all of you. Group disability insurance through an employer is the cheapest you will find. You will want to replace at least 60 percent of your income.

Life insurance needs increase when you have children. When there are just the two of you, if one should die, the surviving spouse can usually fend for herself if young. But if the surviving spouse is young and has children, all bets are off.

Life insurance replaces the loss of a future income stream. Life insurance is needed for both parents, though. If one is staying at home, he or she needs life insurance also. If this parent were to die, there would be expenses for daycare, house cleaning, transportation, and so on that would need to be covered as well as the person's future income stream if he or she were planning to go back to work.

Term insurance is cheap and easy to get. To figure out how much more insurance you now need use the worksheet in Appendix A and check out the following web sites: www.youdecide.com, www.quicken insurance.com, www.moneycentral.com, www.directquote.com, www.insure.com, and www.insweb.com.

If you think education is expensive, try failure.
—John Condry, educator

They all have great calculators and worksheets. Your employer may offer you minimal life insurance as a benefit, but with a family, your insurance needs are increased. You may want to be sure there is enough money to send the kids to college and to pay off the mortgage and any other debts you may have.

Taxes

The good news is that Uncle Sam realizes kids are expensive. The bad news is that Uncle Sam doesn't realize *how* expensive kids are. You are eligible for the child tax credit that is available for children being supported by you if they are under age 17. The credit begins to phase out if your income as a single parent is over $75,000, $110,000 for married filing jointly. The credit is reduced by $50 for every $1,000 of income over the threshold income limit.

Now the credit was $600 per child for the years 2003 and 2004. The new tax law of 2003 accelerates the credit amount to $1,000 for those years and then guess what? Back down it goes. For the years 2005 thru 2008 it will be $700, goes up to $800 in 2009, then reaches the $1000 mark in 2010 and you guessed it. It all changes again, it sunsets in 2010 and goes back to $500 per kid. Only Congress in its infinite wisdom could have thought up this one!

A childcare credit for daycare expenses is also available to you if you work outside your home or are a full-time student. If you have a flexible spending account available at work in which you can set aside a certain amount of money from your paycheck pretax to use for childcare, it's a better deal than the childcare credit.

If your bundle of joy is past needing baby-sitters and is heading to college, there are a few breaks for you there as well. There are two education credits, the Hope Scholarship credit and the Lifetime Learning credit, now available. These credits are mutually exclusive, which in tax speak means that you can't use them for the same kid in the same tax year. So you'll need to do some planning here.

The Hope Scholarship credit is available for the first two years of college. The credit is worth 100 percent of the first $1,000 in tuition

More money is spent on chewing gum than books. But after all, you can borrow a book.

expenses and 50 percent of the next $1,000 for a maximum credit of $1,500.

The Lifetime Learning credit is not just for kids. Anyone who is enrolled in undergraduate or graduate courses or is just taking courses to improve his or her job skills can use the credit. This is a tax credit of 20 percent on up to $5,000 of qualified tuition and fees. The maximum credit is currently $2,000. Both credits have income limits attached and are phased out between $41,000 and $51,000 for a single taxpayer and $82,000 and $102,000 for married folks filing jointly.

There is an adoption credit that is based on your costs to adopt a child. You can claim up to $10,000 of qualified expenses. These fees include reasonable adoption fees, court costs, attorney fees, and legal fees. The credit is phased out for income levels between $75,000 and $115,000 and disallowed once you hit $115,000. You are not eligible for this credit if you are adopting your spouse's child.

The Golden Years or Golden Arches

So what do you do? Save for retirement or save for college for the kids? I vote for retirement! I have checked, and there are no scholarships for retirement given out no matter how smart you are.

You should be fully funding your retirement plans at work, and if your employer matches, be sure you are taking advantage of the match. That money will grow tax deferred until you start to withdraw it in retirement.

If it does become apparent later on that you don't have enough to fund junior's education, you may be able to borrow from your 401(k), 403(b) plan or 457. With your IRAs, you can withdraw funds from the IRA to pay for college expenses for the kids and grandkids before age 59 ½ and you will not be assessed the 10 percent penalty. You *will* owe taxes on the money, though. With Roth IRAs, you have access to the contributions you made because they were made with after-tax dollars, so there's no tax and no penalty.

After paying for the wedding, about the only thing a father has left to give away is the bride.

Social Security

Social Security is not just for retirees. If something should happen to you or your spouse when the kids are small, the surviving spouse could be eligible for survivor benefits, as would the kids. Also, children with special needs are often eligible for benefits from Social Security.

Oh yeah, the kid needs a Social Security number. If you want to claim her on your taxes, you need to have a valid Social Security number because the IRS needs to know she really exists. The easiest way to do this is when you are still in the hospital. Apply for a number when you furnish the information for your baby's birth certificate. You will need your Social Security number and her father's number as well. If you don't do it then, you'll need to go to a Social Security office and apply for a number there.

A Will

One of the biggest stumbling blocks for many couples when they are trying to put together their estate plan is not being able to agree on a guardian for minor children if something should happen to both parents.

You will need to name a guardian, and I would suggest a sibling or a friend might be a good choice, with a parent as a backup. Why? Age! If you are 35 and you name your 65-year-old mother (even though she may be a young 65) and the children are 3 and 6, what happens in 10 years when your mother is not a young 75 and she is dealing with teenagers learning to drive and going to their first prom?

By the way, you should ask your family members or friends before you draw up your will to make sure they would be willing to take on the responsibility of caring for your children if something should happen to you. Diane Keaton starred in a very funny movie, *Baby Boom,* in which she played a single yuppie who found herself the guardian of a six-month-old baby. It changed her lifestyle dramatically, but because it was Hollywood, it had a happy ending.

Children are a great comfort in your old age, and they help you reach it faster.

After you have been through the traumatic experience of finding a guardian, will this same person be the one you want to manage the assets you may be leaving the kids? No? Okay, now what? You will need to find someone who will act as trustee of the trust that will need to be set up for the kids. What trust, you're asking? What about the insurance proceeds? There could be half a million dollars or more. If you have three kids and your sister has two of her own, will she have the time, energy, and inclination to manage your kids' money. Maybe?

When doing estate planning, you do need to plan as if you were to die the day after the documents have been signed. It's not a pleasant thought, I know, but it's much needed reality here. If you have minor children and there is a lot of money involved, you probably don't want them inheriting the money at 21. You may want to consider a trust so that, after college, they can receive some of the money at age 25. This way, they will need to work for their supper for a while, and then the rest can be distributed to them at a later date.

How Much Will It Cost to Raise a Kid?

This is the sort of thing you almost don't want to know. Hang on to your hats! According to the most recent U.S. Department of Agriculture report, the average family (and they define average as a family earning $65,800) will spend about $249,000 in today's dollars to raise a child born in 2002 until she is 17. Now, that number has been adjust for inflation. This is for the food, shelter, and necessities needed to raise a kid. This does not include a college education; I repeat, this does not include a college education. Now add in the college education and if you do that you will remain celibate!

If you have more than one child, you don't just double that number. If you did, you would go into shock and quit this parenting business all together (not that you don't already have sticker shock!). Each child that follows the first is cheaper because there is the economics of scale theory at work here. After the first one, you already have some of the equipment (unless you're like me and have kids six years apart),

When you feel like criticizing the younger generation, just remember who raised them.

you have already moved out of the one-bedroom apartment and into a three-bedroom house, you already own the minivan, and you already have a family plan for your health insurance, and so on.

Increased housing costs are the single largest expenditure, averaging $53,000 over the 17-year period. The cost for food is $25,000 for that same timeframe, but I am sure no one at the Department of Agriculture ever invited my son to dinner. These numbers would indicate an annual expenditure of $1,500 per child for food. That's about $29 week. That wouldn't keep my son in lunch money for the week!

Now, your mother-in-law may have just said that your daughter is priceless and she is, but she does come with a real price tag. So the next time someone says that the bundle of joy you are holding in your arms is worth her weight in gold, you know they are right on the money! For fun, and I do mean just that, check out www.bankrate.com, click on their calculator section, and figure out what it will cost you to raise a child. Here you have the ability to fine-tune the numbers that will fit your individual household. It's a numbing experience!

Paying for College

So now, if we add the cost of college to the cost of raising a child, what do we get? Depressed!

Well, you know you want the kid to go to school, but you have to find something that fits your budget. There are lots of ways to pay for college. Full scholarships are always welcome, but they are few and far between. You might think she's a genius because she could do her numbers with the Count on *Sesame Street* at age 2, but can she score an 800 on her math SAT? If not, start working on a backup plan.

The average tuition and room and board for a four-year private college was $25,000 for the year 2003. For a four-year public college, it was $9,500, and over half of that was for room and board. College costs increased at around 5 percent last year.

Education begins when your mother sends you to college and is completed when you send your daughter there.

These numbers are for only part of the total college package. They don't include fees, books, transportation, computers, clothes, midnight pizza runs, shaving cream, shampoo (yes, some kids do shave and bath), and a cell phone. These need to be factored in, but they are so highly individual that it's hard to come up with an average cost. That's something you will need to work on with your student.

If we take the average cost of tuition and room and board and project forward using a 5 percent inflation rate, the first year of private college for a baby born in 2003 and starting college in 2021 will cost over $60,000. If she attends a state school, it would cost around $23,000. Can you save enough?

Now that you have sticker shock, how are you going to pay for school? There are a variety of new programs to help the beleaguered parent today. I will touch on them briefly so that you are aware of them, but if you are still able to hold that bundle of joy in your arms, you have the advantage of time on your side to begin saving. If your kid is older, its still not too late.

Projected College Costs

(5% inflation)		
Year	Private	Public
2003	25,000	9,500
2004	26,300	10,000
2005	27,600	10,500
2006	28,900	11,000
2007	30,400	11,500
2008	31,900	12,100
2009	33,500	12,700
2010	35,200	13,400
2011	36,900	14,000
2012	38,800	14,700
2013	40,700	15,500
2014	42,800	16,200
2015	44,900	17,100
2016	47,100	17,900
2017	49,500	18,800
2018	52,000	19,700
2019	54,600	20,700
2020	57,300	21,800
2021	60,200	22,900
2022	63,200	24,000
2023	66,300	25,200
2024	69,600	26,500
2025	73,100	27,800
2026	76,800	29,200
2027	80,600	30,600
2028	84,700	32,200
2029	88,900	33,800
2030	93,300	35,500

Ideas are like children—your own are wonderful.

Most parents cannot save enough to pay for college. College expenses are paid for with savings, loans, grants, and current cash flow, both yours and the student's. Hopefully, by the time the kids are in school, your career has taken off, and you have increased earnings that will help. If a spouse stayed home with the kids when they were young, he or she may now be working also. There are three new savings programs that offer parents some help in saving for college. Congress is always changing the rules, so you will need to keep abreast of the changes.

> *If you purchased check writing software from Quicken or Microsoft Money you have the ability to figure out how much you'll need to save for college expenses. There are programs already on your computer to help you with college planning. There are calculators on line as well that will help. Visit www.quicken.com, www.moneycentral.com, and www.financenter.com.*

Paying For Education with Savings Bonds

Both I Bonds and EE Bonds purchased after 1990 can be used for the Education Bond Program, a program designed to allow a tax exclusion for savings bonds' interest when used to pay for qualified college tuition and fees. There are some strict requirements to meet, though. Bonds must be in the parent's name, not the child's. If grandma wants to gives the kids savings bonds for college, she needs to purchase them in your name or your spouse's. You can also use the bonds for your own tuition expenses, but you must be at least 24 years old when you purchase the bonds. The costs of books and room and board are not considered qualified expenses.

You aren't required to indicate that you intend to use the bonds for educational purposes when you buy them. So you can be saving for college in a 529 plan and have EE bonds as a back up. The bonds are in the parent's name so they are not considered an asset owned by the child for financial aid consideration.

There are income limits as to who can use the program. For this year, single taxpayers have the ability to use the bonds tax-free if their

The child who knows the value of a dollar will usually ask for two.

income is under $58,000 and the exclusion phases out for incomes between $58,000 and $73,500. For married couples filing jointly, the exclusion phases out between $87,750 and $117,750. These numbers are indexed for inflation annually.

You are limited to the number of bonds you can purchase annually. $30,000 of face value for each type of bond. There is no limit to the amount you can accumulate though. You can purchase these bonds on line thru the Treasury website www.publicdebt.treas.gov or www.savingsbonds.gov, through payroll direct programs or from your local bank.

Coverdell Educational Savings Account (ESA)

This is not a new plan, just a new name. These were the Educational IRAs that had a name that made no sense. And at one time they were limited to $500. They are now known as ESAs or Educational Savings Accounts.

Today these accounts can be set up for kids under 18 years of age, and there is an annual contribution limit of $2,000 per child. The contribution is not tax deductible, but the earnings will accumulate tax-free and will remain tax-free if used for education expenses. If the money is not used for school, the earnings become taxable. The account is in the child's name using his or her Social Security number.

The individual making the contribution on behalf of the child has income limitations to deal with. For taxpayers filing a joint return, their ability to make the contribution phases out with income between $190,000 to $220,000. For single taxpayers, it is $95,000 to $110,000. As a parent, if your income disqualifies you from setting up a Coverdell Educational Savings Account, someone else such as grandma can set it up for your child as long as grandma meets the income requirements.

The $2,000 limit doesn't sound like very much but it will help! Let's assume you start today when your little one is still in diapers. You will have 18 years to save. Assuming an 8 percent return on the money, there could be $75,000 in the savings account when the kiddo

By the time the average teenager is able to work, she won't.

starts college and the money will be tax free if used for college expenses. You would have invested $36,000 of your money and the account would have earned $39,000. If you were in the 25 percent tax bracket you just saved close to $10,000 in taxes.

ESAs allow the use of the money not just for college expenses. These dollars can be used for K-12 education expenses. Education expenses can include the purchase of a computer.

Prepaid State Tuition Plans (529 Plans)

Prepaid tuition plans have been around for awhile, but in the beginning, they were very limited. They did you allow to lock in tuition costs, but if you didn't use the money, your return was abysmal, usually 3 percent. In 1997, Congress changed the rules. State-run college savings plans can now be set up so that the money is invested in mutual funds and grows tax deferred until the kid starts college. In last year's tax package, Congress sweetened the pie and allowed the earnings to be tax free if used for college expenses thru 2010. After that the earnings will be taxed at the child's rate, which could be as low as 10 percent.

Learning about college aid is only a few keystrokes away. Visit www.petersons.com for information about financial aid as well as information on colleges. Also check out the Department of Education's site at www.ed.gov as well as www.finaid.org.

The new plans are run by financial institutions such as mutual funds companies for the individual states, and each state has a different plan with different rules and different investment options. Many of the states allow nonresidents to invest in the plan, and most states allow the money to be used for schools anywhere within the continental United States.

Visit www.savingforcollege.com for more information on what's available in the state you live in. This site is run by Joe Hurley, author of *The Best Ways to Save for College.* 529 plans are the best savings tools for college that have become available in a very long time.

One way to teach children to count is to give them different allowances.

Teaching Your Kids About Money

Most kids do not know enough about money. That said, how do we fix it? Financial education is not taught in our schools; even graduate students working on their MBAs don't get coursework in personal finance. The media is filling the gap nicely, and there are books, web sites, magazines, newsletters, radio shows, TV shows, and even entire TV channels dedicated to money and personal finance, but most of it is for adults.

Kids need to understand money and how we as adults get it into our hands. Tell a small child that you have no money to buy something, and he or she will tell you to charge it. Kids also think that money comes from the ATM. Most of them have never been inside a bank, just the drive through or the ATM window.

They need to understand the concept of working for money, getting paid for that work, and depositing a paycheck into the bank for safekeeping. This gives us the privilege of going to the ATM to make withdrawals of our money so that we are able to purchase goods and services. Most 6-year-olds are able to grasp this concept.

A really hard concept is charge cards and how they work. These are really just short-term loans that we get when we use our credit card. If we pay if off each month, no interest is charged. The card is our form of identification to show the merchant that the credit card company has money set aside that we can borrow to make our purchases.

Kids should get allowances. It's better to make mistakes at 13 with $30 than at 33 with $30,000. The experts recommend giving a dollar amount to match their ages. So a 10-year old would get $10 and so on. But if you expect them to pay for their entertainment, church contributions, school lunches, and so on, they may need more. Help them set goals and budget their money. Some needs to be set aside for lunches, some should be saved for a rainy-day fund, some should be earmarked for entertainment, some should be saved for the new video game, and so on. It wouldn't hurt to encourage saving some for college

It costs more to amuse a child than it once did to educate her mother.

as well. The college experience is much more meaningful if the kid is paying for part of it.

If they run out money in the middle of the week, don't bail them out. That's not the lesson you want them to learn, that you'll be there with your wallet open to always help. If there is no money left for school lunches, help them make lunch and refrain from making any comments. If they begin to beg or whine that they have no money to go to the mall on Saturday, turn a deaf ear.

Many parents want kids to do chores in exchange for their allowances. I am of the opinion that an allowance is a part of the family expenditures. Kids should be expected to carry their weight in a family and to help out with family chores such as getting dinner, setting the table, cleaning up, and so on. If the kiddo wants to earn more money, then perhaps you pay her extra for raking the leaves or washing the car. It's your call here; you are the parent!

Teaching kids about delaying gratification is very important. We've all witnessed a kid throwing a tantrum in a store and then getting what he or she wanted. For starters, have the kid begin to save for something he or she wants like a video game, a CD, or a scooter. Make it attainable in a couple of weeks; any longer than that and you'll lose 'em. Now, if you want to take this one step further, offer to make the child a loan to help purchase it. Charge interest because that is the cost of borrowing. The child can pay you back a certain amount each week when he or she receives their allowance. Visit www.coolmath4kids.com with your kids. This site has a loan calculator where kids can figure out loan payments once you set the term and interest rate.

> *Two fun web sites for kids to use and learn about money are www.coolbank.com and www.moneyopolis.org.*

Take whatever opportunities come up to teach kids about money. Take them grocery shopping. Give them part of the list and a cart of their own. Encourage them to read the prices and check them against the computer at check out. Here are some other quick and

---

Parents don't bring up children anymore—they finance them

easy lessons: Why do you use coupons? Why do you buy things on sale? Why do you shop at a discount store?

Before your teenager heads off for college, she'll need some lessons on budgeting and credit cards. Help avoid plastic problems. She will start to get pre-approved credit card applications in the mail once she's at school. Credit card companies are smart marketers. They know you would throw them away if they arrived in your mailbox, but she'll open them. She needs to learn about credit long before she starts Psych 101. Maybe you want her to go off to school with a debit card instead of a credit card. Then she can't spend more than what she's got in her account!

Grandparents as Primary Caregivers

Over 11 million grandparents are providing childcare and helping to raise their grandchildren. Almost 4 million children live in grandparent-headed households, and 1.3 million children are being raised solely by their grandparents. These are sobering statistics!

We have boomerang kids today. You know what I mean here; we toss them out on their own, and then they come zooming back when things don't work out well for them. It could be a divorce, an illness, the death of a spouse, the loss of a job, drug abuse. Not only do they come home, they often bring the grandkids with them. So your empty nest that you had just begun to redecorate is now full of boarders again. And indeed, home should be where they flock to in times of need.

I recently met a woman who, at 68, had to go back to work so she could afford the things she and her 12-year-old grandson needed; they couldn't make it on her meager savings and Social Security benefits. There are programs, services, and possible financial support available to help you as a grandparent. Don't go it alone; you just need to know where to look for help. Start with the sites listed here:

Children are not only heirs to your possessions—they are heirs to your values and character.

✔ **AARP:** Go to www.aarp.org and click on "grandparents." This site provides information about services and programs that can help improve the lives of grandparent-headed households. It also provides other information for grandparents.,

✔ **Grand Parent Again:** This site at www.grandparentagain.com offers information about education, legal help, support groups, and links to other organizations for grandparents raising grandchildren.

✔ **Generations United:** This national organization (www.gu.org) focuses solely on promoting intergenerational strategies, programs, and policies.

✔ **Grandsplace:** This site (www.grandsplace.com) is dedicated to supporting grandparents and other relatives raising other people's children.

✔ **Social Security Administration:** (www.socialsecurity.gov) Your grandkids may be eligible for benefits if you are collecting benefits and have legally adopted them or if both parents are deceased or disabled.

The Bottom Line

Parenting doesn't end once the kid is eligible to vote does it? Kids need to learn about money and as parents we need to learn about money. You may find yourself financially responsible for your adult kids and your grandchildren.

If a man empties his purse into his head, no one can take it from him.
—Ben Franklin

Notes:

*W*hen I met Michelle she had one question she wanted answered. She wanted to know how much was enough? She and her partner Lisa wanted to retire early but were unsure about how much they needed to have in their nest egg.

Michelle and Lisa have been in a long-term relationship and want to grow old together. No different than any other couple I speak to who are nearing retirement. Retirement planning is the number one financial issue worrying women. Everyone wants to know when they can retire and if they can retire early? The bull market of the 90s along with the advent of the 401(k) plan has been driving this rage to retire early. But Michelle is even more specific: she wants out at age 55. She would literally like to take the money and run she said. She has the money right now, for she took advantage of the company's cash buy-out plan of her pension, and the money is sitting there waiting for her in an IRA. Lisa's company does not have an early out program available but she was hoping she could join Michelle in a year or two.

A big concern is whether they will have enough money in retirement to maintain their current lifestyle. They are paying off a new car but were wondering about needing another one a couple of years into retirement. How should they be planning for that purchase? Michelle has some stock options that she has not used yet and was wondering if she should use them to pay off the mortgage and car loan?

They proudly told me they had seen an attorney and were taking the steps necessary to get their estate planning done before they retired. They wanted all of their ducks lined up they told me.

Chapter 17

What You Need to Know as Somebody's Partner

● ●

In This Chapter

In this chapter I need to point out to you that as somebody's partner you have very little legal protection. And the
rights and privileges afforded married folk and even
divorced couples don't apply here for you. As a woman you
need to plan if you take on the role of partner.

● ●

Whether you are a heterosexual couple living together because you
have chosen not to marry or you are a same-sex couple living together,
society describes you as domestic partners. You have similar issues
financially and legally, the primary difference is social acceptance. In
our society today it's easier to be a heterosexual couple living together
than a same-sex couple.

In this chapter, I'm going to discuss the finances of living together
and how you protect yourself and your partner legally and financially
while you are alive or upon your death. Society, businesses, and some
parts of our government are recognizing the fact that people do live
together and do need legal protection. A marriage certificate does protect the parties involved and does give each certain rights and privileges that are not available for domestic partners.

---

*I'm going to get out of debt this year if I have to mortgage my
house to do it!*

The IRS does not recognize any category of taxpayers except married, single, or head of household. Less than 10 percent of American families represent the *Ozzie and Harriet* ideal of dad going off to work and mom staying home to raise the kids.

As a couple living together, you have begun to share closet space, but how much more do you want to share or are you willing to share with each other? This has nothing to do with your gender. But there are some things you need to be aware of, for you are in a unique situation.

Applying What You've Learned

Because you are in a unique situation, there are many legal and financial issues. Planning for your future becomes doubly important for you may have to provide the structure and legal protection that normally the government provides for a married couple.

Setting Goals

Goals you establish as a single person could be quite different from those established once you are partnered. What are your financial goals for this relationship? Or are you afraid to look that far ahead?

Establish what you want and what your partner wants. Certainly, you both should be planning for retirement, but what about a house, a family, and an early retirement? Don't allow things to just happen. Communication is key to making this living-together thing work for both of you.

Whose money are you going to use to accomplish these dreams? There is an old adage; "He who has the gold rules." Should it be that way for you? I don't think so, but don't allow yourself to get caught up in that. Money is powerful, and very often, the partner making the most money feels that he or she should have veto power and the most say in decisions. Don't fall into that trap if you want an equal relationship. Maybe you need to keep your goals separate rather than joining forces right now.

If you want to feel rich, just count all of the things that you have that money can't buy.

If you have children from a previous relationship or marriage, there may be goals that involve them for which your new partner doesn't want to accept responsibility. You need to be cognizant of that as you do your own planning and attempt to provide an education for the kids.

Net Worth

You should know what your net worth is and what you are bringing into this relationship. Why? If this domestic partnership ever ends, you will want to walk away with what is yours. I know I am not sounding very romantic, but I have the wisdom of experience, and my job as a financial planner is to bring the practical side into every decision you make. Don't worry, you wouldn't be the first person to call me a "Killjoy."

Where do you stand on this issue? The key here is whether you want to combine your assets and your incomes and make yourselves a financial couple. Or maybe you should just think about sharing living expenses for a while and see where it goes.

As you begin to accumulate major stuff together like appliances, a car, a sound system, and furniture, you need to decide about ownership. Does one of you buy the washer and the other the dryer so that there are clear lines of ownership? Do you both put up money and create a joint purchase agreement? This is a simple agreement that states that you have joint ownership and what should happen if you separate. For example, if you should separate, you would agree on a mutual price, and one of you could buy out the other. You can also put in the agreement that, if you can't agree on a fair price, you will sell it and split the proceeds.

When buying a house, it is very important to have everything in writing. You want a property agreement. How will you split ownership: 50-50, 60-40, depending upon who puts up how much money? Dividing the cost of ownership and upkeep can prove to be one of those really awkward moments in your relationship, but you need to talk about it. If one of you should die, how is that asset going to be

If your outgo is greater than your income, your upkeep will soon be your downfall.

handled? Does the surviving partner inherit the property? Does some-one else inherit the property? Do you designate in your will how the asset should be disposed of, or do you title the property so that, if one of you should die, the survivor has full ownership? Get some professional help with these documents, but do spend some time discussing the issues. It truly will eliminate future problems.

Next is the cash flow worksheet. How much does it cost you both to live together? Where does your money go each paycheck? Do you have two separate checking accounts and a third joint account for household stuff? If you are considering combining checking accounts, get some check-paying software such as Quicken or Microsoft Money to help keep track of your expenses. What do you have left over to save, and where do you save it? All of these are questions you need to answer before you start this process.

If one of you is a spender and the other is a saver, keep separate checkbooks; it will save a lot of future arguments. Use the common checkbook to pay the common bills and use your own checking accounts to keep track of your personal stuff. If your incomes are not equal, you may want to decide to split up the expenses proportionally (60-40 and so on).

Having an emergency fund is important here. You want a stash of cash set aside, and each of you should be responsible for accumulating your own if you are keeping separate accounts. This definitely is not a romantic notion, but you should have enough money to be able to leave this relationship if the need arises. An emergency fund should tide you over if there is an emergency but also if you want to leave your present job or a relationship. This way, you have the dollars to walk. Just consider this your "Go to hell!" money.

Credit and Debt
You may be merging households, but you don't want to merge debt. Each of you should be responsible for your own debt and your own credit card payments. You will not be liable for your partner's debt

---

If money talks, why didn't it cry for help a long time ago?

unless you co-signed a loan or have a joint credit card with both names on it. As a word of caution, before signing anything, read it carefully.

Debt will bury your dreams quicker than anything else. Getting out of debt so that you have the increased cash flow to achieve your dreams should be your number one goal.

Credit cards present a problem because many couples want to share everything. Don't. Even married couples should have their own credit cards. You don't want to co-mingle your credit history if one of you has had credit problems recently. That could present problems down the road if you want to buy a house together. Before you try to get pre-approved for a mortgage, both of you should check your credit history. If you were in a relationship previously, your credit history may be mixed with your former partner's. Clean that up before trying to get a mortgage.

Insurance

Health insurance is a must-have for everyone today. You can't afford to be sick unless you do have insurance. If each of you is working and has your own health insurance through your employer, read no further. It gets sticky, however, if one of you does not have health insurance.

Over 3,500 corporations are now recognizing domestic partnerships and are offering domestic-partner benefits. Some are only being offered to same-sex couples; others are offered to heterosexual couples as well. If you are married and your husband is covered by your employer's health plan that is considered a nontaxable benefit. In a domestic partnership, however, remember that the IRS doesn't recognize this relationship; this benefit is no longer a tax-exempt benefit. It becomes taxable income to you.

If you sign up for the benefit, your partner will have healthcare coverage, but there is a cost attached. You will owe federal income taxes, Medicare taxes, Social Security taxes, and possibly state income taxes on the benefit. So before you sign on the dotted line, understand the tax consequences. There may be cheaper alternatives.

Fools can make money—it takes a wise woman to know how to spend it.

Disability insurance is used to insure your income stream if you are not able to work, and it is really important because, in the eyes of the law, you are two single people living together. There are no Social Security disability benefits available for partners unless you are in a common-law marriage. Check with your employer's benefits department for group policy coverage.

Life insurance is used to insure the loss of your income stream for your dependents if you should die. Many people have minimal life insurance offered as a benefit through their employer, but if you want to protect your partner or you have dependents to be concerned about, get more life insurance. Check Chapter 5, "Protecting Yourself and Your Assets: Buying Insurance," for more details on where to get life insurance and help with estimating how much life insurance you need to purchase.

While you are reviewing your life insurance needs, check the beneficiary designation on any policies you currently own. Life insurance bypasses your will, so whomever you have listed as the beneficiary on your policy will receive the proceeds if you die—no matter what you may have indicated in your will. If you want to protect a new partner, be sure you have specified that person as the beneficiary on your life insurance policy.

Some insurance companies don't allow same-sex partners to name each other as a beneficiary due to a "lack of an insurable interest" because they are not blood relatives or a spouse. You may need to name your estate as the beneficiary and then in your will leave the proceeds to your partner, or you could search out an insurance company that will allow you to name your partner as the beneficiary.

Another way around the lack of insurable interest problem is to name a blood relative as the beneficiary when you first make the application for the insurance. Then, after a few months, change the beneficiary to your partner. Yes, it is a bit of subterfuge, but it will work and get you the desired results.

Long-term-care insurance may be very important for same-sex couples who own a home jointly. You do not have spousal rights if one of

---

Poverty is a state of mind often induced by a friend's new car.

you should need to apply for Medicaid. Medicaid rules state that, in the case of a married couple who own a home and one spouse needs to enter a nursing home, the other spouse can stay in the home. The home doesn't have to be liquidated. However, for same-sex couples, the home must be sold unless the healthy partner can buy out the ill one.

Taxes

The IRS does not recognize same-sex relationships, so you will need to file individual tax returns. A heterosexual couple living in a common-law state can file a joint return if they have a common-law marriage. But you must meet the state's definition of a common-law marriage. The following gives you a general idea of what is expected if your relationship is recognized as a common-law marriage, and all four conditions must exist :

✔ You must be a heterosexual couple living in a state that recognizes common-law marriages: Alabama, Colorado, the District of Columbia, Georgia, Idaho, Iowa, Kansas, Montana, Ohio, Oklahoma, Pennsylvania, Rhode Island, South Carolina, Texas, and Utah. New Hampshire is considered a common law state only for inheritances and Social Security benefits.

> Living Together: A Legal Guide for Unmarried Couples *by Attorneys Ralph Warner, Toni Ihara & Frederick Hertz a must read book. Check out the Nolo website at www.nolo.com for more books and information.*

✔ You must publicly be holding yourselves out as being married. An example of that would be using the same last name.

✔ You must have been together for a significant amount of time. (I know that's nebulous, but it's not any more defined than that.)

✔ You must intend to be married eventually. (Again, this is nebulous, but it also means you cannot be married to anyone else!)

The best things in life may be free, but the things money can buy aren't bad either.

If you do have a common-law marriage, you will need to go through a traditional divorce proceeding to dissolve it. My advice is: if you live in a common-law state and you want to live together, do so. But keep things separate enough so that you are not considered married in the eyes of the law, and if your intention is to get married, get married!

The Golden Years or The Golden Arches

Retirement planning is the key to having a comfortable retirement. You need to plan on your own because, unless you are in a common-law marriage, you have no legal right to your partner's retirement plan. Married couples can inherit each other's IRAs and then can actually roll the IRA into their own. This is only allowed between married spouses. With 401(k) plans, the spouse is the beneficiary unless he or she signs off. The same is true with government pensions.

So you need to do some planning. Be sure that each of you is saving and investing for retirement and that you have designated your partner as the beneficiary on your retirement plans. This is the only way to protect each other. You can also name your estate as the beneficiary and then leave everything to your partner in your will. The problem with that, is if a family member thinks he or she should have inherited your 401(k) plan, the person can contest your will and make things messy because then it will need to decided by the judicial system.

Social Security

In a same-sex partnership, you will be entitled to Social Security benefits based only on your own earnings record. Social Security retirement benefits based on a spouse's earning record are not available in same-sex partnerships. With common-law marriages, the SSA will recognize state law where the worker lived. So if you had a valid common-law marriage and you are the "spouse" of the worker, you may be entitled to benefits. This is very iffy. Head to your nearest Social Security office for help. Call the SSA at 800-772-1213 for the office nearest you. The Social

Prosperity keeps many people in debt.

Security Act is very clear that, in cases like this, the agency is governed by state law and cannot make case-by-case decisions.

Your biological or adopted minor children are entitled to survivor benefits based on your Social Security earnings record if you should die. When the SSA is paying benefits to a minor child, it sends the benefits to a representative payee who is responsible for using the money for the needs of the child. This is usually the surviving parent but may occasionally be someone else.

In the case of a same-sex partnership, the Social Security administration will look to the law of the state where you live to see whether or not a parental relationship has been established under state law. If it's not the biological parent who passes away, then survivor benefits can only be paid to the child if state law recognizes a parental relationship.

A Will

If there's one area of financial planning that you need to know about as a domestic partner, estate planning is it. If you do not have a will, your assets are distributed according to state law, and no state law recognizes life partners as heirs. It recognizes surviving spouses, your children, your parents, your siblings, and so on down the familial chain. Some states recognize common-law marriages, but none recognize same-sex unions. This is an important part of your planning because, if not planned properly, your partner could be left with nothing.

You need a will for starters. Next you need to check everything you own on which you ever designated a beneficiary: your IRAs, 401(k) plan, 403(b) plan, 457 plan, Keogh Plan, SIMPLE-IRA, profit-sharing plan, life insurance policy, or an annuity. These need to be updated. You want them to complement your current thinking and plans. Who do you want to be the beneficiaries? Your partner? Your children? Also, if you have children, who do you want to raise the kids if you are not around? Your partner? Your sister? If you don't specify a guardian, the courts will decide who is to raise your kids.

A durable power of attorney is a very powerful document that will allow you to choose someone to act on your behalf legally and

---

There are bigger things in life than money—bills.

financially. That person will be able to file your tax returns, sell the stocks in your portfolio, collect rent from your tenants, make repairs on your house, and possibly even begin to gift your assets away for you. Choose wisely but do choose someone.

Without this power, if you should become incapacitated, your partner cannot do these things for you even if you own everything jointly. He or she would have to make you a ward of the state by petitioning the courts and then hope that the court would appoint him or her guardian and not a blood relative to look after you.

A second document is a durable power of attorney for healthcare, sometimes referred to as a healthcare proxy, a living will, or a medical directive. This document allows you to choose another person to act on your behalf to make medical decisions for you if you are incapacitated. Your proxy should be willing to be an advocate for you, lobbying on your behalf to carry out your wishes, not his or her own.

The two documents should work together; in some states, they are actually covered in one document. A durable power of attorney for healthcare should be available for free from your local hospital, hospice, or nursing home if you are admitted as a patient.

Powers of attorney are governed by state laws, so there are 50 different sets of laws regarding this topic. If you have moved, your power of attorney may be invalid. Get some professional help with this. If you spend time in two states, you may want to complete documents for both states. Your estate-planning attorney can help you with these. Check out the following sites for help: www.hospiceinfo.org; www.aarp.org; www.agingwithdignity.org; and www.nolo.com.

Trusts are one way that you can tamperproof your estate planning. If you want something that no one can mess with, this is it. A revocable living trust will allow you to set up the trust in your name. You will be the creator of the trust, the trustee, and the beneficiary of the trust. You would name a successor trustee if you could not handle the duties of being trustee, and you would name your heirs as well. Upon your death, the trustee distributes your assets according to your wishes. The trust does not need to go through probate court like a will does, so the

You should not confuse your career with your life.

whole event is kept private, and it becomes much harder for relatives to challenge your decisions.

Estate taxes will need to be paid if your estate exceeds $1 million in 2003. This is your exemption, the amount you are allowed to give away during your lifetime or upon death that is exempt from federal estate taxes. The exemption amount will increase to $3.5 million by the year 2009. Check out Chapter 11 for more details on estate tax changes.

Many states currently do not have an estate tax. That may all change in the future due to the Federal estate tax change which no longer gives the states some of the federal taxes collected. Some states do have an inheritance tax, which is paid by the heirs on the assets they receive. The rates vary from state to state. States that impose inheritance taxes are Connecticut, Delaware, Indiana, Iowa, Kansas, Kentucky, Louisiana, Maryland, Michigan, Montana, Nebraska, New Hampshire, North Carolina, Pennsylvania, South Dakota, and Tennessee. Here's a word of caution: If you are living in one of these states and you bequeath your assets to your partner, who is not a blood relative, your partner will pay a higher inheritance tax than a blood relative. So if you leave your partner assets such as your home, be sure there are also funds available to pay the inheritance tax so that he or she won't have to sell the home to pay the taxes.

Hired Help

The more complicated your life, the more complicated your financial planning will be. You may need some sophisticated help with your investments as well as planning. Certainly look at Chapter 18, "The Hired Help, and ask the planner you are interviewing about the types of clients he or she handles. You want someone who understands and empathizes with your concerns and problems as a domestic partner.

For same-sex partners, you may have to search a bit longer, but there are planners available that specialize in same-sex domestic partnerships. Check out www.gfn.com, which is the Gay Financial Network. Click on the site's professional directory to find a planner or attorney that

Money can't buy happiness; it can, however, rent it.

specializes in same-sex partnerships. This site is a good financial web site that just happens to be dedicated to the gay community. Another source is a new organization, Pride Planners,

> *A resource book to add to your library is Harold Lustig's book* 4 Steps to Financial Security for Lesbian and Gay Couples.

based in Massachusetts. This is a professional organization for financial planners serving the gay and lesbian community. You can reach them at 802-438-2822 or at www.prideplanners.com.

Children

Children are a special concern. If we add children to this equation of two people living together, it becomes froth with emotions, emotions that may not all be positive. Parents in domestic partnerships often do not have the rights that biological/adoptive married parents have.

There are no hard and fast statistics on how many domestic partner relationships break up because there are no tracking mechanisms in place like marriage licenses and divorce decrees. My guess is that they would be at least equal to the divorce rate among heterosexual married couples, so the odds are not with you. Over half of all marriages fail and end up in divorce, and there are many failed marriages that don't end up in divorce, just separate bedrooms. So what happens to the children?

Children are caught in the middle. When you make the decision to have children, your planning should start so that they are protected and so are you. With a heterosexual domestic partnership, make sure both parents' names are on the birth certificate.

Consider a co-parenting agreement with everything spelled out. You want this to be a formal arrangement, so I would suggest getting a lawyer familiar with this type of situation to help. You want to use language to the effect that, if your relationship should break up, you both still want to be involved in raising your child. The courts do seem to favor the biological mother if there is one, but many states

---

It's inflation when you have to be pretty well off just to be poor.

are recognizing the needs of the other parent after a relationship has been dissolved.

Many states allow same-sex adoption, and then both parents have equal legal rights, which include financial support for the child. Biological parents have equal legal rights to a child. The problem often occurs when one parent is the biological mother and the other parent never legally adopted the child but after the breakup still wants to be part of the child's life.

Children need to know they are loved, and they need to know they are not the reason for the breakup. No matter how you feel about each other, remember that the child loves you both and needs you both in his or her life.

Documents That Can Make It Easier

So you thought that living together was going to be simple. Just move in and go with the flow. That would be easy, wouldn't it? But life happens while you're planning it, so you need to be prepared. There are some documents you need to have in a domestic partnership that give you some of the same rights as married folks have. You have to gather them up, though, because the law won't take care of you here. This is still pretty much uncharted territory.

The following is a list of documents that will make things work when the relationship gets bumpy or if something should happen to one of you:

✔ **Relationship agreement.** Check with a family law attorney who works with and understands domestic partners. This can cover everything you would do as a couple legally and financially. Sometimes referred to as a domestic partner agreement.

✔ **Property agreement.** This would spell out how you are going to handle the property you have acquired together or will acquire together and how things will be disposed of in a breakup.

The chief advantage of having money is that you don't have to worry about not having it.

✔ **Co-parenting agreement.** Spells out each parent's rights now and if there is a breakup.

✔ **A will.** This is needed to make it clear to the world how you want your assets distributed and to whom.

✔ **Durable power of attorney.** Allows you to choose someone to act on your behalf legally and financially.

✔ **Durable power of attorney for healthcare.** Allows you to choose someone to act on your behalf medically if you are incapacitated.

✔ **A trust.** An entity that can own property and distribute income and assets to the named beneficiaries. Can be used during your lifetime and, upon death, your assets can pass to your named beneficiary.

The Bottom Line

The only legal protection you will have as a partner is to be sure you have done the planning necessary to make it happen. If there is children involved you need to be even more diligent about planning to protect them and yourself. Find competent help to guide your decisions.

Money isn't everything, usually it isn't even enough.

Notes:

ania had set a goal and when her net worth reached $75,000 she promised herself she was going to find a financial planner to help her invest her money. When she received her account statement recently she had reached that level.

Tania and Billy consider themselves newlyweds, with a new house, new jobs and a new life together. They've been in their home about a year now and used their cash wedding gifts and savings to make the down payment on the house. Tania's parents made them an offer they decided they couldn't afford to pass up. They offered Tania and Billy $30,000 to do with what they wanted, a wedding, a down payment on a house or a combination of the two. Tania and Billy choose the latter and had a small summer wedding in her grandmother's garden.

Tania started a new job recently and rolled over $15,000 from her previous employer's plan into an IRA. But it is sitting in a money market waiting for her to make a decision on where to invest it. Her current 401(k) plan is invested in a bond fund paying less than 1 percent. So her first question for her planner was going to be where to invest her money?

Tania and Billy are both 32 years old. They have lots of questions they wanted help with for it seemed to them that everything in their lives involved money in some way. They would like that elusive American dream and they would like to fill the two empty bedrooms in their new house with kids and be able to put up a white picket fence so the kids will be safe when playing in their own yard. Retiring early and having enough money to retire early also plays into this dream they told me. They have nightmares though; about educating those kids and having enough of a nest egg so they don't outlive their money in retirement.

Tania and Billy realize the importance of financial planning and acknowledge that they don't have all of the answers when it comes to preparing for the future. What they do have is a sense of when to bring in professional help to assist them in reaching their goals.

Chapter 18

Looking at the Bottom Line

* *

In This Chapter

The end is in sight! This is the last chapter and it's all about finding help with your financial planning.

* *

The Hired Help

I applaud you for getting through 17 chapters. This has been hard work: setting goals, getting organized, deciding which investments will be best suited for you, helping your kids learn about money. It's good stuff but nonetheless exhausting. Some of you have been stimulated by it; others have found it to be a necessary chore so that you can reach your goals. By this time, you've realized there is more to personal financial planning than just figuring out what funds you need to choose in your 401(k) plan or who to choose as your beneficiary.

But do you need a financial planner? Would you benefit from some help with your financial planning? In my opinion, everyone would benefit from sitting down with a planner and reviewing their financial strategies. At some point in your life, you may need to engage a financial planner, and the rest of this chapter will tell you how and where to find the best.

Taxation is based on supply and demand—the government demands and we supply.

How Do You Get Good Help Today?

There are many reasons individuals make that initial contact with a planner, and it is usually associated with a life event such as a new job, marriage, birth, divorce, disability, death, receiving an inheritance, losing a job, or after reading this book! You may need advice that is beyond the realm of your experience or that of family and friends. Another reason you may seek out advice is if you find that your simple portfolio has grown and you want some help fine-tuning it or if you want some help managing it because you believe it's more than you can handle.

Good financial advice may be just what the doctor ordered if you find yourself financially overwhelmed. What do you do? Where do you go for help? If you've been there, it may be time to hire an advisor.

What to Expect from the Help

Planners should start out asking lots of questions. They may have you fill out what seems like endless paperwork, but it's actually no more than I asked you to do when you did all your homework. A planner will need to know more about you than your doctor does. To be able to give you good advice and help you strategize, a planner will need to know about your lifestyle, your family, your income, your job, your business, your spending habits, your health, your family's health, your financial situation, and even information about your mom and dad.

Financial planning is a process, and a financial planner should be your personal guide on the trip. Advice should evolve as your situation changes, but there should always be the process. A planner should do the following for you:

1. A planner should assist you in identifying your personal and work goals and then help you make some sense of them. For example, the goal of a comfortable retirement is different for each of you. A planner can help you refine what "comfortable" is. A planner helps you work on the fine details of your goals. Your goals may cover a wide range of needs, from wanting to get out of debt to

---

There is one difference between a tax collector and a taxidermist— the taxidermist leaves the hide. —Mortimer Caplan

that comfortable retirement. A planner should be helping you strategize and prioritize.

2. A planner needs to gather information about you and your situation. This means collecting data on your assets and the ownership of those assets, reviewing important documents such as your will and your estate plan (and perhaps your employment contract), reviewing your retirement plan, and learning about your business if you are self-employed. You should be asked to do a net worth statement and fill out a cash flow worksheet (nothing new here!). The planner will want to know how you are spending your money and if there is a positive cash flow so that you have cash left over to save and invest. Sound familiar?

3. A planner should identify current or future potential problems or obstacles that could prevent you from reaching your goals. The planner should be helping you set a reasonable timeframe for the achievement of your goals.

4. A planner should help you develop a personal spending plan if your cash flow is negative. Again, you'll need to be honest and tell him or her if you are in debt.

5. A planner should provide written recommendations and solutions to your problems. You and the planner may decide that there is a need for a complete financial plan. You might just want a review of your portfolio, so the written recommendations should be customized to your needs.

6. A planner should help you implement the advice he or she has given you. You should not be sitting and staring at your financial plan, wondering how the heck you can accomplish this.

7. A planner should periodically review your plan with you, at least on an annual basis. You should be letting the planner know about any financial changes in your life so that she or he can help.

. . . in this world nothing is certain but death and taxes.
—Benjamin Franklin

Changes would include a death in the family, divorce, marriage, birth, and so on.

What a Planner Expects of You

For financial planners to provide you with good service, they expect you to participate in the financial planning process. A planner looks for honesty in her client. You need to be honest about your situation and give the planner all the facts, even if some of them are painful or awkward. When asked to fill out forms and worksheets, the planner expects you to do your homework honestly. Guessing on the facts or asking the planner to fill them in for you really won't do. A financial planner just may "fire" you as a client as a direct result of your lackadaisical attitude.

The Perfect Planner

The planner you choose should at least be a Certified Financial Planner (CFP) and be schooled in the areas of financial planning. Having credentials doesn't always make a planner better, but the consumer at least has some assurance about the planner's education. A business or finance degree or an MBA is a plus.

A description of the prefect planner, would read like a personal ad for the perfect mate. A Renaissance man or woman would make an ideal planner, look for the following in a planner:

✔ **Educator.** Foremost, a planner needs to be able to educate you on the areas of financial planning and why they are important.

✔ **Communicator.** The ideal planner should be a good one. There will be loads of stuff you won't understand, and you will need someone to translate for you at times.

✔ **Listener.** You want someone who will listen to you, hear you, and understand what questions you are really asking.

Taxes, after all, are the dues that we pay for the privilege of membership in an organized society. —Franklin D. Roosevelt

✔ **Trustworthy.** A planner should earn your trust and confidence. Trust is the number one issue for the financial consumer.

✔ **Competent.** This goes without saying that you want someone who is able to grasp your situation and problems, help you set goals, and implement a financial plan. The planner should have experience and knowledge in all areas of financial planning.

✔ **Commitment.** A planner should be committed to helping and working with her clients so they can be successful in realizing their goals.

✔ **Objectivity.** A planner should have your best interest at heart. You should get objective, unbiased advice and recommendations that are appropriate for your needs.

Paying the Hired Help

Planners are compensated in several different ways. When engaging a planner, understand how he or she is being compensated for working for you. You want objective advice that is not influenced by how much a planner can earn when selling you a variable life insurance product. Ask potential planners how they are compensated; they should fully disclose all fees, commissions, and trailing commissions. If there is a commission product involved, ask if there is any kind of contest going on. That's right, a contest. This is very common with annuity sales. The more they sell they might end up with a trip to Hawaii.

✔ **Fee-only planner.** These planners may charge an hourly fee, a flat fee for a comprehensive financial plan, or they may be retained on an annual basis. Fee-only planners do not earn any compensation from the investments they recommend. Planners that are exclusively fee-only planners are very difficult to find.

✔ **Commission-only planner.** A commission-only planner will review your situation, offer advice, and then earn his or her compensation

The income tax has made more liars out of the American people than golf has. —Will Rogers

when you purchase an insurance product or a financial product such as a mutual fund. When dealing with a commission-only planner, exercise caution because his or her only source of income is the revenues generated from selling.

✔ **Fee and commission planner.** Often referred to as a fee-based planner, these planners are compensated from both sales and fees. This has become the most popular form of financial-planning compensation. You pay an hourly fee to meet with the planner and receive his or her advice. If you choose to purchase financial products from the planner, he or she will earn a commission on the sale of the product.

✔ **Money manager.** Some planners manage your investments for you, charging a percentage of the assets under management for their fee. The fee ranges from 0.5 percent to 2.0 percent. Again, exercise caution when choosing a money manager, and never give someone discretionary power over your money.

What Will It Really Cost?

When hiring a fee-only planner that charges an hourly fee, you can expect to pay anywhere between $75 and $400 an hour. Paying $400 an hour does not necessarily assure you of better advice. Different areas of the country have different pay scales.

A complete financial plan can be had for as little as $275, but it will be a "canned" plan. You will fill out a questionnaire including something about your risk tolerance, and a computer somewhere will spit out a plan for you. Many of the large brokerage firms and mutual fund companies offer these types of plans.

A customized financial plan done by a financial planner could cost anywhere from $1,000 to $5,000, depending on the complexity of your finances. Some planners will offset the price of the plan if you purchase your mutual funds, annuities, or insurance through them.

Planners that charge an annual retainer may charge it on a percentage of assets, including your retirement plans and use assets such

Borrowing is the American way. How else did the national debt get so big?

as your home. Often there is a flat fee ranging from $1,000 to $5,000, depending on your needs.

Planners that manage money charge on the assets (which could include your 401[k] plan) under management. Depending on the size of your portfolio, the fee will be between 0.5 percent to 2.0 percent. The larger the portfolio, the smaller the fee. If the client portfolio does well, the planner does well. For example, if you have $500,000 invested, the planner will probably charge about 1.0 percent, and it will cost you $5,000 in planner fees for the year.

Commissions can be earned on many different types of financial products including mutual funds, stocks, bonds, limited partnerships, annuities, and insurance. Commissions can be paid up front or over a period of time, often referred to as a trailing commission.

At times, added incentives are offered by brokerage firms to the sales people that sell their financial products. A planner may need to sell 15 annuities to win a trip to Hawaii. Always ask a planner how he or she is being compensated. Don't be embarrassed to ask the awkward questions. A Certified Financial Planner (CFP) should be willing to disclose his or her compensation schedule to you. This doesn't mean you can ask to see the person's 1040. It means that planners will tell you what they will earn, usually only in percentages on the products they sell you.

When choosing a planner, first look for the characteristics you want in that person and then consider compensation. There are other issues such as trust, communication, confidence, and education that are just as important or more so. No one way of compensation is all good or all bad. Certainly, the fee-only planner can offer the most objective advice, but purebred fee-only planners are not that easy to find nor are there that many of them. They make up less than 20 percent of the financial-planning profession, and many of the planners who call themselves fee-only are really money managers in drag.

> *According to Dalbar, an opinion research firm in Boston, Massachusetts, the number one issue for a financial consumer when looking for a financial advisor is not compensation but trust. People want a planner they can trust and talk to.*

A bank is a place where they lend you an umbrella in fair weather and ask for it back when it rains. —Robert Frost

Picking and Choosing

Choosing a financial advisor can be one of the most important financial decisions you make; it's certainly more important than what mutual fund you should be buying this month. Finding the right advisor, however, may be difficult.

So where do you begin to look for someone? Begin by asking your friends, work associates, and relatives if they use a financial advisor. Speak with your other professional advisors, such as your attorney and your accountant, and ask whom they would recommend. Several professional organizations listed at the end of the chapter can assist you in your search as well. Just keep asking.

Next you will need to interview several planners, at least three. Interview them before you make a decision to become their client. Many advisors offer an introductory consultation. During this interview, you will have the opportunity to ask questions about the planner and his or her firm. Don't be afraid to ask tough questions. Remember that this is your money, and you will never find anyone as interested in it as you are. Grill them just as you would your daughter's first boyfriend.

The Interview Process

You should be comfortable asking questions, and a planner should be comfortable answering them. If he or she stumbles or hesitates on any of the questions, begin to wonder why. The following is a list of smart questions that you may want to get the answers to during the interview process.

Background and experience

✔ What credentials have they earned?

✔ What are the educational requirements for those credentials. Some credentials just require sending in a fee and you can then use the initials after your name.

Misers aren't much fun to live with, but they do make great ancestors.

✔ What is their educational background?

✔ How long have they been practicing financial planning?

✔ Are they licensed with the state securities division?

✔ Are they registered with the Securities and Exchange Commission?

Services

✔ What kind of services do they offer?

✔ How are they compensated?

✔ Are they licensed to sell products?

✔ Do they sell financial products?

✔ What companies do they represent?

✔ Do they review clients' taxes?

✔ Do they have a minimum account size?

✔ Who do you call if you have a question?

✔ Who will actually handle your account?

Who Can Help You Find Your Planner?

The following organizations will send you names of planners in your geographical area. They also provide consumer publications on financial planning as well as online consumer information.

Financial Planning Association (FPA)
5775 Glenridge Drive, NE
Suite B-300
Atlanta, GA 30328
800-322-4237
www.fpanet.org
(Membership: 35,000)

If your strength is small, don't carry heavy burdens.
If your words are worthless, don't give advice. —Chinese Proverb

American Institute of Certified Public Accountants
Personal Financial Planning Division
(AICPA-PFP Division)
1211 Avenue of the Americas
New York, NY 10036
888-777-7077
www.cpapfs.org

AICPA's personal financial-planning division is made up of CPAs
who have earned a Personal Financial Specialist designation
(Number: 7,000).

National Association of Personal Financial Advisors (NAPFA)
3250 North Arlington Heights Road,
Suite 109
Arlington Heights, IL 60004
800-366-2732
www.napfa.org

(NAPFA has a membership of
fee-only planners. Membership:
1,000+)

*When you begin your search
for a financial planner, don't let
your fingers do the walking. Stay
away from the Yellow Pages. The
Yellow Pages are okay if you're
looking for a pizza shop but not
for someone you are about to
entrust your life savings to.*

Garrett Planning Network
12700 Johnson Drive
Shawnee, KS 66216
866-260-8400
www.garrettplanningnetwork.com

A network of fee-only financial planners willing to work with
consumers on an hourly, as needed basis. This is new organization
with only a small number of planners.

---

*After a while you learn that what you really are is all the experiences
and all the thoughts you've ever had.*

Checking on the Help

If an individual or a firm holds itself out as providing investment advice and if it is managing assets over $25 million, it is required to register with the Securities and Exchange Commission in Washington. Individuals may be covered under blanket registration of the firms they work for.

Planners managing less than $25 million in assets must be registered in the state in which they practice with the appropriate state securities commissioner. Ask for copies of the forms (ADV part II) they file with their respective regulatory bodies. These forms list their education and experience. The only exception to this is the state of Wyoming, which has no state overseer so all planners must be registered with the SEC.

There are various ways you can check out your planner. If he or she has bragged about an MBA from Harvard, check it out. Call Harvard. A diploma on the wall means absolutely nothing. Computers can create anything today. Check the referrals given to you. If the planner claims to be registered with the SEC, check with the SEC. These agencies are there to protect the financial consumer. The following is a list of resources you can use to check out your planner.

The Certified Financial Planner Board of Standards (CFP Board)
1670 Broadway, Suite 600
Denver, CO 80202-4809
888-237-6279
www.cfp-board.org

Consumers can call the CFP Board to confirm whether a financial planner is currently licensed to use the CFP marks, to determine whether a CFP licensee has ever been publicly disciplined, or to lodge a complaint against a Certified Financial Planner.

The road to success is always under construction.

National Association of Insurance Commissioners (NAIC)
2301 McGee Street, Suite 800
Kansas City, MO 64108
816-842-3600
www.naic.org

Contact NAIC to be directed to your state agency that regulates insurance. Then check to see if the financial planner is licensed to sell insurance or has any insurance violations.

National Association of Securities Dealers (NASD)
1735 K Street, NW
Washington, DC 20006
800-289-9999
www.nasdr.com

The NASD is an association of the firms that sell securities, and it is what is referred to as a self-regulatory organization (SRO). This means the association polices its own members (sort of like hiring the fox to guard the hen house). If your advisor sells products, check them out here. You can also check with them to obtain the disciplinary history of registered representatives and broker dealers. This is kept in a central registration depository (CRD file).

North American Securities Administration Association (NASAA)
10 G Street, NE, Suite 710
Washington, DC 20002
202-737-0900
www.nasaa.org

NASSA is an organization of state securities administrators. Consumers can check with NASAA to find out which state agency regulates their state's securities-licensed financial planners. These are planners with less than $25 million under management

---

Tell me and I'll forget; show me and I may remember, involve me and I'll understand. —Chinese Proverb

Securities and Exchange Commission (SEC)
450 5th St., NW
Washington, DC 20549
800-732-0330
www.sec.gov

The SEC is a federal agency that governs the securities industry. It is one of the good guys in Washington because it looks out for the investor. If your planner calls herself an RIA (Registered Investment Advisor) and has more than $25 million under management, she should be registered with the SEC.

The Bottom Line

So much stuff to absorb! The perfect planner's resume should read like a description for a renaissance woman. There are organizations out there to help you find a planner and there are organizations out there that regulate planners. When looking for a planner be sure you interview more than one.

Having more money does not ensure happiness. People with 10 million dollars are no happier than people with 9 million dollars.
—Hobart Brown

APPENDICES

A. Worksheets

B. Exceptional Websites

Net Worth

Date:_____

	Total	Self	Spouse	Joint
Assets (What You Own)				
Cash or Equivalents				
Cash				
Checking accounts				
Savings accounts				
Money market fund				
Certificates of deposit (CDs)				
Savings bonds/treasuries				
Life insurance (cash value)				
Total				
Invested Assets				
Retirement Assets				
IRA accounts				
Pension/profit sharing				
401(k), 403(b), 457 plans				
Keogh accounts				
Annuities (surrender value)				
Other				
Investments				
Stocks				
Bonds				
Mutual funds				
Government securities				
Rental property				
Business equity				
Receivables (money owed you)				
Limited partnerships				
Patents, copyrights				
Trusts				
Other				
Total				

	Total	Self	Spouse	Joint
Use Assets				
Personal Property				
Home				
Vacation home				
Automobiles				
Household furnishings				
Clothes and jewelry				
Antiques, collectibles				
Boats, RVs, etc.				
Other				
Total				
Total assets	$ ___	$ ___	$ ___	$ ___
Liabilities (What You Owe)				
Debts				
Medical/dental				
Taxes owed				
Education loans				
Alimony				
Child support				
Mortgage				
Business loans				
Personal loans				
Pledges				
Contracts				
Property taxes owed				
Mortgage on rental property				
Home-equity loans				
Credit card debt				
Other				
Total liabilities	$ ___	$ ___	$ ___	$ ___
Total assets	$ ___	$ ___	$ ___	$ ___
Minus total liabilities	$ ___	$ ___	$ ___	$ ___
Net worth	$ ___	$ ___	$ ___	$ ___

Cash Flow

	Monthly	Annually	Comments
Salary			
Salary/spouse			
Self-employment income			
Social Security			
Social Security (spouse)			
Pension			
Pension (spouse)			
Rental income			
Interest			
Dividends			
Capital gains			
Alimony received			
Child support			
Other			
Other			

Basic Expenses

Home Expenses			
Mortgage			
Real estate taxes			
Condo/Assoc. fees			
Home-equity loan			
2nd Home Expenses			
Mortgage			
Real estate taxes			
Other Expenses			
Apartment			
Rent			
Parking fees			
Other fees			

Item	Weekly	Monthly	Yearly
Grounds Maintenance			
Lawn service			
Rubbish removal			
Snow removal			
Supplies and equipment			
Tree and shrub care			
Other			
Utilities			
Electric			
Water			
Oil			
Telephone			
Gas			
Insurance			
Homeowners			
Umbrella			
Household			
Groceries			
Cleaning supplies, etc.			
Clothing			
Family			
Dry cleaning			
Healthcare			
Insurance			
Doctor			
Prescriptions/medications			
Dentist			
Other			
Auto Expenses			
Loan payment			
Gasoline			
Repairs and maintenance			
Insurance			
Registration, license, inspection			

Item	Weekly	Monthly	Yearly
Tolls			
Parking			
Other			
Transportation			
Bus, train, subway			
Life Insurance Premiums			
Policy 1			
Policy 2			
Disability Insurance Premiums			
Policy 1			
Alimony and Child Support			
Alimony			
Child support			
Work Related			
Union dues			
Continuing education			
Other			
Childcare			
Daycare			
Miscellaneous			
Bank charge			
Postage			
Financial—tax prep, legal			
Other			

Discretionary Expenses

	Weekly	Monthly	Yearly
Cleaning Expenses			
Weekly			
Food			
Meals out			
Contributions			
Childcare			
Summer camp			
Lessons			

Item	Weekly	Monthly	Yearly
Vacations/Entertainment			
Vacations	_____	_____	_____
Entertainment	_____	_____	_____
Memberships/Dues			
Exercise/health clubs	_____	_____	_____
Country/pool clubs	_____	_____	_____
Other	_____	_____	_____
Subscriptions			
Newspapers	_____	_____	_____
Magazines	_____	_____	_____
Gifts			
Birthdays, anniversaries	_____	_____	_____
Holidays	_____	_____	_____
Personal Care			
Hair salon	_____	_____	_____
Toiletries	_____	_____	_____
Other	_____	_____	_____
Allowances			
Adults	_____	_____	_____
Children	_____	_____	_____
Miscellaneous			
Cable TV	_____	_____	_____
Hobbies	_____	_____	_____
Pet expenses	_____	_____	_____
	_____	_____	_____
	_____	_____	_____
Charge Cards/Loans			
1.	_____	_____	_____
2.	_____	_____	_____
3.	_____	_____	_____
4.	_____	_____	_____

Possible Expenses

Item	Weekly	Monthly	Yearly
Home Expenses—Repair/Replacement			
Furniture	_____	_____	_____
Appliance	_____	_____	_____
Roof, septic, etc.	_____	_____	_____
Other	_____	_____	_____
Education Expenses			
Tuition and fees	_____	_____	_____
Room and board	_____	_____	_____
Books	_____	_____	_____
Transportation	_____	_____	_____
Other	_____	_____	_____

Savings

	Weekly	Monthly	Yearly
Pension/IRA	_____	_____	_____
401(k), 403(b), 457 plan	_____	_____	_____
Self-employment plans	_____	_____	_____
Personal savings	_____	_____	_____
Emergency fund	_____	_____	_____
Other	_____	_____	_____

Taxes

	Weekly	Monthly	Yearly
Federal	_____	_____	_____
State	_____	_____	_____
Social Security	_____	_____	_____
Medicare	_____	_____	_____
Other	_____	_____	_____
Totals	$_____	$_____	$_____

Inventory and Location of Important Documents

Document	Location	Document	Location
Personal Documents			
My birth certificate	_____	Children's Social Security cards	_____
My Social Security card	_____		
Spouse's birth certificate	_____	Divorce/separation records	_____
Spouse's Social Security card	_____	Names and addresses of relatives and friends	_____
Citizenship papers	_____	List of professional advisors	_____
Adoption papers	_____	List of professional memberships	_____
Military discharge papers	_____		
Marriage certificate	_____	Degrees	_____
Children's birth certificates	_____	Organ donor card	_____
Children's adoption papers	_____		
Estate/Legal Planning Document			
My will	_____	Letter of instruction	_____
Copy of my will	_____	Spouse's will	_____
Trust documents	_____	Copy of spouse's will	_____
Power of attorney	_____	Spouse's power of attorney	_____
Medical directives	_____	Spouse's medical directives	_____
Burial instructions	_____	Spouse's burial instructions	_____
Cemetery plot deed	_____	Spouse's letter of instruction	_____
Insurance Records			
Life insurance policy (group)	_____	Auto insurance policy	_____
Life insurance policy (individual)	_____	Homeowners policy	_____
Other death/accidental coverage	_____	Renters policy	_____
Health insurance policy	_____	Umbrella liability policy	_____
Disability policy	_____	Property and casualty policy	_____

Document	Location	Document	Location
Financial Records			
Income tax returns (six years)_____		Annuity contracts _____	
Employment contracts _____		Stock option purchase plan _____	
Partnership agreements _____		Retirement plans _____	
List of checking/savings accounts_____		• 401(k) _____	
Checkbooks, savings passbooks _____		• 403(b) _____	
Bank statements, canceled checks ____		• 457 _____	
List of credit cards _____		• Federal Thrift Savings Plan_____	
Certificates of deposit (CDs) _____		• IRAs _____	
Brokerage account statements _____		• Self-employment plans _____	
Mutual fund statements _____		• Profit-sharing plan _____	
Stock certificates _____		• Pension plan _____	
Bonds _____		Other securities _____	
Ownership Records			
Titles/deeds to real estate _____		Loan agreements _____	
Title insurance _____		Auto title, registration _____	
Mortgage agreement _____		Boat title, registration _____	
Rental property records _____		Warranties _____	
Miscellaneous			
Safe combinations _____		_____	
Passwords for computer _____		_____	
Videotaped inventory of home _____		_____	
Financial-planning worksheets_____		_____	
Contents of safety deposit box_____		_____	
Keys for safety deposit box _____		_____	
Lease agreement _____		_____	

BALLPARK E$TIMATE ©

Planning for retirement is not a one-size-fits-all exercise. The purpose of Ballpark is simply to give you a basic idea of the savings you'll need when you retire.

1. How much annual income will you want in retirement? (Figure 70 percent of your current annual income just to maintain your current standard of living. Really.) $_____

2. Subtract the income you expect to receive annually from:

   ✔ Social Security
   If you make under $25,000, enter $8,000; between $25,000 and $40,000, enter $12,000; over $40,000, enter $14,500. For a more personalized estimate, enter the appropriate benefit figure from your Social Security statement from the Social Security Administration (1-800-772-1213, www.ssa.gov). Ballpark assumes you will begin receiving Social Security Benefits at age 65, however the age for full benefits is rising to 67. Your Social Security statement will provide a personalized benefit estimate based on your actual earning history.   − $_____

   ✔ Traditional Employer Pension—a plan that pays a set dollar amount for life; the dollar amount depends on salary and years of service (in today's dollars)   − $_____

   ✔ Part-time income   − $_____

   ✔ Other   − $_____

   This is how much you need to make up for each retirement year: = $_____

Now you want a ballpark estimate of how much money you'll need in the bank the day you retire. Some accountants went to work and devised this simple formula. For the record, they figure you'll realize a constant real rate of return of 3 percent after inflation, you'll live to age 87, and you'll begin to receive income from Social Security at age 65. If you anticipate living longer than age 87 or earning less than a 3 percent real rate of return on your savings, you'll want to consider using a higher percentage of your current annual gross income as a goal on line 1.

3. To determine the amount you'll need
   to save, multiply the amount you
   need to make up by the factor below: $_____

   Age you expect to retire: Your factor is:

Age you expect to retire:	Your factor is:
55	21.0
60	18.9
65	16.4
70	13.6

4. If you expect to retire before age 65,
   multiply your Social Security benefit from
   line 2 by the following factor: + $_____

Age you expect to retire:	Your factor is:
55	8.8
60	4.7

5. Multiply your savings to date by the factor
   below (include money accumulated in a
   401(k), IRA, or similar retirement plan):   − $_____

If you want to retire in:	Your factor is:
10 years	1.3
15 years	1.6
20 years	1.8
25 years	2.1
30 years	2.4
35 years	2.8
40 years	3.3

Total additional savings needed at retirement: = $_____

Don't panic. These same accountants devised another formula to show you how much to save each year in order to reach your goal amount. They factor in compounding—when your money not only makes interest, your interest starts making interest as well, creating a snowball effect.

6. To determine the ANNUAL amount
   you'll need to save, multiply the TOTAL
   amount by the factor below: = $_____
   If you want to retire in: Your factor is:

If you want to retire in:	Your factor is:
10 yrs.	.085
15 yrs.	.052
20 yrs.	.036
25 yrs.	.027
30 yrs.	.020
35 yrs.	.016
40 yrs.	.013

See? It's not impossible or even particularly painful. It just takes planning. And the sooner you start, the better off you'll be.

The Ballpark Estimate is designed to provide a rough estimate of what you will need to save annually to fund a comfortable retirement. It provides an approximation of projected Social Security benefits and utilizes only one of many possible rates of return on your savings. Ballpark reflects today's dollars and does not account for inflation; therefore, you should recalculate your savings needs on a regular basis and as your salary and circumstances change. You won't want to stop with the Ballpark Estimate; it is only a first step in the retirement planning process. You will need to do further analysis, either by yourself using a more detailed worksheet or computer software, or with the assistance of a financial professional.

Reprinted here with permission from the American Savings Educational Council (ASEC, www.asec.org).

Appendix B: Exceptional Websites

There is no glossary included with this book. That was a conscious decision on my part. I could fill 500 pages with what I would like you to have at your fingertips. Instead I have included five exceptional web sites for you to use. The first four sites also have other financial information as well. Again I apologize to those of you without a computer at your fingertips. Head to your local library for help.

http://www.nyse.com/ (click on glossary)

http://biz.yahoo.com/glossary

http://www.finance-glossary.com

http://www.nasdr.com/glossary/a.asp

http://www.investorwords.com

Index

Notes:

Notes:

Notes:

Notes:

Notes:

Notes:

Notes:

Notes:

Notes:

Notes:

Notes:

Notes:

Notes: